Guess what?

We offer GMAT Prep Classes & Private Tutoring too!

Visit powerscore.com for more information.

  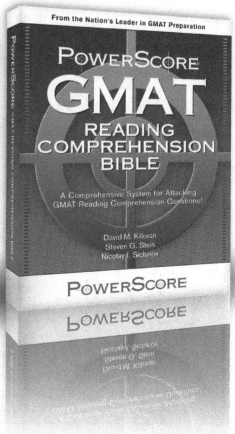

"These books saved my GMAT score."

–J. Wang

PowerScore
GMAT BIBLE SERIES
Complete the Trilogy. Visit powerscore.com.

PowerScore® GMAT CRITICAL REASONING BIBLE

A Comprehensive System for Attacking
GMAT Critical Reasoning Questions!

Copyright © 2005-2017 by PowerScore Incorporated. All Rights Reserved. No part of this publication may be reproduced, stored in a retrieval system, or transmitted in any form or by any means electronic, mechanical, photocopying, recording, scanning, or otherwise, without the prior written permission of the Publisher. Parts of this book have been previously published in other PowerScore publications and on the powerscore.com website.

GMAC, GMAT, and GMATPrep are trademarks of the Graduate Management Admission Council.

PowerScore® is a registered trademark. *The Critical Reasoning Bible*™, *The Sentence Correction Bible*™, *The Reading Comprehension Bible*™, The Three Question Families™, The Critical Reasoning Primary Objectives™, The Conclusion Identification Method™, The Fact Test™, The Idea Umbrella™, The Uniqueness Rule of Answer Choices™, Mistaken Negation™, Mistaken Reversal™, The Supporter/Defender Assumption Model™, The Assumption Negation Technique™, The Opposition Construct™, The Elemental Attack™, Test of Abstraction™, and The Variance Test™ are the exclusive service marked property of PowerScore. Any use of these terms without the express written consent of PowerScore is prohibited.

Published by
PowerScore Publishing, a division of PowerScore Incorporated
57 Hasell Street
Charleston, SC 29401

Author: David M. Killoran

Manufactured in Canada
12 25 20 16

ISBN: 978-0-9721296-3-3

Contents

Chapter One: Introduction

Introduction 3
A Brief Overview of the GMAT 4
The Analytical Writing Assessment 6
The Integrated Reasoning Section 6
The Quantitative Section 6
The Verbal Section 7
Experimental Questions 7
The GMAT CAT Format 8
Special GMAT CAT Considerations 9
Computers and Noteboards 12
The GMAT Scoring Scale 13
The GMAT Percentile Table 13
The Use of the GMAT 14

Chapter Two: The Basics of Critical Reasoning

GMAT Critical Reasoning 17
Critical Reasoning Question Directions 17
The Parts of a Critical Reasoning Question 18
Approaching the Questions 19
Analyzing the Stimulus 21
The Range of Stimulus Topics 22
GMAT Vocabulary 23
Arguments versus Fact Sets 25
Identifying Premises and Conclusions 26
One Confusing Indicator Form 29
Premise and Conclusion Recognition Mini-Drill 30
Additional Premise Indicators 33
Counter-Premise Indicators 34
Additional Premise and Counter-Premise Recognition Mini-Drill 35
Recognizing Conclusions Without Indicators 37
Complex Arguments 38
A Commonly Used Construction 40
Truth versus Validity 41
Argument Analysis 42
Inferences and Assumptions 44

The Mind of a GMAT Author..44
Read the Fine Print...45
Tracking Indicators and Concepts..47
Scope...47
Fluidity of Analysis and Concept Application...48
Final Chapter Note..48
Premise and Conclusion Analysis Drill...49

CHAPTER THREE: THE QUESTION STEM AND ANSWER CHOICES

The Question Stem...57
Analyzing the Question Stem...57
The Ten Critical Reasoning Question Types..58
Question Type Notes...69
Question Type Variety...70
"Most" in Question Stems...70
Question Stem Wording Variations...71
Identify the Question Stem Drill..72
"Except" and "Least" in Question Stems..76
Except and *Least* Identify the Question Stem Mini-Drill.....................................79
Prephrasing Answers..81
The Answer Choices...82
Question Approach Review..85
Final Chapter Note..87

CHAPTER FOUR: MUST BE TRUE QUESTIONS

Must Be True Questions...91
Prephrasing with Must Be True Questions...92
Returning to the Stimulus...96
New Information and the Idea Umbrella..96
Primary Objective #4 and Modifier Words Revisited...98
Language: Negatives and Double Negatives..100
Correct Answers in Must Be True Questions Reviewed.......................................102
Incorrect Answers in Must Be True Questions..102
Stimulus Opinions versus Assertions...105
Conditional Reasoning..106
Three Logical Features of Conditional Reasoning..107
Valid and Invalid Statements..108
Valid and Invalid Statement Recognition Mini-Drill..111
The Multiplicity of Indicator Words...113
How to Recognize Conditionality..115

Sufficient and Necessary Diagramming Drill..116
Final Note..120
Must Be True Question Type Review..121
Must Be True Question Problem Set...123

CHAPTER FIVE: MAIN POINT QUESTIONS

Main Point Questions...131
Two Incorrect Answer Types...132
Fill in the Blank Questions...136
Main Point—Fill in the Blank Questions..136
Final Chapter Note...137
Main Point Question Type Review..138
Fill in the Blank Question Type Review..138
Must Be True and Main Point Question Stem Mini-Drill..................................139
Main Point Question Problem Set...141

CHAPTER SIX: WEAKEN QUESTIONS

Weaken Questions..147
How to Weaken an Argument..149
Common Weakening Scenarios...151
Three Incorrect Answer Traps..152
Weaken Questions Analyzed..153
Final Note..157
Weaken Question Type Review..158
Weaken Question Problem Set...159

CHAPTER SEVEN: CAUSE AND EFFECT REASONING

What is Causality?...169
How to Recognize Causality..169
Causality in the Conclusion versus Causality in the Premises..........................170
Situations That Can Lead to Errors of Causality..172
The Central Assumption of Causal Conclusions...173
How to Attack a Causal Conclusion..174
Diagramming Causality...175
Two Cause and Effect Problems Analyzed..176
Causal Reasoning Review...180
Final Note..181
Causal Reasoning Problem Set...182

Chapter Eight: Strengthen and Assumption Questions

- The Second Family 191
- The Difference Between Strengthen and Assumption Questions 192
- Strengthen Questions 193
- How to Strengthen an Argument 194
- Three Incorrect Answer Traps 195
- Strengthen Questions Analyzed 196
- Causality and Strengthen Questions 198
- Weaken vs Strengthen Questions 201
- Strengthen Question Type Review 202
- Strengthen Question Problem Set 203
- Assumption Questions 206
- The Supporter/Defender Assumption Model™ 208
- The Assumption Negation Technique™ 215
- Negating Statements 216
- Logical Opposition 216
- Statement Negation Drill 219
- Three Quirks of Assumption Question Answer Choices 221
- Assumptions and Causality 222
- Assumption—Fill in the Blank Questions 224
- Assumption Question Type Review 226
- Assumption Question Problem Set 228

Chapter Nine: Resolve the Paradox Questions

- Resolve the Paradox Questions 233
- Stimulus Peculiarities 233
- Question Stem Features 234
- Active Resolution 235
- Address the Facts 237
- Oppositional Circumstances and Cause 239
- Resolve the Paradox Question Review 240
- Resolve the Paradox Question Problem Set 241

Chapter Ten: Method of Reasoning and Flaw in the Reasoning Questions

Method of Reasoning Questions..247
Flaw in the Reasoning Questions..248
Prephrasing in Method and Flaw Questions...249
The Fact Test in Method and Flaw Questions...250
Stimulus Notes...250
Incorrect Answers in Method and Flaw Questions...251
The Value of Knowing Common Errors of Reasoning..252
Common Errors of Reasoning Explained..254
Errors in the Use of Evidence..254
Source Argument..258
Circular Reasoning...259
Errors of Conditional Reasoning..260
Mistaken Cause and Effect...261
Straw Man...262
Appeal Fallacies...263
Survey Errors..265
Errors of Composition and Division..267
Uncertain Use of a Term or Concept...268
False Analogy...268
False Dilemma..269
Time Shift Errors..270
Numbers and Percentages Errors...270
Idea Application: Correct and Incorrect Answers Analyzed......................................271
Method of Reasoning—Bolded Argument Part Questions..273
Method—AP Stimulus Structure...273
A Common Wrong Answer..276
Final Note...276
Method of Reasoning and Flaw in the Reasoning Question Type Review................277
Identify the Flaw in the Argument Drill...279
Method of Reasoning and Flaw in the Reasoning Problem Set.................................288

Chapter Eleven: Parallel Reasoning Questions

Parallel Reasoning Questions..295
Parallel Flaw Questions...295
The Peril of Abstraction...296
Solving Parallel Reasoning Questions...297
What To Do If All Else Fails...305
Parallel Reasoning Question Review..306
Parallel Reasoning Question Problem Set..307

Chapter Twelve: Numbers and Percentages

Numbers and Percentages 313
Must Be True Questions and Numbers and Percentages 319
Markets and Market Share 322
Numbers and Percentages Review 323
Numbers and Percentages Practice Drill 325
Numbers and Percentages Problem Set 329

Chapter Thirteen: Evaluate the Argument, Cannot Be True, and Principle Questions

Evaluate the Argument Questions 335
The Variance Test™ 337
Evaluate the Argument Question Type Review 342
Cannot Be True Questions 343
Two Notable Stimulus Scenarios 344
Cannot Be True Question Review 345
Principle Questions 347
Principle Question Review 349
Final Note 349

Chapter Fourteen: Test Readiness

The day before the test 353
The morning of the test 353
At the test center 354
After the test 354
Afterword 355

Complete Chapter Answer Key

Notes 357
Question Description Legend 357
Question Family Categorization 358
Chapter-by-Chapter Answer Key 359

Glossary and Index

Glossary and Index 363

About PowerScore

PowerScore is one of the nation's most respected test preparation companies. Founded in 1997, PowerScore offers GMAT, GRE, LSAT, SAT, and ACT preparation classes in over 150 locations in the U.S. and abroad. Preparation options include Full-length courses, Accelerated courses, Live Online courses, On Demand courses, private tutoring, and admissions consulting. For more information, please visit our website at www.powerscore.com or call us at (800) 545-1750.

About the Author

Dave Killoran, a graduate of Duke University, is an expert in test preparation with over 20 years of experience teaching classes for graduate school admissions tests. In addition to having written PowerScore's legendary LSAT Bible Series and many other popular publications, Dave has overseen the preparation of thousands of students and founded two national test preparation companies.

Other PowerScore GMAT Books

PowerScore's also offers several other GMAT publications: *The PowerScore GMAT Sentence Correction Bible*, *The PowerScore GMAT Reading Comprehension Bible*, and *The PowerScore GMAT Verbal Bible Workbook*.

Chapter One: Introduction

Chapter One: Introduction

Introduction 3

A Brief Overview of the GMAT 4

The Analytical Writing Assessment 6

The Integrated Reasoning Section 6

The Quantitative Section 6

The Verbal Section 7

Experimental Questions 7

The GMAT CAT Format 8

Special GMAT CAT Considerations 9

Computers and Noteboards 12

The GMAT Scoring Scale 13

The GMAT Percentile Table 13

The Use of the GMAT 14

Introduction

Welcome to the *PowerScore GMAT Critical Reasoning Bible*. We congratulate you on your savvy purchase—you have bought the most advanced book ever published for the GMAT Critical Reasoning section. The purpose of this book is to provide you with a powerful and comprehensive system for attacking the Critical Reasoning section of the Graduate Management Admission Test (GMAT). By thoroughly studying and correctly applying this system we are confident you will increase your Critical Reasoning score.

This book has been carefully designed to reinforce your understanding of the concepts behind the Critical Reasoning section. The concepts and techniques discussed herein are drawn from our experience with GMAT tutoring and coaching, and our live and on-demand GMAT courses, which we feel are the most effective in the world.

In order to apply our methods effectively and efficiently, we strongly recommend that you carefully read and re-read each of the discussions regarding arguments, concepts, and question types. We also suggest that as you finish each question you look at both the explanation for the correct answer choice and the explanations for the incorrect answer choices. Closely examine each problem and determine which elements led to the correct answer, and then study the analyses provided in the book and check them against your own work. By doing so you will greatly increase your chances of recognizing the patterns present in all Critical Reasoning questions.

This book also contains a variety of drills and exercises that supplement the discussion of techniques and question analysis. The drills help strengthen specific skills that are critical for GMAT excellence, and for this reason they are as important as the questions. In the answer keys to these drills we will often introduce and discuss important GMAT points, so we strongly advise you to read through all explanations.

Please note that this book is not a practice guide, but rather a preparation guide. The purpose of the book is to teach you techniques and strategies, and we use a variety of questions to that end. For practice questions, we strongly recommend picking up the Official Guides from GMAC, the makers of the GMAT. Those books contains hundreds of released GMAT questions that are perfect for trying out the approaches taught in this book.

On page 357 there is a complete quick-reference answer key to all problems in this book. The answer key contains a legend of question identifiers, as well as chapter-by-chapter answer keys.

Because access to accurate and up-to-date information is critical, we

If you are looking to further improve your GMAT score, we also recommend that you pick up copies of the renowned PowerScore GMAT Sentence Correction Bible and GMAT Reading Comprehension Bible. When combined with the Critical Reasoning Bible, you will have a formidable methodology for attacking the Verbal portion of the test. The other GMAT Bibles are available through our website at powerscore.com and at fine retailers.

CHAPTER ONE: INTRODUCTION

strongly suggest that all *Critical Reasoning Bible* students visit http://www.mba.com on a frequent basis. MBA.com is the official website of the makers of the test, and they provide a variety of online resources and updates. This is also the website to visit in order to register for the test and to get information about your specific test center.

Because access to accurate and up-to-date information is critical, we have devoted a section of our website to *Critical Reasoning Bible* students. This free online resource area offers supplements to the book material, answers questions posed by students, and provides updates as needed. There is also an official book evaluation form that we strongly encourage you to use. The exclusive *GMAT Critical Reasoning Bible* online area can be accessed at:

powerscore.com/crbible

If we can assist you in your GMAT preparation in any way, or if you have any questions or comments, please do not hesitate to contact us via email at:

crbible@powerscore.com

We look forward to hearing from you!

A Brief Overview of the GMAT

The Graduate Management Admission Test is required for admission at over 1000 business schools worldwide. According to the Graduate Management Admission Council (GMAC), the makers of the test, "The GMAT is specifically designed to measure the verbal, quantitative, and writing skills of applicants for graduate study in business. It does not, however, presuppose any specific knowledge of business or other specific content areas, nor does it measure achievement in any particular subject areas." The GMAT is given in English, and consists of the following four separately timed sections:

- **Analytical Writing Assessment.** 1 essay, 30 minutes. The essay asks for an analysis of an argument.

- **Integrated Reasoning Section.** 12 questions, 30 minutes; four question types: Graphics Interpretation, Two-Part Analysis, Table Analysis, and Multi-Source Reasoning.

When you take an actual GMAT, you must present an ID. They will also take your picture and digitally scan your palm vein pattern. These steps are taken in order increase test security and to eliminate problems.

- **Quantitative Section.** 37 multiple-choice questions, 75 minutes; two question types: Problem Solving and Data Sufficiency.

- **Verbal Section.** 41 multiple-choice questions, 75 minutes; three question types: Reading Comprehension, Critical Reasoning, and Sentence Correction.

An optional break of 8 minutes is allowed before and after the Quantitative section, and so the order of the test sections is always identical:

Analytical Writing Assessment		
Analysis of an Argument	30 minutes	1 question
Integrated Reasoning		
Graphics Interpretation	30 minutes	12 questions
Two-Part Analysis		
Table Analysis		
Multi-Source Reasoning		
Break	8 minutes	
Quantitative Section		
Data Sufficiency	75 minutes	37 questions
Problem Solving		
Break	8 minutes	
Verbal Section		
Critical Reasoning	75 minutes	41 questions
Reading Comprehension		
Sentence Correction		

Although the 8-minute breaks are optional, you should always take the entire break time in order to avoid fatigue.

CHAPTER ONE: INTRODUCTION

The Analytical Writing Assessment

The Analytical Writing Assessment (AWA) appears at the beginning of the GMAT, immediately after the computer tutorial. The AWA consists of one essay, and you have thirty minutes to complete the essay. The essay topic is called Analysis of an Argument.

The AWA was developed in 1994 in response to requests from business schools to add a writing component to the GMAT. Studies had shown that strong writing and communication abilities are critical for strong business performance, and business schools wanted to have a means of assessing candidates' communication abilities. According to GMAC, "The AWA is designed as a direct measure of your ability to think critically and to communicate your ideas...The Analysis of an Argument task tests your ability to formulate an appropriate and constructive critique of a specific conclusion based upon a specific line of thinking."

The Analytical Writing Assessment essay is initially scored on a 0 to 6 scale in half-point increments by two readers—one human reader, and one machine reader. The two scores are averaged to produce a final score for the essay.

The Integrated Reasoning Section

The Integrated Reasoning section was introduced in June 2012 in response to surveys that indicated what business schools felt were important skills for incoming students.

12 questions are presented in one of four formats: Graphics Interpretation, Two-Part Analysis, Table Analysis, and Multi-Source Reasoning. The questions focus on your data-handling skills, and feature unique elements of computer interaction. For example, you must synthesize and evaluate information from a variety of sources, organize and combine information in order to understand relationships, and manipulate information in order to solve problems.

A separate Integrated Reasoning score from 1 to 8 in single-point increments is produced based on your performance in this section.

The Quantitative Section

The Quantitative section of the GMAT is comprised of questions that cover mathematical subjects such as arithmetic, algebra, and geometry. There are two question types—Problem Solving and Data Sufficiency.

Problem Solving questions contain five separate answer choices, each of which offers a different solution to the problem. Approximately 22 of the 37 Quantitative section questions will be in the Problem Solving format.

At the conclusion of the GMAT you have the option to cancel your score. Previously, there was no way to determine exactly what your score would be before cancelling, but now you can preview your unofficial score (excluding the Writing score) and then decide to keep or cancel them.

Data Sufficiency questions consist of a question followed by two numbered statements. You must determine if the numbered statements contain sufficient information to solve the problem—individually, together, or not at all. Each Quantitative section contains approximately 15 Data Sufficiency questions, and this type of problem is unique to the GMAT and can be exceptionally challenging.

The Verbal Section

The GMAT Verbal section is a test of your ability to read for content, analyze argumentation, and to recognize and correct written errors. Accordingly, there are three types of problems—Reading Comprehension, Critical Reasoning, and Sentence Correction.

Reading Comprehension questions examine your ability to analyze large amounts of material for content and understanding. Passages range up to 350 words in length, and each passage is accompanied by 3 to 8 questions. Passage topics are drawn from a variety of areas, including business, science, politics, law, and history.

Critical Reasoning questions present a short argument followed by a question such as: "Which of the following weakens the argument?" "Which of the following parallels the argument?" or "Which of the following must be true according to the argument?" The key to these questions is understanding the reasoning types and question types that frequently appear. Within the Verbal Section you will encounter approximately 10 to 14 Critical Reasoning questions.

Critical Reasoning has been on the GMAT since 1988.

Each Sentence Correction problem presents a sentence containing an underlined section. Five answer choices follow the problem, and each suggests a possible phrasing of the underlined section. The first answer choice is a repeat of the underlined section, and the remaining four answers are different from the original. Your task is to analyze the underlined section and determine which of the answers offers the best phrasing.

Experimental Questions

During the GMAT you will encounter questions that will not contribute to your score. These questions, known as "experimental" or "pre-test" questions, are used on future versions of the GMAT. Unfortunately, you will not be informed during the test as to which questions do not count, so you must give your best performance on each question.

About 1/4 of the questions on the GMAT are experimental.

The GMAT CAT Format

As opposed to the traditional paper-and-pencil format used by many other tests, the GMAT is administered on a computer. Consequently, only one question at a time is presented, the order of questions is not predetermined, and the test actually responds to your answers and shapes the exam in order to most efficiently arrive at your proper score. This format is known as a Computer Adaptive Test, or CAT.

For example, the first question in the Verbal or Quantitative section will be a medium difficulty question. If answered correctly, the computer will supply a somewhat harder question on the assumption that your score is somewhere above that level. If this next question is answered correctly, the following question will again be more difficult. This process continues until a question is missed. At that point, the test will supply a somewhat easier question as it tries to determine if you have reached your score "ceiling." By increasing or decreasing the difficulty of the questions based on prior response, the test attempts to quickly pinpoint your appropriate score level and then confirm that level. Consequently, the first several questions are used to broadly establish your general scoring range:

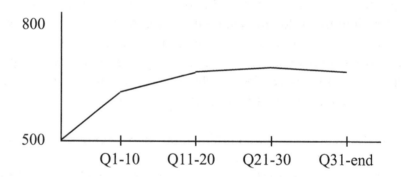

In the diagram above, correct responses to the first several questions lead to significant jumps in score, whereas later questions make smaller adjustments. A strong beginning followed by a weak finish will produce a higher score than a weak beginning followed by a strong finish. For this reason it is essential that your performance early in the section be as strong as possible, even if this requires using more than the average time allotted per question.

Special GMAT CAT Considerations

The CAT format has certain features that appreciably alter the testing experience:

- The CAT format does not allow you to "skip" a question; that is, you cannot leave a question blank nor can you come back to a question. In order to move forward in the test you *must* answer the question on the screen. If you do not know the answer, you must make an educated guess. And since the test adapts to your previous responses, once you complete a question, you cannot return to that question.

- You cannot write on the computer screen, but a booklet of five noteboards will be given to you. You may not erase your notes, but you can request additional noteboards.

- Facility with a computer is clearly an advantage; fast typing is also an advantage in the Analytical Writing Section where your response must be typed into the computer.

- The test penalizes examinees who do not finish all the questions in the section. Thus, since the number of questions answered is incorporated into the calculation of scores, it is helpful that you complete every question in each section. There can be a strong penalty for leaving questions unanswered, and so it is typically better to miss a question than to leave it unanswered. See the *Critical Reasoning Bible* booksite for more information on guessing strategy!

- The results of your test (excluding the Writing score) are available at the conclusion of the exam.

Question Difficulty Matters

Complicating the GMAT CAT scoring system is that question difficulty affects your overall score. Each question is assigned a predetermined "weight," and more difficult questions have a greater weight. Consequently, it is important that you answer difficult questions and not just "skip" any question that appears difficult. Answering fifteen easy questions will produce a lower score than answering fifteen difficult questions.

General Pacing

Since completing every question in a section is critical, pacing is equally important. Based purely on the number of questions and the total time per section, the following lists the average amount of time you can spend per question:

Integrated Reasoning Section	12 questions, 30 minutes
Average time per question	*2 minutes, 30 seconds*
Quantitative Section	37 questions, 75 minutes
Average time per question	*2 minutes, 1 second*
Verbal Section	41 questions, 75 minutes
Average time per question	*1 minute, 49 seconds*

Score-Specific Pacing

The following references provide alternate Quantitative and Verbal pacing strategies depending on desired score.

Basic Quantitative Strategy for various scoring ranges:		
700-800	Complete every question	average of just under 2 minutes per question
600-690	Attempt to complete every question	average of 2 minutes, 15 seconds per question, keep enough time to guess on uncompleted questions
500-590	Attempt to complete at least 75% of questions	average of 2 minutes, 35 seconds per question, keep enough time to guess on uncompleted questions

Basic Verbal Strategy for various scoring ranges:		
700-800	Complete every question	average of 1 minute, 45 seconds per question
600-690	Attempt to complete every question	average of 2 minutes per question, keep enough time to guess on uncompleted questions
500-590	Attempt to complete at least 75% of questions	average of 2 minutes, 20 seconds per question, keep enough time to guess on uncompleted questions

However, since the questions at the start of each section are more critical than later questions, a greater amount of time than the average can be allotted to the early questions, and then the pace can be accelerated as the sections proceeds.

Timing Your Practice Sessions

One of the most important tools for test success is a timer. When working with paper tests or the *Official Guide for GMAT Review,* your timer should be a constant companion during your GMAT preparation.

Although not all of your practice needs to be timed, you should attempt to do as many questions as possible under timed conditions. Time pressure is the top concern cited by test takers, and practicing with a timer will help acquaint you with the challenges of the test. After all, if the GMAT was a take-home test, no one would be too worried about it.

When practicing with a timer, keep notes about how many questions you complete in a given amount of time. You should vary your approach so that practice does not become boring. For example, you could track how long it takes to complete 3, 5, or 8 questions. Or you could see how many questions you can complete in 6 or 10 minutes. Trying different approaches will help you get the best sense of how fast you can go while still maintaining a high degree of accuracy.

A timer is invaluable because it is both an odometer and speedometer for your practice. With sufficient practice you will begin to establish a comfortable Critical Reasoning speed and the timer allows you to make sure you are maintaining this pace. Whether you use a watch, stopwatch, or kitchen timer is irrelevant; just make sure you time yourself rigorously.

When you learn a new concept or are practicing with a certain technique, you should begin by doing the first several problems untimed in order to get a feel for how the idea operates. Once you feel comfortable with the concept, begin tracking the time it takes you to complete each question. At first, do not worry about completing the question within a specified time frame, but rather examine how long it takes you to do each question when you are relaxed. After doing another 3 or 4 questions in this fashion, then begin attempting to complete each question in the time frame allowed on the test. Thus, you can "ramp up" to the appropriate time per question.

Excellent silent countdown timers can be purchased through our website at powerscore.com.

CHAPTER ONE: INTRODUCTION

Computers and Noteboards

Taking a standardized test on a computer is an unusual experience. The natural tendency to mark up the page is thwarted since you cannot write on the computer screen. Consequently, using the noteboards provided is an important aid to smooth test performance. Five noteboards will be supplied by the test administrator. You may not erase your work, but you can request more noteboards during the test if you run out of space.

During the pre-test tutorial, use part of one noteboard to quickly draw out the following chart:

A							
B							
C							
D							
E							

As you progress though each question, you can use the chart to keep track of eliminated answer choices as is necessary. For example, if you are certain answer choices (A) and (C) are incorrect in problem #2, simply "X" them out on the chart:

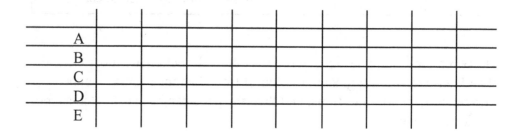

	2						
A	X						
B							
C	X						
D							
E							

In this fashion you can overcome the inability to physically mark out answer choices on the computer screen.

You should also familiarize yourself with GMAT CAT computer controls since computer aptitude is clearly an advantage. The test is given on standard computers, and the free GMATPrep Software contains test tutorials to help you gain experience with the GMAT computer controls. In addition, in the Analytical Writing Section, your typing ability affects overall performance, and thus you must have at least basic typing skills.

The GMAT Scoring Scale

Every GMAT score report contains five sections:

- An Integrated Reasoning Score—on a scale of 1 to 8
- A Quantitative Score—on a scale of 0 to 60
- A Verbal Score—on a scale of 0 to 60
- A Total Score—on a scale of 200 to 800
- An Analytical Writing Assessment Score—on a scale of 0 to 6

The Quantitative and Verbal scores are combined to create the Total Score. The Total Score is the one most familiar to GMAT test takers, and it is given on the famous 200 to 800 scale, with 200 being the lowest score and 800 the highest score.

The Integrated Reasoning Score is scaled in 1-point increments, and does not contribute to your Total Score.

The Analytical Writing Assessment essay is initially scored on a 0 to 6 scale (in half-point increments) by two readers—one human reader, and one machine reader (basically, a computer scoring program). The two scores are averaged to produce a final score for your essay. Approximately 90% of all test takers receive a score of 3.5 or higher.

Your AWA score has no effect on your Total Score.

The GMAT Percentile Table

It is important not to lose sight of what the GMAT Total Score actually represents. The 200 to 800 test scale contains 61 different possible scores. Each score places a student in a certain relative position compared to other test takers. These relative positions are represented through a percentile that correlates to each score. The percentile indicates where the test taker ranks in the overall pool of test takers. For example, a score of 700 represents the 90th percentile, meaning a student with a score of 700 scored better than 90 percent of the people who have taken the test in the last two years. The percentile is critical since it is a true indicator of your positioning relative to other test takers, and thus business school applicants.

It is important to remember that you do not have to answer every question correctly in order to receive an excellent GMAT score. There is room for error, and accordingly you should never let any single question occupy an inordinate amount of your time.

Charting out the entire percentage table yields a rough "bell curve." The number of test takers in the 200s and 700s is very low (only 10% of all test takers receive a score in the 700s; only 3% in the 200s), and most test takers are bunched in the middle, comprising the "top" of the bell. In fact, approximately 30% of all test takers score between 450 and 550 inclusive, and about 50% of all test takers score between 400 and 600 inclusive.

The median score on the GMAT scale is roughly 550. The median, or middle, score is the score at which approximately 50% of test takers have a lower score and 50% of test takers have a higher score.

CHAPTER ONE: INTRODUCTION

The Use of the GMAT

The use of the GMAT in business school admissions is not without controversy. Experts agree that your GMAT score is one of the most important determinants of the type of school you can attend. At many business schools an "admissions index" consisting of your GMAT score and your undergraduate grade point average is used to help determine the relative standing of applicants, and at some schools a sufficiently high admissions index virtually guarantees your admission.

For all the importance of the GMAT, the exam is not without flaws. As a standardized test currently given in the computer adaptive format there are a number of skills that the GMAT cannot measure, including listening skills, note-taking ability, perseverance, etc. GMAC is aware of these limitations and on an regular basis they warn all business school admission offices about using the GMAT scores as the sole admission criterion. Still, because the test ultimately returns a number for each student, the tendency to rank applicants is strong. Fortunately, once you get to business school the GMAT is forgotten. For the time being consider the test a temporary hurdle you must leap in order to reach the ultimate goal.

For more information on the GMAT, or to register for the test, contact the Graduate Management Admission Council at their website at www.mba.com.

Chapter Two:
The Basics of Critical Reasoning

Chapter Two: The Basics of Critical Reasoning

GMAT Critical Reasoning 17
Critical Reasoning Question Directions 17
The Parts of a Critical Reasoning Question 18
Approaching the Questions 19
Analyzing the Stimulus 21
The Range of Stimulus Topics 22
GMAT Vocabulary 23
Arguments versus Fact Sets 25
Identifying Premises and Conclusions 26
One Confusing Indicator Form 29
Premise and Conclusion Recognition Mini-Drill 30
Additional Premise Indicators 33
Counter-Premise Indicators 34
Additional Premise and Counter-Premise Recognition Mini-Drill 35
Recognizing Conclusions Without Indicators 37
Complex Arguments 38
A Commonly Used Construction 40
Truth versus Validity 41
Argument Analysis 42
Inferences and Assumptions 44
The Mind of a GMAT Author 44
Read the Fine Print 45
Tracking Indicators and Concepts 47
Scope 47
Fluidity of Analysis and Concept Application 48
Final Chapter Note 48
Premise and Conclusion Analysis Drill 49

GMAT Critical Reasoning

The focus of this book is on GMAT Critical Reasoning, and each Verbal section contains a total of 10 to 14 Critical Reasoning questions. When the total time allotted is weighed against the total number of questions in the Verbal section, you have an average of approximately one minute and forty-nine seconds to complete each question. Of course, the amount of time you spend on each question will vary with the difficulty of each question. For virtually all students the time constraint is a major obstacle, and as we progress through this book we will discuss time-saving techniques that you can employ within the section.

On average, you have 1 minute and 49 seconds to complete each question.

Critical Reasoning Question Directions

The general directions for Critical Reasoning problems are short and seemingly simple:

"For each question, select the best of the given answer choices."

Because these directions always precede first question in the Verbal section, you should familiarize yourself with them now. Once the GMAT begins, *never* waste time reading the question directions in any section.

Let's examine the directions more closely. Consider the following phrase: "select the best of the answer choices given." By stating up front that answers have comparative value and some are better than others, the makers of the test compel you to read every single answer choice before making a selection. If you read only one or two answer choices and then decide you have the correct one, you could end up choosing an answer that has some merit but is not as good as a later answer. One of the test makers' favorite tricks is to place a highly attractive wrong answer choice immediately before the correct answer choice in the hopes that you will pick the wrong answer choice and then move to the next question without reading any of the other answers.

Always read each of the five answer choices before deciding which answer is correct.

What is notable about the directions is what is *not* stated. No mention is made of whether to accept all statements as true, nor is any comment made about what you should assume about each question. A bit later in this chapter we will address the truth of the statements in each passage, but let's take a moment to talk about the assumptions that underlie each problem. In general, standardized tests such as the GMAT operate on "common sense" grounds; that is, you should only assume things that would be considered common sense or widely known to the general public. The implication is that you can make some assumptions when working with questions, but not other assumptions. Of course, the GMAC does not hand out a list of what constitutes a reasonable assumption!

Assumptions are a critical part of GMAT Critical Reasoning, and we will talk about assumptions in more detail in a later chapter.

CHAPTER TWO: THE BASICS OF CRITICAL REASONING

Even outside of the GMAT, the test makers do not clearly state what assumptions are acceptable or unacceptable for you to make, mainly because such a list would be almost infinite. For GMAT purposes, as you approach each question you can take as true any statement or idea that an average person would be expected to believe on the basis of generally known and accepted facts. For example, in a question you can assume that the sky sometimes becomes cloudy, but you cannot assume that the sky is always cloudy (unless stated explicitly by the question). GMAT questions will *not* require you to make assumptions based on extreme ideas (such as that it always rains in Seattle) or ideas not in the general domain of knowledge (such as the per capita income of residents of France). Please note that this does not mean that the GMAT cannot set up scenarios where they discuss ideas that are extreme or outside the bounds of common knowledge. Within a Critical Reasoning question, the test makers can and do discuss complex or extreme ideas; in these cases, they will give you context for the situation by providing additional information. However, be careful about assuming something to be true (unless you believe it is a widely accepted fact or the test makers indicate you should believe it to be true). This last idea is one we will discuss in much more detail as we look at individual question types.

Here's a good example of what they expect you to assume: when "television" is introduced in a stimulus, they expect you to know, among other things, what a TV show is, that TV can portray the make-believe or real, what actors do, and that TV is shown by transmitting signals into TV sets in homes and elsewhere.

The Parts of a Critical Reasoning Question

Every Critical Reasoning question contains three separate parts: the stimulus, the question stem, and the five answer choices. The following diagram identifies each part:

The question to the right is presented for demonstration purposes only. For those of you who wish to try the problem now, the correct answer is listed in the first sidebar on the next page.

1. No accountant at Merge Company is an executive, but all the executives at the company graduated from Blesston College, and every Blesston graduate is female. ←——— Stimulus

   Each of the following must be true on the basis of the statements above EXCEPT? ←——— Question Stem

   (A) Every Merge Company executive is female.
   (B) Most Blesston graduates are not accountants.
   (C) There are no male executives at Merge Company.   ←——— Answer Choices
   (D) Some Blesston College graduates are not accountants.
   (E) Some females are not accountants.

As a technical note, on the GMAT CAT an empty answer bubble appears next to each answer, and there is no letter in the bubble. However, for the convenience of discussion, throughout this book we will present problems with the answer choices lettered (A) through (E).

Approaching the Questions

When examining the three parts, students sometimes wonder about the best strategy for attacking a question: should I read the question stem first? Should I preview the five answer choices? The correct answer is *Read the parts in the order given*. That is, first read the stimulus, then read the question stem, and finally read each of the five answer choices. Although this may seem like a reasonable, even obvious, approach we mention it here because some GMAT texts advocate always reading the question stem before reading the stimulus. We are certain that these texts are seriously mistaken, and here are a few reasons why:

1. Understanding the stimulus is the key to answering any question, and reading the question stem first tends to undermine the ability of students to fully comprehend the information in the stimulus. On easy questions this distraction tends not to have a significant negative impact, but on more difficult questions the student often is forced to read the stimulus twice in order to get full comprehension, thus wasting valuable time. Literally, by reading the question stem first, students are forced to juggle two things at once: the question stem and the information in the stimulus. That is a difficult task when under time pressure. The bottom line is that any viable strategy must be effective for questions at all difficulty levels, but when you read the question stem first you cannot perform optimally. True, the approach works with the easy questions, but those questions could have been answered correctly regardless of the approach used.

2. Reading the question stem first often wastes valuable time since the typical student will read the stem, then read the stimulus, and then read the stem again. Unfortunately, there simply is not enough time to read every question stem twice.

3. Some question stems refer to information given in the stimulus, or add new conditions to the stimulus information. Thus, reading the stem first is of little value and often confuses or distracts the student when he or she goes to read the stimulus.

4. On stimuli with two questions, reading one stem biases the reader to look for that specific information, possibly causing problems while doing the second question, and reading both stems before reading the stimulus wastes entirely too much time and leads to confusion.

5. For truly knowledgeable test takers there are situations that arise where the question stem is fairly predictable. One example—and there are others—is with a question type called Resolve the Paradox. Usually, when you read the stimulus that accompanies these questions, an obvious paradox or discrepancy is presented. Reading the question

The correct answer to the problem on the previous page is answer choice (B).

On those rare occasions when the question stem is presented before the stimulus, read the question stem first (since it appears first). This happens primarily with Fill in the Blank questions (which will be covered in later chapters).

In our experience, the vast majority of high-scoring GMAT takers read the stimulus first.

CHAPTER TWO: THE BASICS OF CRITICAL REASONING

stem beforehand does not add anything to what you would have known just from reading the stimulus. In later chapters we will discuss this situation and others where you can predict the question stem with some success.

6. Finally, one of the main principles underlying the read-the-question-stem-first approach is flawed. Many advocates of the approach claim that it helps the test taker identify and skip (by simply guessing instead of doing the question) the "harder" question types such as Parallel Reasoning or Method of Reasoning. However, test data show that questions of any type can be hard or easy. Some Parallel Reasoning questions are phenomenally easy whereas some Parallel Reasoning questions are extremely difficult. In short, the question stem is a poor indicator of difficulty because question difficulty is more directly related to the complexity of the stimulus and the corresponding answer choices.

Understandably, reading the question stem before the stimulus sounds like a good idea at first, but for the majority of students (especially those trying to score in the 600s and above), the approach is a hindrance, not a help. Solid test performance depends on your ability to quickly comprehend complex argumentation; do not make your task harder by reading the question stem first.

A combined glossary and index appears at the end of this book, on page 363. Use it to look up any term you do not understand, or to find the page references where a concept is discussed in detail.

Analyzing the Stimulus

As you read the stimulus, initially focus on making a quick analysis of the topic under discussion. What area has the author chosen to write about? You will be more familiar with some topics than with others, but do not assume that everything you know "outside" of the stimulus regarding the topic is true and applies to the stimulus. For example, say you work in a real estate office and you come across a GMAT question about property sales. You can use your work experience and knowledge of real estate to help you better understand what the author is discussing, but do not assume that things will operate in the stimulus exactly as they do at your workplace. Perhaps property transactions in your state or country are different from those in other states or countries, or perhaps protocols followed in your office differ from those elsewhere. In a GMAT question, look carefully at what the author says about the topic at hand; statements presented as facts on the GMAT can and do vary from what occurs in the "real world." This discrepancy between the "GMAT world" and the "real world" is one you must always be aware of: although the two worlds overlap, things in the GMAT world are often very different from what you expect. From our earlier discussion of common sense assumptions we know that you can assume that basic, widely-held facts will hold true in the GMAT world, but by the same token, you cannot assume that specialized information that you have learned in the real world will hold true on the GMAT. We will discuss "outside information" in more detail when we discuss GMAT question types.

Next, make sure to read the entire stimulus very carefully. The makers of the GMAT have extraordinarily high expectations about the level of detail you should retain when you read a stimulus. Many questions will test your knowledge of small, seemingly nitpicky variations in phrasing, and reading carelessly is GMAT suicide. In many respects, the requirement forced upon you to read carefully is what makes the time constraint so difficult to handle. Every test taker is placed at the nexus of two competing elements: the need for speed (caused by the timed element) and the need for patience (caused by the detailed reading requirement). How well you manage these two elements strongly determines how well you perform. In the previous chapter we discussed how to practice using time elements, so make sure to use those ideas as you work through practice questions both in this book and in your other test materials.

Reading closely is a critical GMAT skill.

Finally, analyze the structure of the stimulus: what pieces are present and how do those pieces relate to each other? In short, you are tasked with knowing as much as possible about the statements made by the author, and in order to do so, you must understand how the test makers create GMAT arguments. We will discuss argumentation in more detail in a moment.

GMAT argumentation is one of the main topics of this book, and will be discussed in every chapter.

CHAPTER TWO: THE BASICS OF CRITICAL REASONING

The Range of Stimulus Topics

The spectrum of topics covered by Critical Reasoning stimuli is quite broad. Previous stimuli topics have ranged from art to business to medicine and science. According to the makers of the test, "Because the Verbal section includes content from a variety of topics, you may be generally familiar with some of the material; however, neither the passages nor the questions assume knowledge of the topics discussed."

Despite the previous statement, many GMAT students come from a humanities or business background and these test takers often worry about stimuli containing scientific, medical or even technological topics. Remember, the topic of a stimulus does *not* affect the underlying logical relationship of the argument parts. And, the GMAT will not assume that you know anything about advanced technical or scientific ideas. For example, while the GMAT may discuss mathematicians or the existence of a difficult problem in math, you will not be asked to make calculations nor will you be assumed to understand esoteric terminology. Any element beyond the domain of general public knowledge will be explained for you, as in the following example:

Some specific topics do recur, and we will note those in future chapters.

> Researcher: Einstein's *Annus Mirabilis Papers*, the 1905 works that introduced some of his most notable and recognizable theories, were at first overlooked by many physicists of the time, and flatly rejected by others. These works were so important, however, that years...

The stimulus above, although reproduced only in part, is a good example of how the test makers will supply information they feel is essential to understanding the question. In this case, the reader is not expected to understand either the content or historical importance of Einstein's *Annus Mirabilis Papers*, and so the test makers conveniently furnish that information. Thus, although on occasion you will see a stimulus that references an ominous looking word or idea (examples include *high-density lipoprotein*, *aphasia*, and *pironoma*), you will not need to know or be assumed to know anything more about those elements than what you are told by the test makers.

When you read a science-based stimulus, focus on understanding the relationship of the ideas and do not be intimidated by the terminology used by the author. As we will ultimately find, reading a GMAT stimulus is about seeing past the topic to analyze the structural relationships present in the stimulus. Once you are able to see these relationships, the topic will become less important.

GMAT Vocabulary

Continuing the theme from the prior section, students are often concerned that success on GMAT Critical Reasoning questions requires an especially large vocabulary, or perhaps a working knowledge of logical terms. In fact, much of the language featured on the GMAT is made up of common, familiar terms (such as "city," "job," and "fuel") that most native English speakers would not find challenging, and that non-native speakers would largely find familiar. Of course, it's not the simple words that worry most people. It's the comparatively small number of less familiar terms that tend to cause the most concern. Challenging GMAT vocabulary thus falls into three distinct categories:

1. Advanced Words

    "Advanced words" are the high-level vocabulary words that you rarely encounter in daily life. Examples (not from the GMAT) would include words such as "tenebrous" or "recondite." Those are words that you just do not hear in normal conversation with your friends, classmates, or coworkers! Fortunately, words that are this obscure almost never appear on the GMAT, and generally the most difficult vocabulary words that appear on the test are challenging but somewhat more common—words such as "discord" or "forage" (both of which *have* been used on the GMAT).

    Tenebrous: gloomy or dark

    Recondite: beyond ordinary understanding

    When considering what vocabulary level is required for a strong GMAT performance, let's consider what the test makers have to say about the issue. According to GMAC, "The GMAT test is administered in English and is designed for programs that teach in English. But the exam requires just enough English to allow us to adequately and comprehensively assess Verbal reasoning, Quantitative reasoning and Integrated Reasoning skills." So, there is no expectation of a high-level vocabulary, but there is no precise definition as to what that means, and certainly no published list of words that do and do not constitute an adequate vocabulary.

    So, should you study a list of hard vocabulary words in preparation for the GMAT? The answer is No. First, you would likely be wasting a huge amount of time preparing for words that you most likely would not see on the test. Second, and more importantly, there is a compensation when challenging vocabulary is used: when this happens, GMAT authors generally either define such terms or provide sufficient context in the passage to determine what the word means. For example, a GMAT question about land used the word "arid," but then followed that usage by referring to the use of water in the area being strictly controlled. Thus, even without knowing the meaning of "arid," you could infer that

CHAPTER TWO: THE BASICS OF CRITICAL REASONING

it was related to a lack of water, and thus still easily complete the question. The bottom line is that in most cases, when you encounter what would be termed as higher-level vocabulary, there will be information around that usage that helps you to understand the meaning of the given term.

2. Scientific/Technical/Legal Jargon

    As mentioned previously, specialized terminology can be among the scariest vocabulary you encounter on the GMAT. Seeing terms such as "pellagra," "irradiation," or "pineal gland" will cause most test takers to pause for a moment. However, such specialized terms are beyond the general vocabulary of almost every GMAT taker, so GMAC would not expect test takers to be familiar with them. In each instance, a definition or usage information will be supplied in the stimulus. Although definitions are often in the immediate vicinity of the first appearance of the word, in some cases (notably in Reading Comprehension passages) the definition is provided a number of lines later. Regardless, when you see terms of this type, you should begin looking for the definition that will almost certainly be provided (and relax, because you will not have to guess at the meaning of the word).

3. Logical Terminology

    While the GMAT does not require you to understand specific terms from the scientific, medical, technical, or legal worlds, some GMAT Critical Reasoning questions do hinge on your knowledge of certain words or phrases that are part of the logical canon of the test. Most of the words that present problems are not specialized logic terms, though, and thus you will not be expected to know the meaning of specialized terms such as "ad hominem" or "syllogism." Instead, you will at times be required to be familiar with argument terms such as "conclusion" or "analogy." Later in this book we will cover each of those terms (and many more!) in greater detail.

Arguments versus Fact Sets

GMAT stimuli fall into two distinct categories: those containing an argument and those that are just a set of facts. Logically speaking, an argument can be defined as a set of statements wherein one statement is claimed to follow from or be derived from the others. Consider the following short example of an argument:

> All professors are ethical. Mason is a professor. So Mason is ethical.

The first two statements in this argument give the reasons (or "premises") for accepting the third statement, which is the conclusion of the argument.

Fact sets, on the other hand, are a collection of statements without a conclusion, as in the following example:

> "The Jacksonville area has just over one million residents. The Cincinnati area has almost two million residents. The New York area has almost twenty million residents."

The three sentences above do *not* constitute an argument because no conclusion is present and an argument, by definition, requires a conclusion. The three sentences merely make a series of assertions without making a judgment. Notice that reading these sentences does not cause much of a reaction in most readers. Really, who cares about the city sizes? This lack of a strong reaction is often an indication that you are not reading an argument and are instead reading just a set of facts.

When reading Critical Reasoning stimuli, you should seek to make several key determinations, which we call the Critical Reasoning Primary Objectives™.

Your first task is to determine if you are reading an argument or a fact set.

Primary Objective #1: Determine whether the stimulus contains an argument or if it is only a set of factual statements.

To achieve this objective, you must recognize whether a conclusion is present. Let us talk about how to do this next.

There are many books on logic and argumentation. In this book we attempt to concisely spell out what you need to know to succeed on the GMAT. This is different from philosophical logic, and therefore this section will not teach you argumentation as it is taught in a university.

Fact sets rarely cause a strong reaction in the reader because no persuasion is being used. When an author attempts to persuade you to believe a certain conclusion, there tends to be a noticeable reaction.

Identifying Premises and Conclusions

For GMAT purposes, a premise can be defined as:

"A fact, proposition, or statement from which a conclusion is made."

A premise gives a reason why something should be believed.

Premises support and explain the conclusion. Literally, the premises give the reasons why the conclusion should be accepted. To identify premises, ask yourself, "*What reasons has the author used to persuade me? Why should I believe this argument? What evidence exists?*"

A conclusion can be defined as:

"A statement or judgment that follows from one or more reasons."

A conclusion is the point the author tries to prove by using another statement.

Conclusions, as summary statements, are supposed to be drawn from and rest on the premises. To identify conclusions, ask yourself, "*What is the author driving at? What does the author want me to believe? What point follows from the others?*"

Because language is the test maker's weapon of choice, you must learn to recognize the words that indicate when a premise or conclusion is present. In expressing arguments, authors often use the following words or phrases to introduce premises and conclusions:

Make sure to memorize these word lists. Recognizing argument elements is critical!

Remember that words can be used in different ways. Thus, a word can appear on this list and not be used as a premise or conclusion indicator.

Premise Indicators	Conclusion Indicators
because	thus
since	therefore
for	hence
for example	consequently
for the reason that	as a result
in that	so
given that	accordingly
as indicated by	clearly
due to	must be that
owing to	shows that
this can be seen from	conclude that
we know this by	follows that
	for this reason

26   THE POWERSCORE GMAT CRITICAL REASONING BIBLE

Because there are so many variations in the English language, these lists cannot be comprehensive, but they do capture many of the premise and conclusion indicators used by GMAT authors. As for frequency of appearance, the top two words in each list are used more than any of the other words in the list.

Arguments can contain more than one premise and more than one conclusion.

When you are reading, always be aware of the presence of the words listed above. These words are like road signs; they tell you what is coming next. Consider the following example:

> Humans cannot live on Venus because the surface temperature is too high.

As you read the first portion of the sentence, "Humans cannot live on Venus," you cannot be sure if you are reading a premise or conclusion. But, as soon as you see the word "because"—a premise indicator—you know that a premise will follow, and at that point you know that the first portion of the sentence is a conclusion. In the argument above, the author wants you to believe that humans cannot live on Venus, and the reason is that the surface temperature is too high.

About 80% to 85% of GMAT stimuli contain arguments. The remainder are fact sets.

In our daily lives, we make and hear many arguments. However, unlike on the GMAT, the majority of these arguments occur in the form of conversations (and when we say "argument," we do not mean a fight!). Any GMAT argument can be seen as an artificial conversation, even the basic example above:

> Author: "Humans cannot live on Venus."
>
> Respondent: "Really? Why is that?"
>
> Author: "The surface temperature of Venus is too high."

One way to visualize the relationship of premises and conclusions is to think of an argument as a house. The premises are like the walls of the house, and the conclusion is like the roof—supported by those walls. Another analogy that might help you to visualize the relationship is that of a table: the premises are the legs, and the conclusion is the tabletop.

If at first you struggle to identify the pieces of an argument, you can always resort to thinking about the argument as an artificial conversation and that may assist you in locating the conclusion.

Here are more examples of premise and conclusion indicators in use:

1. "The economy is in tatters. Therefore, we must end this war."

    "Therefore" introduces a conclusion; the first sentence is a premise.

CHAPTER TWO: THE BASICS OF CRITICAL REASONING

Important note: premises and conclusions can be constructed without indicator words present.

2. "We must reduce our budget due to the significant cost overruns we experienced during production."

"due to" introduces a premise; "We must reduce our budget" is the conclusion.

3. "Fraud has cost the insurance industry millions of dollars in lost revenue. Thus, congress will pass a stricter fraud control bill since the insurance industry has one of the most powerful lobbies."

This argument contains two premises: the first premise is the first sentence and the second premise follows the word "since" in the second sentence; the conclusion is "congress will pass a stricter fraud control bill."

Order of presentation has no effect on the logical structure of the argument. The conclusion can appear at the beginning, the middle, or the end of the argument.

Notice that premises and conclusions can be presented in any order—the conclusion can be first or last, and the relationship between the premises and the conclusion remains the same regardless of the order of presentation. For example, if the order of the premise(s) and conclusion was switched in any of the examples above, the logical structure of the argument would not change.

Also notable is that the premises and the conclusion can appear in the same sentence, or be separated out into multiple sentences. Whether the ideas are together or separated has no effect on the logical structure of the argument.

If a conclusion is present, you *must* identify the conclusion prior to proceeding on to the question stem. Often, the reason students miss questions is because they have failed to fully and accurately identify the conclusion of the argument.

Remember, a fact set does not contain a conclusion; an argument must contain a conclusion.

Primary Objective #2: If the stimulus contains an argument, identify the conclusion of the argument. If the stimulus contains a fact set, examine each fact.

One Confusing Indicator Form

Because the job of the test makers is to determine how well you can interpret information, they will sometimes arrange premise and conclusion indicators in a way that is designed to be confusing. One of their most confusing forms places a conclusion indicator and premise indicator back-to-back, separated by a comma, as in the following examples:

"Therefore, since..."

"Thus, because..."

"Hence, due to..."

This form is called the "conclusion/premise indicator form."

A quick glance would seemingly indicate that what will follow is both a premise and a conclusion. In this instance, however, the presence of the comma creates a clause that, due to the premise indicator, contains a premise. The end of that premise clause will be closed with a second comma, and then what follows will be the conclusion, as in the following:

"Therefore, since higher debt has forced consumers to lower their savings, banks now have less money to loan."

"Higher debt has forced consumers to lower their savings" is the premise; "banks now have less money to loan" is the conclusion. So, in this instance "therefore" still introduces a conclusion, but the appearance of the conclusion is interrupted by a clause that contains a premise.

CHAPTER TWO: THE BASICS OF CRITICAL REASONING

Premise and Conclusion Recognition Mini-Drill

Each of the following problems contains a short argument. For each argument, identify the conclusion and the premise(s). *Answers on page 31*

1. "Given that the price of steel is rising, we will no longer be able to offer discounts on our car parts."

2. "The political situation in Somalia is unstable owing to the ability of individual warlords to maintain powerful armed forces."

3. "Since we need to have many different interests to sustain us, the scientists' belief must be incorrect."

4. "So, as indicated by the newly released data, we should push forward with our efforts to recolonize the forest with snowy tree crickets."

5. "Television has a harmful effect on society. This can be seen from the poor school performance of children who watch significant amounts of television and from the fact that children who watch more than six hours of television a day tend to read less than non-television watching children."

6. "The rapid diminishment of the ecosystem of the Amazon threatens the entire planet. Consequently, we must take immediate steps to convince the Brazilian government that planned development projects need to be curtailed for the simple reason that these development projects will greatly accelerate the loss of currently protected land."

Premise and Conclusion Recognition Mini-Drill Answer Key

1. Features the premise indicator "given that."

    Premise: "Given that the price of steel is rising,"

    Conclusion: "we will no longer be able to offer discounts on our car parts."

2. Features the premise indicator "owing to."

    Premise: "owing to the ability of individual warlords to maintain powerful armed forces."

    Conclusion: "The political situation in Somalia is unstable"

3. Features the premise indicator "since."

    Premise: "Since we need to have many different interests to sustain us,"

    Conclusion: "the scientists' belief must be incorrect."

4. Features the conclusion/premise form indicator "So, as indicated by."

    Premise: "as indicated by the newly released data"

    Conclusion: "we should push forward with our efforts to recolonize the forest with snowy tree crickets."

Premise and Conclusion Recognition Mini-Drill Answer Key

5. Features the premise indicator "this can be seen from." The second sentence contains two premises.

    Premise 1:   "This can be seen from the poor school performance of children who watch significant amounts of television"

    Premise 2:   "and from the fact that children who watch more than six hours of television a day tend to read less than non-television watching children."

    Conclusion: "Television has a harmful effect on society." Note how this sentence does not contain a conclusion indicator. Yet, we can determine that this is the conclusion because the other sentence contains two premises.

6. Features the conclusion indicator "consequently" and the premise indicator "for the simple reason that." There are also two premises present.

    Premise 1:   "The rapid diminishment of the ecosystem of the Amazon threatens the entire planet."

    Premise 2:   "for the simple reason that these development projects will greatly accelerate the loss of currently protected land."

    Conclusion: "we must take immediate steps to convince the Brazilian government that planned development projects need to be curtailed"

Additional Premise Indicators

Aside from previously listed premise and conclusions indicators, there are other argument indicator words you should learn to recognize. First, in argument forms, sometimes the author will make an argument and then for good measure add another premise that supports the conclusion but is sometimes non-essential to the conclusion. These are known as *additional premises*:

Additional Premise Indicators
Furthermore
Moreover
Besides
In addition
What's more
After all

Additional premises are still, of course, premises. They may be central to the argument or they may be secondary. To determine the importance of the premise, examine the remainder of the argument.

Following are two examples of additional premise indicators in use:

1. "Every professor at Fillmore University teaches exactly one class per semester. Fillmore's Professor Jackson, therefore, is teaching exactly one class this semester. Moreover, I heard Professor Jackson say she was teaching only a single class."

    The first sentence is a premise. The second sentence contains the conclusion indicator "therefore" and is the conclusion of the argument. The first sentence is the main proof offered by the author for the conclusion. The third sentence begins with the additional premise indicator "moreover." The premise in this sentence is non-essential to the argument, but provides additional proof for the conclusion and could be, if needed, used to help prove the conclusion separately (this would occur if an objection was raised to the first premise).

2. "The city council ought to ease restrictions on outdoor advertising because the city's economy is currently in a slump. Furthermore, the city should not place restrictions on forms of speech such as advertising."

    The first sentence contains both the conclusion of the argument and the main premise of the argument (introduced by the premise indicator "because"). The last sentence contains the additional premise indicator "furthermore." As with the previous example, the additional premise in this sentence is non-essential to the argument but provides additional proof for the conclusion.

CHAPTER TWO: THE BASICS OF CRITICAL REASONING

Counter-Premise Indicators

Counter-premises, also called adversatives, bring up points of opposition or comparison.

When creating an argument, an author will sometimes bring up a counter-premise—a premise that actually contains an idea that is counter to the argument. At first glance, this might seem like an odd thing for an author to do. But by raising the counter-premise and then addressing the complaint in a direct fashion, the author can minimize the damage that would be done by the objection if it were raised elsewhere.

Counter-premises can also be ideas that compare and contrast with the argument, or work against a previously raised point. In this sense, the general counter-premise concept discusses an idea that is in some way different from another part of the argument.

Note that some terms, such as "After all," can appear on multiple indicator lists because the phrase can be used in a variety of ways. As a savvy GMAT taker, it is up to you to identify the exact role that the phrase is playing in the argument.

Counter-premise Indicators
But
Yet
However
On the other hand
Admittedly
In contrast
Although
Even though
Still
Whereas
In spite of
Despite
After all

Following is an example of a counter-premise indicator in use:

1. "The United States prison population is the world's largest, and consequently we must take steps to reduce crime in this country. Although other countries have higher rates of incarceration, their statistics have no bearing on the dilemma we currently face."

    The first sentence contains a premise and the conclusion (which is introduced by the conclusion indicator "consequently"). The second sentence offers up a counter-premise as indicated by the word "although."

Additional Premise and Counter-Premise Recognition Mini-Drill

Each of the following problems contains a short argument. For each argument, identify the conclusion, the premise(s), and any additional premises or counter-premises. *Answers on page 36*

1. Wine is made by crushing grapes and eventually separating the juice from the grape skins. However, the separated juice contains impurities and many wineries do not filter the juice. These wineries claim the unfiltered juice ultimately produces a more flavorful and intense wine. Since these wine makers are experts, we should trust their judgment and not shy away from unfiltered wine.

2. Phenylketonurics are people who cannot metabolize the amino acid phenylalanine. There are dangers associated with phenylketonuria, and products containing phenylalanine must carry a warning label that states, "Phenylketonurics: contains phenylalanine." In addition, all children in developed societies receive a phenylketonuria test at birth. Hence, at the moment, we are doing as much as possible to protect against this condition.

3. During last night's robbery, the thief was unable to open the safe. Thus, last night's robbery was unsuccessful despite the fact that the thief stole several documents. After all, nothing in those documents was as valuable as the money in the safe.

Additional Premise and Counter-Premise Recognition Mini-Drill Answer Key

1. Features the counter-premise indicator "however" and the premise indicator "since."

    Premise: "Wine is made by crushing grapes and eventually separating the juice from the grape skins."

    Counter-premise: "However, the separated juice contains impurities and many wineries do not filter the juice."

    Premise: "These wineries claim the unfiltered juice ultimately produces a more flavorful and intense wine."

    Premise: "Since these wine makers are experts,"

    Conclusion: "we should trust their judgment and not shy away from unfiltered wine."

2. Features the additional premise indicator "in addition" and the conclusion indicator "hence." In this problem the additional premise is central to supporting the conclusion.

    Premise: "Phenylketonurics are people who cannot metabolize the amino acid phenylalanine."

    Premise: "There are dangers associated with phenylketonuria, and products containing phenylalanine must carry a warning label that states, 'Phenylketonurics: contains phenylalanine.'"

    Additional Premise: "In addition, all children in developed societies received a phenylketonuria test at birth."

    Conclusion: "Hence, at the moment, we are doing as much as possible to protect against this condition."

3. Features the counter-premise indicator "despite"; the additional premise indicator "after all"; and the conclusion indicator "thus." The additional premise serves to downplay the counter-premise.

    Premise: "During last night's robbery, the thief was unable to open the safe."

    Counter-premise: "despite the fact that the thief stole several documents."

    Additional Premise: "After all, nothing in those documents was as valuable as the money in the safe."

    Conclusion: "Thus, last night's robbery was unsuccessful."

Recognizing Conclusions Without Indicators

Many of the arguments we have encountered up until this point have had conclusion indicators to help you recognize the conclusion. And, many of the arguments you will see on the GMAT will also have conclusion indicators. But you will encounter arguments that do not contain conclusion indicators. Following is an example:

> The best way of eliminating traffic congestion will not be easily found. There are so many competing possibilities that it will take millions of dollars to study every option, and implementation of most options carries an exorbitant price tag.

An argument such as the above can be difficult to analyze because no indicator words are present. How then, would you go about determining if a conclusion is present, and if so, how would you identify that conclusion? Fortunately, there is a fairly simple trick that can be used to handle this situation, and any situation where you are uncertain of the conclusion (even those with multiple conclusions, as will be discussed next).

Aside from the questions you can use to identify premises and conclusions (described earlier in this chapter), the easiest way to determine the conclusion in an argument is to use the Conclusion Identification Method™:

> Take the statements under consideration for the conclusion and mentally place them in an arrangement that forces one to be the conclusion and the other(s) to be the premise(s). Use premise and conclusion indicators to achieve this end. Once the pieces are arranged, determine if the arrangement makes logical sense. If so, you have made the correct identification. If not, reverse the arrangement and examine the relationship again. Continue until you find an arrangement that is logical.

Let us apply this method to the argument at the top of this page. For our first arrangement we will make the first sentence the premise and the second sentence the conclusion, and supply indicators (in italics):

> *Because* the best way of eliminating traffic congestion will not be easily found, *we can conclude that* there are so many competing possibilities that it will take millions of dollars to study every option, and implementation of most options carries an exorbitant price tag.

Does that sound right? No. Let us try again, this time making the first sentence the conclusion and the second sentence the premise:

CHAPTER TWO: THE BASICS OF CRITICAL REASONING

Because there are so many competing possibilities that it will take millions of dollars to study every option, and implementation of most options carries an exorbitant price tag, *we can conclude that* the best way of eliminating traffic congestion will not be easily found.

Clearly, the second arrangement is far superior because it makes sense. In most cases when you have the conclusion and premise backward, the arrangement will be confusing. The correct arrangement always sounds more logical.

Complex Arguments

Up until this point, we have only discussed simple arguments. Simple arguments contain a single conclusion. While many of the arguments that appear on the GMAT are simple arguments, there are also a fair number of complex arguments. Complex arguments contain more than one conclusion. In these instances, one of the conclusions is the main conclusion, and the other conclusions are subsidiary conclusions (also known as sub-conclusions).

A simple argument does not mean that the argument is easy to understand! Simple in this context means that the argument contains only a single conclusion.

While complex argumentation may sound daunting at first, you make and encounter complex argumentation every day in your life. In basic terms, a complex argument makes an initial conclusion based on a premise. The author then uses that conclusion as the foundation (or premise) for another conclusion, thus building a chain with several levels. Let us take a look at the two types of arguments in diagram form:

In abstract terms, a simple argument appears as follows:

As discussed previously, the premise supports the conclusion, hence the arrow from the premise to the conclusion. By comparison, a complex argument takes an initial conclusion and then uses it as a premise for another conclusion:

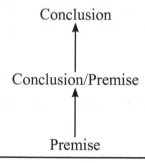

Thus, a statement can be both a conclusion for one argument and a premise for another. In this sense, a complex argument can appear somewhat like a ladder, where each level or "rung" is used to build the next level. Given enough time you could build an argument with hundreds of levels. On the GMAT, however, there are typically three or four levels at most. Let us look at an example of a complex argument:

> Because Germany has the best goalkeeper in soccer, they therefore have the best defense in soccer. Because they have the best defense in football, they will win the next World Cup.

In this argument, the first sentence contains a premise followed by a conclusion. This initial conclusion is then used in the second sentence as a premise to make a larger conclusion:

Premise: "Because Germany has the best goalkeeper in soccer,"

Sub-Conclusion (conclusion of the previous premise/Premise for the following conclusion): "they therefore have the best defense in soccer."

Main Conclusion: "they will win the next World Cup."

The makers of the GMAT love to use complex argumentation because the presence of multiple conclusions tends to confuse students, making attractive wrong answer choices easier to create.

As we will see in Chapter Ten while discussing Method of Reasoning questions, one of the most commonly used complex argument forms is to place the main conclusion in the first sentence of the argument, and then to place the sub-conclusion in the last sentence of the argument, preceded by a conclusion indicator. This form is quite useful since it tends to trick students into thinking the last sentence is the main conclusion.

Another form of complex argumentation occurs with two-speaker stimuli. In these questions, two separate speakers are identified, and each presents his or her own argument or comment. Here is an example:

Kimiko: Instead of spending additional monies on carbon-based technologies, the company should pursue "green" initiatives such as windpower. A simple step such as adding wind turbines to the top of the building would be cheaper than any carbon-based solution.

Tarik: The problem with your proposal is that, while environmentally sound, the wind turbines would not produce nearly enough power to supply the company's manufacturing operations. The company must pursue more reliable energy output options.

In the argument above, each speaker presents premises and a conclusion. As often occurs with this form of question, the two speakers disagree.

One of the benefits of a two-speaker stimulus is that the test makers can introduce multiple viewpoints on the same subject. As you might imagine, the presence of multiple viewpoints tends to be confusing, and the extra viewpoints offer the test makers the opportunity to ask a wider variety of questions.

A Commonly Used Construction

Even within a single-speaker stimulus the test makers can raise alternate viewpoints. One of the most frequently used constructions is to raise a viewpoint at the beginning of the stimulus and then disagree with it immediately thereafter. This efficiently raises two opposing views in a very short paragraph. These stimuli are recognizable because they often begin with the phrase, "Some people claim..." or one of the many variations on this theme, including but not limited to the following:

Although this construction typically appears at the beginning of a stimulus, it can appear later in the stimulus as well.

"Some people propose..."
"Many people believe..."
"Some argue that..." or "Some people argue that..."
"Some critics claim..."
"Some critics maintain..."
"Some scientists believe..."

The structure of this opening sentence is remarkably consistent in form, and adheres to the following formula:

A *number* (some, many, etc.) of *people* (critics, students, teachers, legislators, vegetarians, psychologists etc.) *believe* (claim, propose, argue, etc.) that...

Of course, there are exceptions, as with these opening sentences:

"Although some people claim..."   (starts with "although")
"It has been claimed that..."   (drops the *number* and *people*)
"Cigarette companies claim that..."   (drops the *number*)

The author can also break up the idea, by inserting contextual information, as in the following example:

"Some critics of space exploration programs claim that..."

The use of this device to begin a stimulus almost always leads to the introduction of the opposing view, as in the following partial stimulus:

> Politician: Some people claim that the best way to overcome the current economic recession is to decrease taxes and thus stimulate spending. This approach, however, is rather misguided...

The politician uses the "Some people claim" device to introduce one opinion of taxes and then in the following sentence counters the idea with the view that turns out to be the politician's main point ("This approach, however..."). The remainder of the problem went on to explain the reasoning behind the politician's view.

Given the frequency with which this construction appears at the beginning of stimuli, you should learn to begin recognizing it now. We will again discuss this device in the Main Point section.

Truth versus Validity

So far, we have only identified the parts that are used to construct arguments. We have not made an analysis of the reasonableness or soundness of an argument. But, before moving on to argument analysis, you must be able to distinguish between two commonly confused concepts: validity and truth.

When we evaluate GMAT arguments, we are primarily concerned with validity. That is, what is the logical relationship of the pieces of the argument and how well do the premises, if accepted, prove the conclusion? We are less concerned with the absolute, real world truthfulness of either the premises or the conclusion. Some students will at first try to analyze every single GMAT statement on the basis of whether it is an absolutely true statement (does it happen as stated in the real world). For the most part, that is wasted effort. GMAT Critical Reasoning is primarily focused on whether the conclusion follows logically from a set of given premises. In many cases, the GMAT makers will let you work under a framework where the premises are simply accepted as factually accurate, and then you must focus solely on the method used to reach the conclusion. In a sense this could be called relative truthfulness—you are only concerned about whether the conclusion is true relative to the premises, not whether the conclusion is true in an absolute, real world sense. This is obviously a critical point, and one we will analyze later as we discuss different question types.

Logicians spend a great deal of time discussing validity and truth, even going so far as to create complex truth tables that analyze the validity of arguments. We are not concerned with such methods because they do not apply to the GMAT.

CHAPTER TWO: THE BASICS OF CRITICAL REASONING

In logic, the terms "strong/weak," "good/bad," "valid/invalid," and "sound/unsound" are used to evaluate arguments. For our purposes, "strong," "good," "valid," and "sound" will be interchangeable and all terms refer to the logical structure of the argument. The same holds true for "weak," "bad," "invalid," and "unsound."

An argument can be valid without being true. For example, the following has a valid argument structure but is not "true" in a real world sense:

"All birds can fly. An ostrich is a bird. Therefore, an ostrich can fly."

When flaws are present in GMAT stimuli, the error usually occurs when the author draws a conclusion from the premises.

Argument Analysis

Once you have determined that an argument is present and you have identified the conclusion, you must determine if the argument is a good one or a bad one. This leads to the third Primary Objective:

Primary Objective #3: If the stimulus contains an argument, determine whether the argument is strong or weak.

To determine the strength of the argument, consider the relationship between the premises and the conclusion—do the premises strongly suggest that the conclusion would be true? Does the conclusion feel like an inevitable result of the premises? Or does the conclusion seem to go beyond the scope of the information in the premises? How persuasive does the argument seem to you? When evaluating argument validity, the question you must always ask yourself is: Do the given facts support the conclusion?

To better understand this concept we will examine two sample arguments. The following argument uses the fact set we used before, with the addition of a conclusion:

> "The Jacksonville, Florida area has just over one million residents. Cincinnati, Ohio has almost two million residents. The New York City area has almost twenty million residents. Therefore, we should move to Jacksonville."

The last sentence contains the conclusion, and makes this an argument. Notice how the presence of the conclusion causes you to react more strongly to the stimulus. Now, instead of just reading a set of cold facts, you are forced to consider whether the premises have proven the given conclusion. In this case the author asks you to accept that a move to Jacksonville is in order based on the population of the city. Do you think the author has proven this point?

When considering the above argument, most people simply accept the premises as factually accurate. There is nothing wrong with this (and indeed in the real world they are true, although this fact is irrelevant). As mentioned moments ago, in GMAT argumentation the makers of the test largely allow authors to put forth their premises unchallenged. The test makers are far more concerned about whether those premises lead to the conclusion presented. In the argument above, there is no reason to doubt the accuracy of the premises, but even if we accept the premises as accurate, we still do not have to accept the conclusion.

Most people reading the previous argument would agree that the reasoning is weak. Even though the premises are perfectly acceptable, by themselves they do not prove that "we should move to Jacksonville." The typical reader will experience a host of reactions to the conclusion: Why Jacksonville—why not a city that is even smaller? What about a larger city? What is so important about population? What about considerations other than population size? Because questions of this nature point to flaws in the argument, we would classify the argument as a poor one. That is, the premises do not prove the conclusion. As shown by this example, the acceptability of the premises does not automatically make the conclusion acceptable. The reverse is also true—the acceptability of the conclusion does not automatically make the premises acceptable.

Questions such as the ones posed in this paragraph suggest that the author has made unwarranted assumptions while constructing the argument. We will discuss assumptions in more detail later.

The following is an example of a strong argument:

> "Trees that shed their foliage annually are deciduous trees. Black Oak trees shed their leaves every year. Therefore, Black Oak trees are deciduous."

In this argument, the two premises lead directly to the conclusion. Unlike the previous argument, the author's conclusion seems reasonable and inevitable based on the two premises. Note that the strength of this argument is based solely on the degree to which the premises prove the conclusion. The truth of the premises themselves is not an issue in determining whether the argument is valid or invalid.

When analyzing GMAT arguments, track the strength of the conclusion relative to the premises. A conclusion can, independent of the premises, be strong or weak.

Note that the premises in an argument do not have to *prove* the conclusion for the conclusion to be valid. There are a number of conclusions which are just *probably true* based on the evidence provided. This is not a flaw in and of itself, because the author believes there is a good chance that the conclusion is true (for example: "The Post Office on Main Street has been closed every Sunday since 1956, so it will probably be closed this Sunday as well." Note that this is not flawed reasoning, because the use of the term "probably" allows for the possibility of other outcomes.). The idea of probability is one that can play an important role in GMAT argumentation, and you should always note the language used in conclusions, and how strongly that conclusion follows from the premises.

In this section, we touch on the ideas of inductive and deductive arguments, but you will not need to know those terms for the GMAT.

CHAPTER TWO: THE BASICS OF CRITICAL REASONING

Inferences and Assumptions

When glancing through GMAT questions, you will frequently see the words *inference* and *assumption*. Let us take a moment to define the meaning of each term in the context of GMAT argumentation.

Most people have come to believe that the word *inference* means probably true or likely to be true. Indeed, in common usage *infer* is often used in the same manner as *imply*. On the GMAT these uses are incorrect. In logic, an inference can be defined as something that *must be true*. Thus, if you are asked to identify an inference of the argument, you must find an item that must be true based on the information presented in the argument.

Earlier we discussed assumptions in the context of commonsense assumptions that you can bring into each problem. In argumentation, an assumption is simply the same as an *unstated* premise—what must be true in order for the argument to be true. Assumptions can often have a great effect on the validity of the argument.

Assumptions are a part of every argument, and we will discuss them in detail in Chapter Nine.

Separating an inference from an assumption can be difficult because the definition of each refers to what "must be true." The difference is simple: an inference is what follows from an argument (in other words, a conclusion) whereas an assumption is what is taken for granted while making an argument. In one sense, an assumption occurs "before" the argument, that is, while the argument is being made. An inference is made "after" the argument is complete, and follows from the argument. Both concepts will be discussed in more detail in later chapters, but for the time being you should note that all authors make assumptions when creating their arguments, and all arguments have inferences that can be derived from the argument.

The Mind of a GMAT Author

Let us take a moment to differentiate the makers of the test from the author of each stimulus. The maker of the test is the GMAC, the organization that oversees the protocols under which the GMAT is constructed, administers the test, and processes and distributes the results. The stated purpose of the test makers is to examine your ability to analyze arguments, in an attempt to assess your suitability for business school. The author of the stimulus is the person from whose point of view each piece is written or the source from which the piece is drawn. Sometimes the persona of the author is made abundantly clear to you because the stimulus is prefaced by a short identifier, such as *Division Manager* or *Reviewer*, or even a proper name such as *Roland* or *Sharon*. The source of a stimulus can also be made clear by similar identifiers, such as *Advertisement* or *Editorial*.

Actually, the GMAC is just the "producer" of the GMAT. The actual question construction is done by outside companies such as Pearson VUE and ACT, Inc.

GMAT students sometimes confuse the aim of the test makers with the way those aims are executed. We know that the GMAC has an active interest in testing your ability to discern both good and bad reasoning. The makers of the exam intentionally present flawed arguments because they want to test whether you are easily confused or prone to be swayed by illogical arguments. This often raises situations where you are presented with arguments that are false or seemingly deceptive in nature. This does not mean that the *author* of the piece is part of the deception. The role of a GMAT author is simply to present an argument or fact set. GMAT authors (as separated from the test makers) do *not* try to deceive you with lies. Although GMAT authors may end up making claims that are incorrect, this is not done out of a willful intention to deceive. Deception on the *author's* part is too sophisticated for the GMAT—it is beyond the scope of GMAT stimuli, which are too short to have the level of complexity necessary for you to detect deception if it was intended. So, you need not feel as if the author is attempting to trick you in the making of the argument. This is especially true when premises are created. For example, when a GMAT author makes a premise statement such as, "19 percent of all research projects are privately funded," this statement is likely to be accurate. A GMAT author would not *knowingly* create a false premise, and so, when examining arguments the likelihood is that the premises are not going to be in error and you should not look at them as a likely source of weakness in the argument. This does not mean that authors are infallible. GMAT authors make plenty of errors, but most of those mistakes are errors of reasoning that occur in the process of making the conclusion.

Not only do GMAT authors not attempt to deceive you, they believe (in their GMAT-world way) that the arguments they make are reasonable and solid. *When you read a GMAT argument from the perspective of the author, he or she believes that their argument is sound.* In other words, they do not knowingly make errors of reasoning. This is a fascinating point because it means that GMAT authors, as part of the GMAT world, function as if the points they raise and the conclusions they make have been well-considered and are airtight. This point will be immensely useful when we begin to look at certain forms of reasoning.

Read the Fine Print

One of the aims of the GMAT is to test how closely you read. This is obviously an important skill for anyone in business (who wants an employee who makes a critical mistake in a big negotiation?). One of the ways the GMAT tests whether you have this skill is to probe your knowledge of exactly what the author said. Because of this, you must read all parts of a problem incredibly closely, and you must pay special attention to words that describe the relationships under discussion. For example, if an author concludes, "Therefore, the refinery can achieve a greater operating efficiency," do not make the mistake of thinking the author implied that greater operating efficiency *will* or *must* be achieved.

Consider the following argument: "My mail was delivered yesterday, so it will also be delivered today."

Although this argument is flawed (it could be Sunday and the mail will not be delivered), the author has not intentionally made this error. Rather, the author has made the conclusion without realizing that he has committed an error.

CHAPTER TWO: THE BASICS OF CRITICAL REASONING

The GMAT makers love to examine your comprehension of the exact words used by the author, and that leads to the fourth Primary Objective:

Primary Objective #4: Read closely and know precisely what the author said. Do not generalize!

When it comes to relationships, the makers of the GMAT have a wide variety of modifiers in their arsenal. The following are two lists of words that should be noted when they appear, regardless of whether they appear in the premises or conclusion.

Quantity Indicators	Probability Indicators
all	must
every	will
most	always
many	not always
some	probably
several	likely
few	would
sole	not necessarily
only	could
not all	rarely
none	never

These word lists do not require memorization. They are presented to give you a broad idea of the type of words that can take on an added importance in GMAT questions.

Quantity indicators refer to the amount or quantity in the relationship, such as "some people" or "many of the laws." Probability indicators refer to the likelihood of occurrence, or the obligation present, as in "The Mayor should resign" or "The law will never pass." Many of the terms fit with negatives to form an opposing idea, for example, "some are not" or "would not."

Words such as the Quantity and Probability Indicators are critical because they are a ripe area for the GMAT makers to exploit. There are numerous examples of incorrect answer choices that attempt to capitalize on the meaning of a single word in the stimulus, and thus you must commit yourself to a careful examination of every word on the test.

Tracking Indicators and Concepts

Earlier in this chapter, on page 27, we mentioned that premise and conclusion indicators operate, in a sense, as road signs that tell you what is coming next in the argument. The driving/road signs analogy has some additional relevance to how you should think about GMAT Critical Reasoning questions. As you progress through each question, you must pay close attention to the words used by the test makers, the strength and direction of those words, and what those words tell you about the topic at hand (which is much the same way you drive down a road observing the road signs and other conditions).

Concepts within a stimulus can even be compared to other cars on the road. Every stimulus contains concepts or ideas that play a larger or smaller role in solving the question. Similarly, of the cars on a road, some are a danger to you and must be observed closely, and others present no threat at all and require only minimal attention. The cars (or ideas) you need to pay attention to are the ones that present a danger to you (cars very close to you, erratic drivers, etc). When you first begin driving, everything looks dangerous, but over time you begin to recognize which cars are real threats and which probably are not. The same holds true for Critical Reasoning: at first it can be difficult to distinguish what is important and what isn't, but over time you develop the skills and knowledge to recognize what elements will play an important role in answering the question. So, as you progress through this book, pay close attention to the discussions about concepts, and then when you are practicing, observe when they play a role, and when they do not. In this way, you can become a master at navigating the challenging roads of GMAT Critical Reasoning.

Throughout this book we will discuss the elements that are important and unimportant in GMAT argumentation. Using the driving analogy, the goal is for you to naturally keep your eyes on the road while maintaining an awareness of potential hazards—but not be distracted by every tree that you pass.

Scope

One topic you often hear mentioned in relation to argumentation is scope. The scope of an argument is the range to which the premises and conclusion encompass certain ideas. For example, consider an argument discussing a new surgical technique. The ideas of surgery and medicine are within the scope of the argument. The idea of federal monetary policy, on the other hand, would not be within the scope of the argument.

Arguments are sometimes described as having a narrow (or limited) scope or a wide (or broad) scope. An argument with a narrow scope is definite in its statements, whereas a wide scope argument is less definite and allows for a greater range of possibility. When we begin to examine individual questions, we will return to this idea and show how it can be used to help consider answer choices in certain situations.

Scope can be a useful idea to consider when examining answer choices, because some answer choices go beyond the bounds of what the author has established in the argument. However, scope is also a concept that is overused in modern test preparation. One test preparation company used to tell instructors that if they could not answer a student's question, they should just say that the answer was out of the scope of the argument! As we will see, there are always definite, identifiable reasons that can be used to eliminate incorrect answer choices.

Fluidity of Analysis and Concept Application

When students first begin studying for the GMAT, the cascade of information in individual questions can be unnerving—there seems to be too much going on, all at once. Thus, when first analyzing GMAT questions (and later, GMAT concepts), we break the process into component parts. By recognizing each individual component you can more easily gain an understanding and mastery of the argument as a whole.

Because the analysis of these arguments is broken down into pieces, this may give the impression that as you move through a stimulus and answer choices you are taking deliberate steps, each with a defined beginning and end. That is not the case. Instead, the analysis you apply will often feel more like a waterfall, with all of the pieces rapidly flowing together and quickly coalescing into a clearer understanding of what has been said, and what you should do. It takes time to become comfortable with this process. You have to first learn a concept, then see how it is used in questions, and then finally be able to identify it and understand it with lightning speed.

One of the goals of this book is to teach you to recognize all of the elements involved in solving LSAT questions and answers.

One of your goals should be to learn those pieces so well that you do not have to stop during the test, but instead can simply recognize what you are seeing and react accordingly.

As you learn each technique, work with it repeatedly so that you can apply it effortlessly and effectively. It takes time and practice, but the potential rewards are great.

Final Chapter Note

The discussion of argumentation in this chapter is, by design, not comprehensive. The purpose of this chapter is to give you a broad overview of the theory underlying GMAT arguments. In future chapters we will apply those theories to specific questions and continue to expand upon the discussion in this chapter. The vast majority of students learn best by examining the application of ideas, and we believe the great bulk of your learning will come by seeing these ideas in action.

Premise and Conclusion Analysis Drill

For each stimulus, identify the conclusion(s) and supporting premise(s), if any. The answer key will identify the conclusion and premises of each argument, the logical validity of each argument, and also comment on how to identify argument structure.
Answers on page 52

1. Admittedly, the practice of allowing students to retake a class they previously failed and receive a new grade is controversial. But the mission of any school or university is to educate their students, and allowing students to retake courses supports this mission. Therefore, for the time being, our school should continue to allow students to retake previously failed courses and receive a new grade.

    A. What is the conclusion of the argument, if any?

    B. What premises are given in support of this conclusion?

    C. Is the argument strong or weak? If you think that the argument is weak, please explain why.

2. While it was once believed that the health of the human body was dependent on a balance between four substances, or "humors," the advent of medical research in the nineteenth century led to the understanding that this view was both simplistic and inaccurate. Thereafter, physicians—especially those in Europe, such as Edward Jenner—began formulating theories of treatment that are now the foundation of modern medicine.

    A. What is the conclusion of the argument, if any?

    B. What premises are given in support of this conclusion?

    C. Is the argument strong or weak? If you think that the argument is weak, please explain why.

CHAPTER TWO: THE BASICS OF CRITICAL REASONING

Premise and Conclusion Analysis Drill

3. If Ameer is correct, either the midterm is cancelled or the final is cancelled. But the professor said in class last week that she is considering cancelling both tests and instead having students submit a term paper. Because the professor has final authority over the class schedule and composition, Ameer is probably incorrect.

    A. What is the conclusion of the argument, if any?

    B. What premises are given in support of this conclusion?

    C. Is the argument strong or weak? If you think that the argument is weak, please explain why.

4. Every endeavor that increases one's self-awareness is an endeavor worth trying. Therefore, even though some ventures are dangerous and even life-threatening, any person would be well-served to undertake any endeavor presented to them, no matter how dangerous. After all, it is only through increasing self-awareness that one can discover the value and richness of life.

    A. What is the conclusion of the argument, if any?

    B. What premises are given in support of this conclusion?

    C. Is the argument strong or weak? If you think that the argument is weak, please explain why.

Premise and Conclusion Analysis Drill

5. Cookiecutter sharks feed on a variety of fishes and mammals by gouging round plugs of flesh out of larger animals. Although attacks on humans are documented, they are rare, and thus these sharks are rightly classified as only a minor threat to people. As many fishes that are not a threat to humans are not endangered, there should be no objection to the new ocean exploration and drilling project, which threatens a cookiecutter shark breeding ground.

   A. What is the conclusion of the argument, if any?

   B. What premises are given in support of this conclusion?

   C. Is the argument strong or weak? If you think that the argument is weak, please explain why.

6. Hog farming is known to produce dangerous toxic runoff, which enters the surrounding ecosystem and contaminates the environment. Despite this, however, hog farming practices should not be more closely regulated because research has shown there is no better method for dispersing effluent from hog farms.

   A. What is the conclusion of the argument, if any?

   B. What premises are given in support of this conclusion?

   C. Is the argument strong or weak? If you think that the argument is weak, please explain why.

CHAPTER TWO: THE BASICS OF CRITICAL REASONING

Premise and Conclusion Analysis Drill Answer Key

Question #1.

    Conclusion: Therefore, for the time being, our school should continue to allow students to retake previously failed courses and receive a new grade.

    Premise: Admittedly, the practice of allowing students to retake a class they previously failed and receive a new grade is controversial.

    Premise: But the mission of any school or university is to educate their students, and allowing students to retake courses supports this mission.

The conclusion is introduced by the indicator "Therefore." "Admittedly" introduces a counter-premise that the author then addresses in the following sentence.

The argument is reasonably strong. A practice is stated as being controversial, but then a reasonable statement is made in support of the practice. The conclusion then advocates continuing an already-existing practice. As no viable reason has been presented against the practice, and a viable reason has been given for the practice, it is not unreasonable to conclude that the practice should continue for the time being.

Question #2.

    Premise: While it was once believed that the health of the human body was dependent on a balance between four substances, or "humors," the advent of medical research in the nineteenth century led to the understanding that this view was both simplistic and inaccurate.

    Premise: Thereafter, physicians—especially those in Europe, such as Edward Jenner—began formulating theories of treatment that are now the foundation of modern medicine.

Careful! The stimulus is only a fact set and does not contain a conclusion. Therefore, there is no argument present and no evaluation of argument validity can be made.

Premise and Conclusion Analysis Drill Answer Key

Question #3.

> Conclusion: Ameer is probably incorrect.
>
> Premise: If Ameer is correct, either the midterm is cancelled or the final is cancelled.
>
> Premise: But the professor said in class last week that she is considering cancelling both tests and instead having students submit a term paper.
>
> Premise: Because the professor has final authority over the class schedule and composition,

The conclusion is introduced in the last sentence, and is preceded by a premise introduced by the word "because."

The argument is weak. Ameer has asserted that at least one of the two tests will be cancelled, and the professor is apparently considering cancelling both. No evidence is presented to contradict Ameer's assertion, so there is no reason to conclude that Ameer is incorrect. Note: the "either…or" construction can be tricky, and the GMAT definition is "at least one possibly both." Thus, unless stated otherwise, both events in an "either...or" statement could occur. This tends to be different from how the phrase is used in everyday language, however, and thus should be noted.

Question #4.

> Conclusion: Any person would be well-served to undertake any endeavor presented to them, no matter how dangerous.
>
> Premise: Every endeavor that increases one's self-awareness is an endeavor worth trying.
>
> Premise: Even though some ventures are dangerous and even life-threatening.
>
> Premise: After all, it is only through increasing self-awareness that one can discover the value and richness of life.

The conclusion is introduced by the device "therefore, even though" and follows the inserted premise.

The argument is weak. Although the premise indicates that *every endeavor that increases one's self-awareness* is worth trying, the conclusion goes too far in saying any person should undertake *any* endeavor because not every endeavor might increase self-awareness.

The last sentence serves as an additional premise that does not affect the reasoning in the prior sentences.

Premise and Conclusion Analysis Drill Answer Key

Question #5.

Conclusion:	There should be no objection to the new ocean exploration and drilling project.
Premise:	Cookiecutter sharks feed on a variety of fishes and mammals by gouging round plugs of flesh out of larger animals.
Premise:	Although attacks on humans are documented, they are rare.
Premise:	Thus these sharks are rightly classified as only a minor threat to people.
Premise:	As many fishes that are not a threat to humans are not endangered.
Premise:	[The project] threatens a cookiecutter shark breeding ground.

This is a fairly lengthy and complex argument. The main conclusion is contained in the last sentence. There is another minor conclusion, presented in the second sentence.

The argument is weak. The author simply notes that many fishes that are not threats are not endangered, but no information is given that establishes whether the cookiecutter shark is endangered. Without that information, the author cannot conclude that there should be no objection to the new drilling project, which is a direct threat to at least one cookiecutter shark breeding ground.

Question #6.

Conclusion:	Despite this, however, hog farming practices should not be more closely regulated.
Premise:	Hog farming is known to produce dangerous toxic runoff, which enters the surrounding ecosystem and contaminates the environment.
Premise:	Research has shown there is no better method for dispersing effluent from hog farms.

The argument is somewhat weak. Just because there is not a better method of dispersing effluent does not mean there should not be more regulation. Considering current regulations, it may be the case that closer monitoring or further regulation is required in order to provide sufficient oversight.

A final note about the indicator lists. On the GMAT, there are frequently exceptions to the general rule. There are many different ways that the English language can be used, and this usage variety is one of the main weapons of the test makers. Thus, a good GMAT taker cannot just rely on a memorized list of words, and you should strive to understand the different ways each word can be used. At the same time, the lists provide a fantastic foundation for understanding what typically happens on the GMAT. The lists help you to more easily understand the argument, but you will see some exceptions where the indicators appear to be used in atypical ways.

Chapter Three:
The Question Stem and Answers

Chapter Three: The Question Stem and Answers

The Question Stem 57

Analyzing the Question Stem 57

The Ten Critical Reasoning Question Types 58

Question Type Notes 69

Question Type Variety 70

"Most" in Question Stems 70

Question Stem Wording Variations 71

Identify the Question Stem Drill 72

"Except" and "Least" in Question Stems 76

Except and *Least* Identify the Question Stem Mini-Drill 79

Prephrasing Answers 81

The Answer Choices 82

Question Approach Review 85

Final Chapter Note 87

The Question Stem

The question stem follows the stimulus and poses a question directed at the stimulus. In some ways the question stem is the most important part of each problem because it specifies the task you must perform in order to get credit for the problem.

GMAT question stems cover a wide range of tasks, and will variously ask you to:

- identify details of the stimulus

- describe the structure of the argument

- strengthen or weaken the argument

- identify inferences, main points, and assumptions

- recognize errors of reasoning

- reconcile conflicts

- find arguments that are identical in structure

On average, you have 1 minute and 49 seconds to complete each Critical Reasoning question.

Analyzing the Question Stem

When examining a typical Critical Reasoning section, you may come to the conclusion that there are dozens of different types of question stems. The test makers create this impression by varying the words used in each question stem. As we will see shortly, even though they use different words, many of these question stems are identical in terms of what they ask you to do.

In order to easily handle the different questions, we categorize the question stems that appear on the GMAT. Fortunately, every question stem can be defined as a certain type, and the more familiar you are with the question types, the faster you can respond when faced with individual questions. Thus, one of your tasks is to learn each question type and become familiar with the characteristics that define each type. We will help you accomplish this goal by including a variety of question type identification drills, and by examining each type of question in detail. This leads to the fifth Primary Objective:

Primary Objective #5: Carefully read and identify the question stem. Do not assume that certain words are automatically associated with certain question types.

Make sure to read the question stem very carefully. Some stems direct you to focus on certain aspects of the stimulus and if you miss these clues you make the problem much more difficult.

You must correctly analyze and classify every question stem because the question stem ultimately determines the nature of the correct answer choice. A mistake in analyzing the question stem almost invariably leads to a missed question. As we will see, the test makers love to use certain words—such as "support"—in different ways because they know some test takers will automatically assume these words imply a certain type of question. Properly identifying the question stem type will allow you to proceed quickly and with confidence, and in some cases it will help you determine the correct answer before you read any of the five answer choices.

The Ten Critical Reasoning Question Types

Each question stem that appears in the Critical Reasoning section of the GMAT can be classified into one of ten different types:

1. Must Be True/Most Supported
2. Main Point
3. Assumption
4. Strengthen/Support
5. Resolve the Paradox
6. Weaken
7. Method of Reasoning
8. Flaw in the Reasoning
9. Parallel Reasoning
10. Evaluate the Argument

Question stems contain criteria that must be met. This criteria could be to weaken the argument, find the method of reasoning, etc.

Occasionally, students ask if we refer to the question types by number or by name. We always refer to the questions by name as that is an easier and more efficient approach. Numerical question type classification systems force you to add two unnecessary levels of abstraction to your thinking process. For example, consider a question that asks you to "weaken" the argument. In a numerical question classification system, you must first recognize that the question asks you to weaken the argument, then you must classify that question into a numerical category (say, Type 6), and then you must translate Type 6 to mean "Weaken." Literally, numerical classification systems force you to perform an abstract, circular translation of the meaning of the question, and the translation process is both time-consuming and valueless.

In the following pages we will discuss each question type in brief. Later we will examine each question type in its own chapter.

1. Must Be True/Most Supported

   This category is simply known as "Must Be True." Must Be True questions ask you to identify the answer choice that is best proven by the information in the stimulus. Question stem examples:

   "If the statements above are true, which of the following must also be true?"

   "Which of the following can be properly inferred from the passage?"

2. Main Point

   Main Point questions are a variant of Must Be True questions. As you might expect, a Main Point question asks you to find the primary conclusion made by the author. Question stem example:

   "The main point of the argument is that"

3. Assumption

   These questions ask you to identify an assumption of the author's argument. Question stem example:

   "The argument in the passage relies on which of the following assumptions?"

4. Strengthen/Support

   These questions ask you to select the answer choice that provides support for the author's argument or strengthens it in some way. Question stem examples:

   "Which of the following, if true, most strengthens the argument?"

   "Which of the following, if true, would most strongly support the position above?"

CHAPTER THREE: THE QUESTION STEM AND ANSWERS

5. Resolve the Paradox

Every Resolve the Paradox stimulus contains a discrepancy or seeming contradiction. You must find the answer choice that best resolves the situation. Question stem example:

"Which of the following, if true, would most help to explain the rise in revenues last year?"

6. Weaken

Weaken questions ask you to attack or undermine the author's argument. Question stem example:

"Which of the following, if true, most seriously weakens the argument above?"

7. Method of Reasoning

Method of Reasoning questions ask you to describe, in abstract terms, the way in which the author made his or her argument. Question stem example:

"Which of the following describes how the argument above is developed?"

8. Flaw in the Reasoning

Flaw in the Reasoning questions ask you to describe, in abstract terms, the error of reasoning committed by the author. Question stem example:

"The reasoning in the chemist's argument is flawed primarily because this argument"

In the answer key to this book, all questions are classified as one of these ten types. There are also additional indicators designating reasoning type, etc.

9. Parallel Reasoning

Parallel Reasoning questions ask you to identify the answer choice that contains reasoning most similar in structure to the reasoning presented in the stimulus. Question stem example:

"Which of the following arguments is most similar in its pattern of reasoning to the argument above?"

10. Evaluate the Argument

With Evaluate the Argument questions you must decide which answer choice will allow you to determine the logical validity of the argument. Question stem example:

"The answer to which of the following questions would contribute most to an evaluation of the argument?"

Other question type elements will be discussed, most notably question variants (such as Argument Part questions). Those will be discussed in later chapters.

> **Important Note:** Although there are ten separate question types on the GMAT, each question type does *not* appear with the same frequency. The most popular question types are Weaken, Must Be True, Assumption, Strengthen, and Resolve. If your GMAT test date is approaching quickly and you have little time to study, go directly to those chapters and study those question types first.

Although each of these question types is distinct, they are related in terms of the root function you are asked to perform. Questions that appear dissimilar, such as Must Be True and Method of Reasoning, are actually quite similar when considered in terms of how you work with the question. All question types are variations of three main question "families," and each family is comprised of question types that are similar to each other.

On the next page, we delineate the three families using box-and-arrow diagrams that reflect the flow of information between the stimulus and the answer choices.

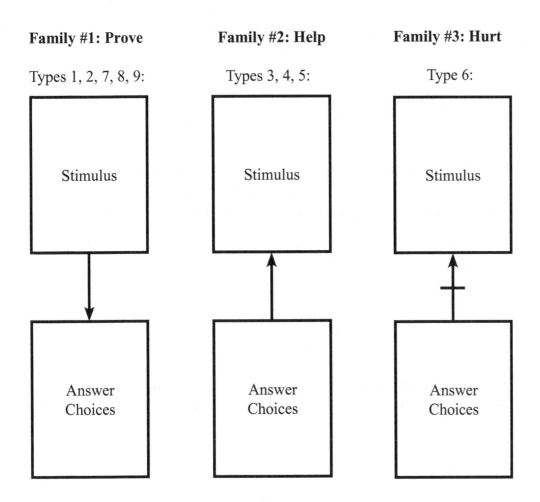

Family #1, also known as the Must Be or Prove Family, consists of the following question types:

(1) Must Be True
(2) Main Point
(7) Method of Reasoning
(8) Flaw in the Reasoning
(9) Parallel Reasoning

Family #2, also known as the Help Family, consists of the following question types:

(3) Assumption
(4) Strengthen/Support
(5) Resolve the Paradox

CHAPTER THREE: THE QUESTION STEM AND ANSWERS

Family #3, also known as the Hurt Family, consists of the following question type:

(6) Weaken

There is one remaining question type not listed above, and that is Evaluate the Argument. Evaluate the Argument questions are a unique combination of the second and third question families, and thus appear as follows:

Family #2 (Help) and Family #3 (Hurt) combine to create the following question type:

(10) Evaluate the Argument

Evaluate questions operate in an unusual manner, and we will discuss those questions in more detail in Chapter Thirteen.

The boxes on the preceding page represent the stimulus and answer choices for any given Critical Reasoning question. The arrows represent the flow of information; one part of the problem is simply accepted and the other part is affected. There are two basic rules to follow when analyzing the diagrams:

1. The part (stimulus or answer choices) at the start of the arrow is accepted as is, and no additional information (aside from general domain assumptions) can be brought in.

2. The part (stimulus or answer choices) at the end of the arrow is what is affected or determined (for example, are you asked to Weaken the argument or determine which answer Must Be True?).

One of the signature features of the three question families is that they define the parameters of what you can do with the information in each question.

In very rough terms, the part at the start of the arrow is taken for granted and the part at the end of the arrow is under suspicion. While this characterization may sound a bit vague, this occurs because there are three different types of relationships, and the details vary from type to type.

Part of the purpose of classifying questions into these three categories is to understand the fundamental structure of Critical Reasoning problems. Many students ask the following two questions upon seeing Critical Reasoning questions for the first time:

1. Should I simply accept every statement in the stimulus as true?

2. Can the answer choices bring in information that is off-the-page, that is, ideas and concepts not stated in the stimulus?

The answer to both questions depends on the question stem and corresponding question family. Let us examine each question family and address these questions in more detail.

The First Question Family

The First Question Family is based on the principle of using the information in the stimulus to prove that one of the answer choices must be true.

In the First Family diagram, the arrow points downward from the stimulus to the answer choices. Hence, the stimulus is at the start of the arrow, and the answer choices are at the end of the arrow. According to the rules above, whatever is stated in the stimulus is simply accepted as given, with no additional information being added. And, because the arrow points to the answer choices, the answer choices are "under suspicion," and the information in the stimulus is used to prove one of the answer choices correct.

Because the stimulus is accepted as stated (even if it contains an error of reasoning), you cannot bring in additional information off the page—you can only use what is stated in the stimulus. Thus, in a Must Be True question, only what the author states in the stimulus can be used to prove one of the answer choices. This reveals the way the arrow works: you start at the stimulus and then use only that information to separate the answers. If an answer choice references something that is not included or encompassed by the stimulus, it will be incorrect. In a Method of Reasoning question, for example, the process works the same. If one of the answers references some method of argumentation that did not occur in the stimulus, then the answer is automatically incorrect. The test makers do not hide this relationship. Most question stems in this family (especially Must Be True) will contain a phrase similar to, "The information *above, if true*..." (italics added). In this way the test makers are able to indicate that you should accept the statements in the stimulus as given and then use them to prove one of the answer choices.

The following rules apply to the First Question Family:

1. You must accept the stimulus information—even if it contains an error of reasoning—and use it to prove that one of the answer choices must be true.

2. Any information in an answer choice that does not appear either directly in the stimulus or as a combination of items in the stimulus will be incorrect.

These rules will be revisited in more detail once we begin analyzing individual Critical Reasoning questions.

The Second Question Family

The Second Question Family is based on the principle of assisting or helping the author's argument or statement in some way, whether by revealing an assumption of the argument, by resolving a paradox, or in some other fashion.

As opposed to the First Family, in this family the arrow points upward to the stimulus. This reverses the flow of information: the answer choices are at the start of the arrow, and the stimulus is at the end of the arrow. Functionally, this means you must accept the answer choices as given, and the stimulus is under suspicion. Accepting the answer choices as given means you cannot dispute their factual basis, even if they include elements not mentioned in the stimulus (we often call this "new" or "outside" information). The test makers make this principle clear because most question stems in this family contain a phrase similar to, "Which of the *following, if true,*..." (italics added). By including this phrase, the test makers indicate that they wish you to treat each answer choice as factually correct. Your task is to examine each answer choice and see which one best fits the exact criteria stated in the question stem (strengthen, resolve, etc.).

In this question grouping, the stimulus is under suspicion. Often there are errors of reasoning present, or leaps in logic, and you are asked to find an answer choice that closes the hole. When you encounter a question of this category, immediately consider the stimulus—were there any obvious holes or gaps in the argument that could be filled by one of the answer choices? Often you will find that the author has made an error of reasoning and you will be asked to eliminate that error.

The following rules apply to the Second Question Family:

1. The information in the stimulus is suspect. There are often reasoning errors present, and depending on the question, you will help shore up the argument in some way.

2. The answer choices are accepted as given, even if they include "new" information. Your task is to determine which answer choice best meets the question posed in the stem.

CHAPTER THREE: THE QUESTION STEM AND ANSWERS

The Third Question Family

The Third Question Family consists of only one question type—Weaken. Accordingly, you are asked to attack the author's argument.

Compared to the Second Question Family, the only difference between the diagrams is that the third family diagram has a bar across the arrow. This bar signifies a negative: instead of strengthening or helping the argument, you attack or hurt the argument. In this sense the third family is the polar opposite of the second family; otherwise the two question families are identical.

For the Third Question Family, the following rules apply:

1. The information in the stimulus is suspect. There are often reasoning errors present, and you will further weaken the argument in some way.

2. The answer choices are accepted as given, even if they include "new" information. Your task is to determine which answer choice best attacks the argument in the stimulus.

As you might expect, there are deeper relationships between the individual question types and the question families. As we discuss the mechanics of individual questions we will further explore these relationships.

Question Type Notes

The following is a collection of notes regarding the Ten Question Types. These notes help clear up some questions that typically arise when students are learning to identify the question types. In the chapters that discuss each question type we will reintroduce each of these points.

- Must Be True and Resolve the Paradox questions are frequently connected to stimuli that do *not* contain conclusions. All remaining question types must be connected to stimuli with conclusions (unless a conclusion is added by the question stem, as sometimes occurs). Hence, when a stimulus without a conclusion appears on the GMAT, only two types of questions can be posed to you: Must Be True or Resolve the Paradox. Question types such as Weaken or Method of Reasoning do not generally appear because no argument or reasoning is present, and those question types ask you to address reasoning. Generally, Resolve the Paradox questions are easy to spot because they contain a paradox or discrepancy. Thus, if you encounter a stimulus without a conclusion and without a paradox, you are most likely about to see a Must Be True question stem.

- Weaken and Strengthen are polar opposite question types, and both are often based on flawed or weak arguments that contain holes that must be closed or opened further.

- Method of Reasoning and Flaw in the Reasoning questions are a brother/sister pair. The only difference between the two is that Flaw in the Reasoning question stems explicitly note that the stimulus contains an error of reasoning. In a Method of Reasoning question the stimulus contains valid or invalid reasoning.

- Parallel Reasoning questions are a one-step extension of Method of Reasoning questions in that you must first identify the type of reasoning used and then parallel it. Method of Reasoning and Parallel Reasoning questions both have a strong Must Be True element.

- Main Point, Method of Reasoning, Flaw in the Reasoning, Parallel Reasoning, and Evaluate the Argument appear the *least* frequently on the GMAT.

Question Type Variety

One of the aims of the test makers is to keep you off-balance. An unsettled, frustrated test taker is prone to making mistakes. By mixing up the types of questions you face, the makers of the test can keep you from getting into a rhythm. Imagine how much easier the Critical Reasoning questions would be if you faced only Must Be True questions. For this reason, you will always see a spread of question types among the Critical Reasoning questions, and you will rarely see the same question type twice in a row. Since this situation is a fact of the GMAT, before the test begins prepare yourself mentally for the quick shifting of mental gears that is required to move from question to question (and, also required to move between the various types of Verbal questions: Critical Reasoning, Sentence Correction, and Reading Comprehension).

"Most" in Question Stems

Of course, every once in a while two answer choices achieve the desired goal; in those cases you simply choose the better of the two answers. Normally, the difference between the two answers is significant enough for you to make a clear distinction as to which one is superior.

Many question stems—especially Strengthen and Weaken stems—contain the qualifier "most." For example, a typical question stem will state, "Which one of the following, if true, most weakens the argument above?" Astute test takers realize that the presence of "most" opens up a Pandora's box of sorts: by including "most," there is a possibility that other answer choices will also meet the criteria of the question stem (Strengthen, Weaken, etc.), albeit to a lesser extent. In other words, if a question stem says "most weakens," the possibility is that every answer choice weakens the argument, and you would be in the unenviable task of having to choose the best of a bunch of good answer choices. *Fortunately, this is not how it works.* Even though "most" will appear in many stems, you can rest assured that only one answer choice will meet the criteria. So, if you see a "most weakens" question stem, only one of the answers will weaken the argument. So, then, why does "most" appear in so many question stems? Because in order to maintain test integrity the test makers need to make sure their credited answer choice is as airtight and defensible as possible. Imagine what would occur if a question stem, let us say a Weaken question, did not include a "most" qualifier: any answer choice that weakened the argument, even if only very slightly, could then be argued to meet the criteria of the question stem. A situation like this would make constructing the test exceedingly difficult because any given problem might have multiple correct answer choices. To eliminate this predicament, the test makers insert "most" into the question stem, and then they can always claim there is one and only one correct answer choice.

Question Stem Wording Variations

Earlier in this chapter, we noted that the test makers use a variety of word choices to give the impression that there are many different types of question stems. Additionally, we noted that you cannot make simple word associations permanently connecting particular words to specific question types. For example, the word "support" is most often used in connection with Strengthen questions, as in the following example:

> Which of the following, if true, provides the most support for the argument?

However, this same word can be used in an entirely different type of question, one in the Must Be True vein:

> The statements above, if true, most strongly support which of the following claims?

If, during the test, you were to read the second question stem too quickly, you might mistakenly conclude that you were facing a Strengthen question, when that is not the case at all.

Of course, "support" is not the only word used in this fashion, and in recent years the test makers have made a concerted effort to create question stems that are generally more challenging to identify (in the process, words such as "infer" and "justify" have been used in ways completely different from how they are normally used).

The inclination to make rigid word-to-question-type connections is strong, but the test makers take steps to avoid being too predictable, so you must remain prepared for unexpected usages as you work through the section. When we later discuss each question type individually, this issue will be raised again, but in the meantime make sure to carefully read each stem, and do not assume that a particular word always indicates a certain question type.

Identify the Question Stem Drill

Each of the following items contains a question stem. In the space provided, categorize each stem into one of the ten Critical Reasoning Question Types: Must Be True, Main Point, Assumption, Strengthen, Resolve the Paradox, Weaken, Method of Reasoning, Flaw in the Reasoning, Parallel Reasoning, or Evaluate the Argument. While we realize that you have not yet worked directly with each question type, by considering the relationships now you will have an advantage as you attack future questions. In later chapters we will present more Identify the Question Stem drills to further strengthen your abilities. *Answers on page 74*

1. Question Stem: "Which of the following, if true, most helps to explain the viewpoint described above?"

    Question Type: _____

2. Question Stem: "Which of the following can be properly inferred from the historian's statement?"

    Question Type: _____

3. Question Stem: "Which of the following, if true, most seriously weakens the reasoning above?"

    Question Type: _____

4. Question Stem: "Which of the following is an assumption required by the argument above?"

    Question Type: _____

5. Question Stem: "Which of the following is most like the argument above in its logical structure?

    Question Type: _____

6. Question Stem: "Of the following, which one most accurately expresses the main point of the argument?"

    Question Type: _____

Identify the Question Stem Drill

7. Question Stem: "Which of the following statements, if true, would provide the most support for the scientists' assertion?"

   Question Type: _____

8. Question Stem: "The argument is flawed because it"

   Question Type: _____

9. Question Stem: "The advertisement proceeds by"

   Question Type: _____

10. Question Stem: "The answer to which of the following questions would most help in evaluating the philosopher's argument?"

    Question Type: _____

11. Question Stem: "Mary challenges Shaun's reasoning by"

    Question Type: _____

12. Question Stem: "The statements above, if true, most strongly support which of the following?"

    Question Type: _____

Identify the Question Stem Drill Answer Key

The typical student misses about half of the questions in this drill. Do not worry about how many you miss; the point of this drill is to acquaint you with the different question stems. As you see more examples of each type of question, your ability to correctly identify each stem will improve.

1. Question Type: Resolve the Paradox

The presence of the phrase "Which of the following, if true," indicates that this question stem must be from either the second or third question family. Because the third family is Weaken, and the question stem asks you to "explain," the question cannot be from the third family. Thus, the question must be from the second family and can only be an Assumption, Strengthen, or Resolve question. The idea of explaining is most closely aligned with Resolving the Paradox.

2. Question Type: Must Be True

The word "inferred" means "must be true," hence that is the classification of this question.

3. Question Type: Weaken

The presence of the phrase "Which of the following, if true," indicates that this question stem must be from either the second or third question family. The presence of the word "weakens" indicates that this is a Weaken question.

4. Question Type: Assumption

The key words in this stem are "required" and "assumption," making this an Assumption question.

5. Question Type: Parallel

The key phrases in this stem are "most like...in logical structure" and "the argument above." Because the argument in the stimulus is used as a model for one of the answers, this is a Parallel Reasoning question.

6. Question Type: Main Point

Because the stem asks you to find the main point, this question is categorized as Main Point.

Identify the Question Stem Drill Answer Key

7. Question Type: Strengthen

The presence of the phrase "Which one of the following, if true," indicates that this question stem must be from either the second or third question family. Because the third family is Weaken, and the question stem asks you to "support," the question cannot be from the third family. Thus, the question must be from the second family and can only be an Assumption, Strengthen, or Resolve question. The idea of supporting is the same as Strengthening.

8. Question Type: Flaw

The presence of the word "flawed" could indicate either a Weaken question or a Flaw in the Reasoning question. In this case, the stem requests you to identify the flaw in the argument (or reasoning), hence this question is a Flaw in the Reasoning question.

9. Question Type: Method

By asking how the advertisement "proceeds," the test makers wish to know the way in which the argument is made, in other words, the method of the reasoning.

10. Question Type: Evaluate

The key phrase is "evaluating the philosopher's argument," which indicates that the test makers require you to find the question that would best help in evaluating the author's argument. Thus, the question is classified as Evaluate the Argument.

11. Question Type: Method

Although the question stem uses the word "challenges," this is not a Weaken question because the stem asks for a description of the way Shaun's reasoning was challenged. Thus, you are asked to identify Mary's method of reasoning.

12. Question Type: Must Be True

The phrase "The statements above, if true," indicates that this question must come from the first question family. In this case, the "most strongly support" is used with the intent of proving one of the answers as correct. Hence, this is a Must Be True question. Note how the use of the word "support" in this question stem differs from the usage in problem #7.

"Except" and "Least" in Question Stems

The word "except" has a dramatic impact when it appears in a question stem. Because "except" means "other than," when "except" is placed in a question it negates the logical quality of the answer choice you seek. Literally, it turns the intent of the question stem upside down. For example, if a question asks you to weaken the argument, the one correct answer weakens the argument and the other four answers do not weaken the argument. If "except" is added to the question stem, as in "Each of the following weakens the argument EXCEPT," the stem is turned around and instead of the correct answer weakening the argument, the four incorrect answers weaken the argument and the one correct answer does not weaken the argument.

Many students, upon encountering "except" in a question stem, make the mistake of assuming that the "except" charges you with seeking the polar opposite. For example, if a question stem asks you to weaken the argument, some students believe that a "Weaken EXCEPT" question stem actually asks you to strengthen the argument. This is incorrect. Although weaken and strengthen are polar opposites, because except means "other than," when a "Weaken EXCEPT" question stem appears, you are asked to find any answer choice other than Weaken. While this could include a strengthening answer choice, it could also include an answer choice that has no effect on the argument. Thus, in a "Weaken EXCEPT" question, the four incorrect answers Weaken the argument and the one correct answer does not weaken the argument (could strengthen or have no effect). Here are some other examples:

1. "Which of the following, if true, strengthens the argument above?"

    One correct answer: Strengthen
    Four incorrect answers: Do not Strengthen

    "Each of the following, if true, strengthens the argument above EXCEPT:"

    One correct answer: Does not Strengthen
    Four incorrect answers: Strengthen

The true effect of "except" is to logically negate the question stem. We will discuss Logical Negation in more detail in the Assumption question chapter.

2. "Which of the following, if true, would help to resolve the
apparent discrepancy above?"

>One correct answer: Resolves the Paradox
>Four incorrect answers: Do not Resolve the Paradox

"Each of the following, if true, would help to resolve the apparent discrepancy above EXCEPT:"

>One correct answer: Does not Resolve the Paradox
>Four incorrect answers: Resolve the Paradox

As you can see from the two examples, the presence of except has a profound impact upon the meaning of the question stem. Because "except" has this powerful effect, it always appears in all capital letters whenever it is used in a GMAT question stem.

The word "least" has a similar effect to "except" when it appears in a question stem. Although "least" and "except" do not generally have the same meaning, when "least" appears in a question stem you should treat it *exactly the same* as "except." Note: this advice holds true only when this word appears in the question stem! If you see the word "least" elsewhere on the GMAT, consider it to have its usual meaning of "in the lowest or smallest degree."

Let us look more closely at how and why "least" functions identically to "except." Compare the following two question stems:

>"Which of the following, if true, would help to resolve the apparent discrepancy above?"
>
>>One correct answer: Resolves the Paradox
>>Four incorrect answers: Do not Resolve the Paradox
>
>"Which of the following, if true, helps LEAST to resolve the apparent discrepancy described above?"
>
>>One correct answer: Does not Resolve the Paradox
>>Four incorrect answers: Resolve the Paradox

By asking for the question stem that "least" helps resolve the paradox, the test makers indicate that the four incorrect answers will more strongly help resolve the paradox. But, in practice, when "least" is used, all five answer choices do *not* resolve the paradox to varying degrees. Instead,

---

Some GMAT Critical Reasoning sections feature "except" questions very heavily, especially as you encounter higher-difficulty problems.

"Except" is used far more frequently in GMAT question stems than "least."

four answers resolve the paradox and the one correct answer does *not* resolve the paradox. Why do the test makers do this? Because the test makers cannot afford to introduce uncertainty into the correctness of the answers. If all five answer choices resolve the paradox, then reasonable minds could come to a disagreement about which one "least" resolves the paradox. In order to avoid this type of controversy, the test makers simply make sure that exactly one answer choice does not resolve the paradox (and, because that answer choice does not resolve the paradox it automatically has the "least" effect possible). In this way, the test makers can present a seemingly difficult and confusing task while at the same time avoiding a test construction problem. Because of this situation, any time you encounter "least" in a question stem, simply recognize that four of the answers will meet the stated criteria (weaken, strengthen, resolve, etc.) and the one correct answer will not. Thus, you will not have to make an assessment based on degree of correctness.

Here is another example comparing the use of the word "least:"

"Which one of the following, if true, would most strengthen the argument above?"

One correct answer: Strengthens
Four incorrect answers: Do not Strengthen

"Which one of the following, if true, LEAST strengthens the argument above?"

One correct answer: Does not Strengthen
Four incorrect answers: Strengthen

Because "least," like "except," has such a strong impact on the meaning of a question stem, the test makers kindly place "least" in all capital letters when it appears in a question stem.

In the answer keys to this book, we will designate questions that contain "except" or "least" by placing an "X" at the end of the question stem classification. For example, a "Weaken EXCEPT" question stem would be classified as "WeakenX." A "Strengthen EXCEPT" question stem would be classified as "StrengthenX" and so on.

Except and *Least* Identify the Question Stem Mini-Drill

Each of the following items contains a question stem. In the space provided, categorize each stem into one of the ten Critical Reasoning Question Types: Must Be True, Main Point, Assumption, Strengthen, Resolve the Paradox, Weaken, Method of Reasoning, Flaw in the Reasoning, Parallel Reasoning, or Evaluate the Argument, and notate any Except (X) identifier you see. *Answers on page 80*

1. Question Stem: "Each of the following, if true, supports the claim above EXCEPT:"

    Question Type: _____

2. Question Stem: "Each of the following, if true, weakens the conclusion above EXCEPT:"

    Question Type: _____

3. Question Stem: "Which one of the following, if all of them are true, is LEAST helpful in establishing that the conclusion above is properly drawn?"

    Question Type: _____

4. Question Stem: "Each of the following describes a flaw in the author's reasoning EXCEPT:"

    Question Type: _____

5. Question Stem: "Which one of the following, if true, does NOT help to resolve the apparent discrepancy between the two surveys discussed?"

    Question Type: _____

CHAPTER THREE: THE QUESTION STEM AND ANSWERS

Except and *Least* Identify The Question Stem Mini-Drill Answer Key

1. Question Type: StrengthenX

The four incorrect answer choices Strengthen the argument; the correct answer choice does not Strengthen the argument.

2. Question Type: WeakenX

The four incorrect answer choices Weaken the argument; the correct answer choice does not Weaken the argument.

3. Question Type: StrengthenX

The four incorrect answer choices Strengthen the argument ("helpful in establishing the conclusion" is the same as Strengthen); the correct answer choice does not Strengthen the argument. The "LEAST" in the stem functions in the same fashion as "EXCEPT."

4. Question Type: FlawX

The four incorrect answer choices describe a Flaw in the Reasoning; the correct answer choice does not describe a Flaw in the Reasoning.

5. Question Type: ResolveX

Although this question stem uses neither "except" nor "least," the use of the word "NOT" indicates that the four incorrect answer choices Resolve the Paradox and the correct answer choice does not Resolve the Paradox. Hence, this question is classified ResolveX.

Prephrasing Answers

Most students tend to simply read the question stem and then move on to the answer choices without further thought. This is disadvantageous because these students run a greater risk of being tempted by the expertly constructed incorrect answer choices. One of the most effective techniques for quickly finding correct answer choices and avoiding incorrect answer choices is prephrasing. Prephrasing an answer involves quickly speculating on what you expect the correct answer will be based on the information in the stimulus.

Prephrasing is the GMAT version of the old adage, "An ounce of prevention is worth a pound of cure."

Although every answer you prephrase may not be correct, there is great value in considering for a moment what elements could appear in the correct answer choice. Students who regularly prephrase find that they are more readily able to eliminate incorrect answer choices, and of course, many times their prephrased answer is correct. And, as we will see in later chapters, there are certain stimulus and question stem combinations on the GMAT that yield predictable answers, making prephrasing even more valuable. In part, prephrasing puts you in an attacking mindset: if you look ahead and consider a possible answer choice, you are forced to involve yourself in the problem. This process helps keep you alert and in touch with the elements of the problem.

All high-scoring test takers are active and aggressive. Passive test takers tend to be less involved in the exam and therefore more prone to make errors.

Primary Objective #6: Prephrase: after reading the question stem, take a moment to mentally formulate your answer to the question stem.

Keep in mind that prephrasing is directly related to attacking the stimulus; typically, students who closely analyze the stimulus can more easily prephrase an answer.

CHAPTER THREE: THE QUESTION STEM AND ANSWERS

When we speak of opposites on the GMAT, we mean logical opposites. For example, what is the opposite of "wet?" Most people would say "dry." But, that is the polar opposite, not the logical opposite. The logical opposite of "wet" is "not wet." Logical opposites break the topic under discussion into two parts. In this case, everything in the spectrum of moisture would be classified as either "wet" or "not wet."

The Answer Choices

All GMAT questions have five answer choices and each question has only one correct, or "credited," response. As with other sections, the correct answer in a Critical Reasoning question must meet the Uniqueness Rule of Answer Choices™, which states that "Every correct answer has a unique logical quality that meets the criteria in the question stem. Every incorrect answer has the opposite logical quality." The correctness of the answer choices themselves conforms to this rule: there is one correct answer choice; the other four answer choices are the opposite of correct, or incorrect. Consider the following specific examples:

1. Logical Quality of the Correct Answer: Must Be True

    Logical Quality of the Four Incorrect Answers:
    the opposite of Must Be True = Not Necessarily True (could be not necessarily the case or never the case)

2. Logical Quality of the Correct Answer: Strengthen

    Logical Quality of the Four Incorrect Answers:
    the opposite of Strengthen = not Strengthen (could be neutral or weaken)

3. Logical Quality of the Correct Answer: Weaken

    Logical Quality of the Four Incorrect Answers:
    the opposite of Weaken = not Weaken (could be neutral or strengthen)

There may be times when you would not read all five answer choices, for example, if you only a short amount of time left in the section and you determine that answer choice (B) is clearly correct. In that case, you would choose answer choice (B) and then move on to the next question.

Even though there is only one correct answer choice and this answer choice is unique, you still are faced with a difficult task when attempting to determine the correct answer. The test makers have the advantage of time and language on their side. Because identifying the correct answer at first glance can be quite hard, you must always read all five of the answer choices. Students who fail to read all five answer choices open themselves up to missing questions without ever having read the correct answer. There are many classic examples of GMAC placing highly attractive wrong answer choices just before the correct answer. If you are going to make the time investment of analyzing the stimulus and the question stem, you should also make the wise investment of considering each answer choice.

Primary Objective #7: Always read each of the five answer choices.

As you read through each answer choice, sort them into contenders and losers. If an answer choice appears somewhat attractive, interesting, or even confusing, keep it as a contender and move on to the next answer choice. You do not want to spend time debating the merits of an answer choice only to find that the next answer choice is superior. However, if an answer choice immediately strikes you as incorrect, classify it as a loser and move on. Once you have evaluated all five answer choices, return to the answer choices that strike you as most likely to be correct and decide which one is correct.

Primary Objective #8: Separate the answer choices into Contenders and Losers. After completing this process, review the contenders and decide which answer is the correct one.

The Contender/Loser separation process is exceedingly important, primarily because it saves time. Consider two students—1 and 2—who each approach the same question, one of whom uses the Contender/Loser approach and the other who does not. Answer choice (D) is correct:

Student 1 (using Contender/Loser)

> Answer choice A: considers this answer for 15 seconds, keeps it as a Contender.
>
> Answer choice B: considers this answer for 10 seconds, eliminates it as a Loser.
>
> Answer choice C: considers this answer for 20 seconds, eliminates it as a Loser.
>
> Answer choice D: considers this answer for 20 seconds, keeps it as a Contender, and mentally notes that this answer is preferable to (A).
>
> Answer choice E: considers this answer for 15 seconds, would normally keep as a contender, but determines answer choice (D) is superior.

You will occasionally hear that only two of the five answer choices have merit. This type of "rule" is valueless because only one answer choice can be correct; the other four answers can be eliminated for concrete and identifiable reasons.

After a quick review, Student 1 selects answer choice (D) and moves to the next question. Total time spent on the answer choices: 1 minute, 20 seconds (irrespective of the time spent on the stimulus).

Student 2 (considering each answer choice in its entirety)

> Answer choice A: considers this answer for 15 seconds, is not sure if the answer is correct or incorrect. Returns to stimulus and spends another 20 seconds proving the answer is wrong.
>
> Answer choice B: considers this answer for 10 seconds, eliminates it.
>
> Answer choice C: considers this answer for 20 seconds, eliminates it.
>
> Answer choice D: considers this answer for 20 seconds, notes this a good answer, then spends an additional 10 seconds returning to the stimulus to prove the answer correct.
>
> Answer choice E: considers this answer for 15 seconds, but determines answer choice (D) is superior.

After a quick review, Student 2 selects answer choice (D) and moves to the next question. Total time spent on the answer choices: 1 minute, 50 seconds.

Comparison: both students answer the problem correctly, but Student 2 takes 30 more seconds to answer the question than Student 1.

Some students, on reading this comparison, note that both students answered the problem correctly and that the time difference was small, only 30 seconds more for Student 2 to complete the problem. Doesn't sound like that big a difference, does it? But, the extra 30 seconds was for just one problem. Imagine if that same thing occurred on every single Critical Reasoning problem in the section: that extra 30 seconds per question would translate to a loss of 5 to 7 minutes when multiplied across 10 to 14 questions in the section! And that lost time would mean that student 2 would get to several questions than Student 1 in this section. This example underscores an essential GMAT truth: little things make a big difference, and every single second counts. If you can save even five seconds by employing a certain method, then do so!

Occasionally, students will read and eliminate all five of the answer choices. If this occurs, return to the stimulus and re-evaluate the argument.

Remember—the information needed to answer the question always resides in the stimulus, either implicitly or explicitly. If none of the answers are attractive, then you must have missed something key in the stimulus.

Primary Objective #9: If all five answer choices appear to be Losers, return to the stimulus and re-evaluate the argument.

Question Approach Review

Take a moment to review the methods discussed in Chapters Two and Three. Together, these recommendations form a cohesive strategy for attacking any Critical Reasoning question. Let us start by reviewing the Primary Objectives™:

Primary Objective #1: Determine whether the stimulus contains an argument or if it is only a set of factual statements.

Primary Objective #2: If the stimulus contains an argument, identify the conclusion of the argument. If the stimulus contains a fact set, examine each fact.

Primary Objective #3: If the stimulus contains an argument, determine if the argument is strong or weak.

Primary Objective #4: Read closely and know precisely what the author said. Do not generalize!

Primary Objective #5: Carefully read and identify the question stem. Do not assume that certain words are automatically associated with certain question types.

Primary Objective #6: Prephrase: after reading the question stem, take a moment to mentally formulate your answer to the question stem.

Primary Objective #7: Always read each of the five answer choices.

Memorize this process and make it second nature! These steps constitute the basic approach you must use to attack each question.

Primary Objective #8: Separate the answer choices into Contenders and Losers. After you complete this process, review the Contenders and decide which answer is the correct one.

Primary Objective #9: If all five answer choices appear to be Losers, return to the stimulus and re-evaluate the argument.

As you attack each problem, remember that each question stem governs the flow of information within the problem:

- The First family uses the stimulus to prove one of the answer choices must be true. No information outside the sphere of the stimulus is allowed in the correct answer choice.

- The Second Family takes the answer choices as true and uses them to help the stimulus. Information outside the sphere of the stimulus is allowed in the correct answer choice.

- The Third Family takes the answer choices as true and uses them to hurt the stimulus. Information outside the sphere of the stimulus is allowed in the correct answer choice.

By consistently applying the points above, you give yourself the best opportunity to succeed on each question.

Final Chapter Note

The individuals who construct standardized tests are called *psychometricians*. Although this job title sounds ominous, breaking this word into its two parts reveals a great deal about the nature of the GMAT. Although we could make a number of jokes about the *psycho* part, this portion of the word refers to psychology; the *metrician* portion relates to metrics or measurement. Thus, the purpose of these individuals is to create a test that measures you in a precise, psychological way. As part of this process, the makers of the GMAT carefully analyze reams of data from every test administration in order to assess the tendencies of test takers. As Sherlock Holmes observed, "You can, for example, never foretell what any one man will do, but you can say with precision what an average number will be up to." By studying the actions of all past test takers, the makers of the exam can reliably predict where you will be most likely to make errors. Throughout this book we will reference those pitfalls as they relate to specific question and reasoning types. For the moment, we would like to highlight one mental trap you must avoid at all times in any GMAT section: the tendency to dwell on past problems. Many students fall prey to "answering" a problem, and then continuing to think about it as they start the next problem. Obviously, this is distracting and creates an environment where missing the next problem is more likely. When you finish a problem, you must immediately put it out of your mind and move to the next problem with 100% focus. If you let your mind wander back to previous problems, you fall into a deadly trap.

This concludes our general discussion of Critical Reasoning questions. In subsequent chapters we will deconstruct each question type and some of the reasoning types frequently used by the test makers. At all times we will use the principles presented in these first chapters. If, in the future, you find yourself unclear about some of these ideas, please return to these chapters and re-read them.

If you feel as if you are still hazy on some of the ideas discussed so far, do not worry. When discussing the theory that underlies all questions, the points can sometimes be a bit abstract and dry. In the remaining chapters we will discuss the application of these ideas to real questions, and working with actual questions often helps a heretofore confusing idea become clear.

Chapter Four:
Must Be True
Questions

Chapter Four: Must Be True Questions

Must Be True Questions	91
Prephrasing with Must Be True Questions	92
Returning to the Stimulus	96
New Information and the Idea Umbrella	96
Primary Objective #4 and Modifier Words Revisited	98
Language: Negatives and Double Negatives	100
Correct Answers in Must Be True Questions Reviewed	102
Incorrect Answers in Must Be True Questions	102
Stimulus Opinions versus Assertions	105
Conditional Reasoning	106
Three Logical Features of Conditional Reasoning	107
Valid and Invalid Statements	108
Valid and Invalid Statement Recognition Mini-Drill	111
The Multiplicity of Indicator Words	113
How to Recognize Conditionality	115
Sufficient and Necessary Diagramming Drill	116
Final Note	120
Must Be True Question Type Review	121
Must Be True Question Problem Set	123

Must Be True Questions

Must Be True questions require you to select an answer choice that is proven by the information presented in the stimulus. The correct answer choice can be a paraphrase of part of the stimulus or it can be a logical consequence of one or more parts of the stimulus. However, when selecting an answer choice, you must find the proof that supports your answer in the stimulus. We call this the Fact Test™:

First Family Information Model:

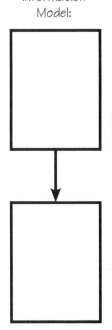

> The correct answer to a Must Be True question can always be proven by referring to the facts stated in the stimulus.

The test makers will try to entice you by creating incorrect answer choices that could possibly occur or are likely to occur, but are not certain to occur. You must avoid those answers and select the answer choice that is most clearly supported by what you read. Do not bring in information from outside the stimulus (aside from commonsense assumptions); all of the information necessary to answer the question resides in the stimulus.

Must Be True question stems appear in a variety of formats, but one or both of the features described below appear consistently:

1. The stem often indicates the information in the stimulus should be taken as true, as in:

    > "If the statements above are true..."
    > "The statements above, if true..."
    > "If the information above is correct..."

    This type of phrase helps indicate that you are dealing with a First Family question type.

2. The stem asks you to identify a single answer choice that is proven or supported, as in:

    > "...which of the following must also be true?"
    > "...which of the following conclusions can be properly drawn on the basis of it?"
    > "...most strongly support which of the following?"
    > "Which of the following can be properly inferred..."

Because Must Be True is the first question type under discussion, we will make test-taking comments that relate to other question types as well.

CHAPTER FOUR: MUST BE TRUE QUESTIONS

In each case, the question stem indicates that one of the answer choices is proven by the information in the stimulus.

Here are several Must Be True question stem examples:

"If the statements above are true, which of the following must be true?"

"Which of the following conclusions is best supported by the statements above?"

"The statements above, if true, best support which of the following assertions?"

"Which of the following can be correctly inferred from the statements above?"

"Which of the following is most strongly supported by the information above?"

Must Be True questions are considered the foundation of the GMAT because the skill required to answer a Must Be True question is also required for every other GMAT Critical Reasoning question. Must Be True questions require you to read text and understand the facts and details that logically follow. To Weaken or Strengthen an argument, for example, you first need to be able to ascertain the facts and details. The same goes for every other type of question. Because every question type relies on the fact-finding skill used to answer Must Be True questions, your performance on Must Be True questions is often a predictor of your overall Critical Reasoning score. For this reason you must lock down the understanding required of this question category: what did you read in the stimulus and what do you know on the basis of that reading?

Prephrasing with Must Be True Questions

When you read an argument, you are forced to evaluate the validity of a conclusive statement generated by a framework designed to be persuasive (that is, after all, what argumentation is all about). When judging an argument, people tend to react with agreement or disagreement depending on the persuasiveness of the conclusion. Fact sets do not engender that same level of response because no argument is present, and, as mentioned in Chapter Two, most Must Be True stimuli are fact sets. Because prephrasing relies in part on your reaction to what you read, prephrasing Must Be True questions can often be difficult. There are exceptions, but if you find yourself having difficulty prephrasing an answer to a Must Be True question, do not worry.

Remember, "infer" means "must be true."

Although difficult questions can appear under any type, Must Be True questions are often considered one of the easier question types.

The following question will be used to further discuss prephrasing. Please take a moment to read through the problem and corresponding answer choices:

1. Neither punishment nor reward is, by itself, enough to raise a well-rounded child. Both are required because punishment alone creates resentment and fear, and reward alone distorts a child's perceptions of the value of things.

   If the statements above are true, then an appropriate test of a parent's ability to raise a well-rounded child is his or her ability to

   (A) punish a child and offer proper reward
   (B) avoid creating a distorted perception of the value of things within the child
   (C) avoid creating resentment and fear within the child
   (D) create an appropriate perception of the value of things within the child
   (E) create contentment and calm within the child

Applying Primary Objective #1, we can see there is a conclusion in the argument: "Both are required." Note how this phrase is followed by the word "because," which indicates that a premise is about to be presented. In an argument, if a premise is presented then there must also be a conclusion present. In this case, the conclusion is presented prior to presentation of the premise. This "reversed" order of conclusion-premise is not uncommon on the GMAT, and it is one of the tricks that the test makers use to keep students off-balance.

In this case the stimulus is short, and applying Primary Objective #2 breaks the argument into three components:

> First Statement: Neither punishment nor reward is, by itself, enough to raise a well-rounded child.
>
> Second Statement: Both are required
>
> Third Statement: because punishment alone creates resentment and fear, and reward alone distorts a child's perceptions of the value of things.

Remember, you can often predict the occurrence of Must Be True questions because the stimulus of most Must Be True questions does not contain a conclusion. This is not one of those cases.

Review the Primary Objectives on page 85!

CHAPTER FOUR: MUST BE TRUE QUESTIONS

Reconstituted into argument form, the three components appear as follows:

> Premise/First Statement: Neither punishment nor reward is, by itself, enough to raise a well-rounded child.
>
> Premise/Third Statement: because punishment alone creates resentment and fear, and reward alone distorts a child's perceptions of the value of things.
>
> Conclusion/Second Statement: Both are required

The question stem is a Must Be True because it asks you determine what is needed to raise a well-rounded child based on the statements in the stimulus, which you are told to accept as true.

Next, to apply Primary Objective #6 (Prephrasing), take a moment to consider what the elements in the stimulus add up to. To do so, consider the premises together, and look for the connection between the elements. The first and third premises explain how punishment and how reward each operate: neither is enough on its own to raise a well-rounded child because if only one of the two is used, then there are negative consequences to that application. On this basis, the author then concludes that you need both elements to raise a well-rounded child.

The question stem asks you to determine an "appropriate test of a parent's ability to raise a well-rounded child," and based on the conclusion, this ability must rest on applying both punishment and reward. Note that there is no claim made on the amounts or the degree to which each should be applied, just that both are "required."

We can now attack the five answer choices with this prephrase in mind. Note that if you did not see that connection between the premises, you would simply move on and attack each answer choice with the facts at hand.

Answer choice (A): This answer is the closest to our prephrase, and this is the correct answer. Notice how the language of this answer choice—"punish a child and offer proper reward"—matches the prephrase discussion above.

With this answer, some students pause for a moment, thinking that the language is too clearly reflective of the terminology of the stimulus. While this may cause momentary concern, simply apply Primary Objective #4 and make sure that the language in the stimulus matches the language in the answer choice.

The scope of the stimulus— especially if that scope is broad— often helps eliminate one or more of the answer choices.

This is not an overly difficult question, but we wanted to use a fairly simple example in order to make this idea crystal clear.

Answer choice (B): This is an interesting answer choice, and most people take a moment before categorizing this as a Loser. The answer choice reflects an idea within the stimulus ("avoid creating a distorted perception of the value of things" appears in the third statement), but distortion is indicated to be a consequence of using reward alone. Simply avoiding that distortion is not what one would use to raise a well-rounded child according to the statements in the stimulus.

Thus, even though the answer uses elements of the stimulus, the idea in this answer does not meet the criteria in the question stem.

Answer choice (C): This answer is also a Loser. This answer acts in exactly the same manner as answer choice (B), but in this instance the focus is on the negative consequences of using punishment alone. Just as avoiding the use of reward alone is not a good test (as in (B)), avoiding the use of punishment alone is not a good test.

Answer choice (D): Many people hold this answer as a Contender and then move on to answer choice (E). As it will turn out, this answer is incorrect because the language is opposite that in the stimulus, which only spoke about creating a distorted perception of the value of things. In this sense, this is an Opposite answer.

However, this answer is quite attractive because the idea is a common sense one: if we wish to create a well-rounded child, one would expect such a child to have an appropriate perception of the value of things. Remember, any answer choice you select must not be selected on the basis that it "sounds good." Use the Fact Test to differentiate between answers that are based on the stimulus and answers that simply make common sense outside the realm of the question.

Answer choice (E): Just as answers (B) and (C) are similar, answer (D) and (E) are also similar. In this instance, the use of punishment alone creates fear and resentment. This answer uses the idea of "contentment and calm," which are rough opposites of the fear and resentment. But, creating a well-rounded child is about applying two different methods of control—punishment and reward—and not so much about creating the opposite result of what would occur if one alone were used.

Of course, as with (D), this answer is quite attractive because the idea is a common sense one that we would expect to be associated with a well-rounded child.

If you did not follow this exact pattern of analysis, or if you classified some answers as Contenders when we classified them as Losers, do not worry. Everyone has their own particular style and pace for attacking questions. The more questions you complete, the better you will get at understanding why answers are correct or incorrect.

This advice also holds true for Reading Comprehension questions.

In Must Be True questions you are like the detective Sherlock Holmes, looking for clues in the stimulus and then matching those clues to the answer choices.

Returning to the Stimulus

As you attack the answer choices, do not be afraid to return to the stimulus to re-read and confirm your perceptions. Most GMAT stimuli contain a large amount of tricky, detailed information, and it is difficult to gain a perfect understanding of many of the stimuli you encounter. There is nothing wrong with quickly looking back at the stimulus, especially when deciding between two or more answer choices.

Please note that there is a difference between returning to the stimulus and re-reading the entire stimulus. On occasion, you will find yourself with no other option but to re-read the entire passage, but this should not be your normal mode of operation.

New Information and the Idea Umbrella

Previously in this chapter—and in reference to all First Family questions—the point has been made that you must refer to the statements in the stimulus to prove the correct answer. Because this is such a critical point, let us take a moment to further explore the full meaning of that advice. When reduced to its component parts, in Must Be True questions there are four classifications of *information* that can be used to prove that an answer choice is correct:

This section discusses the types of information that can be used to prove that an answer choice is correct. In a few pages, we'll discuss different types of answers that are correct and incorrect.

1. The actual statements of the stimulus

    This category of information is probably fairly obvious: in Must Be True questions, you can use the statements of the author without reservation.

2. Commonsense assumptions

    As discussed in Chapter 2 on page 18, GMAC expects you to make certain assumptions that would reflect information that the average person would be expected to know. For example, GMAC considers it common knowledge (and thus assumes everyone knows) that Canada and China are on different continents, that dryness is a lack of moisture, and so on. This is the sort of common knowledge that all test takers should have and are consistently asked to use.

3. Consequences of the statements presented in the stimulus

    Two or more pieces of information in the stimulus can combine to logically produce what appears to be a "new" idea, but in fact is not. For example, a stimulus might mention that a farmer has two fields of corn and three fields of carrots, followed by an answer choice that refers to the farmer's "five" crops. While "five" does not appear in the stimulus, this would not be "new" information given the nature of the statements in the stimulus.

Or, a stimulus might say that "all runners are prone to long-term knee problems, and Jim is a runner," and the right answer could refer to the fact that "Jim is prone to long-term knee problems." Again, combining the statements produces what is technically a new statement, but one that is supported clearly and directly by the stimulus.

4. Information under the "umbrella" of the statements in the stimulus

    Certain concepts act as an umbrella, and as such they automatically imply other things. For example, a discussion of "all animals" thereby includes cats, zebras, lizards, etc. In this way, elements that are not explicitly mentioned in the stimulus can still validly appear in the right answer choice. As another example, if a stimulus talks about a "bank," then, if the information is presented properly, the answers could then refer to "vaults," "currency," etc.

Note that, technically, items 3 and 4 above trade on the common sense information referenced in item 2, and are derived directly from the information cited in item 1.

Each of the above classifications meets the Fact Test ("The correct answer to a Must Be True question can always be proven by referring to the facts stated in the stimulus"), because each refers directly to the facts of the stimulus or to immediate consequences of those facts. So, as you analyze each answer choice, make certain to consider whether a statement that appears "new" might actually be derived from one of the sources of information discussed above.

Primary Objective #4 and Modifier Words Revisited

Primary Objective #4 states: "Read closely and know precisely what the author said. Do not generalize!" This is especially important in Must Be True questions because the details are all the test makers have to test you on. Consider the following stimulus:

2. To be considered for this year's Perfect Student Scholarship, a student needs to have received an A in every class, and to have achieved a perfect attendance record for this year. Torrey is the only student in this school who has received As in all of her classes, but she has been absent three times this year.

When reading the stimulus, your eye should be drawn to the modifier and indicator words, which are underlined below:

> To be considered for this year's Perfect Student Scholarship, a student <u>needs</u> to have received an A in <u>every</u> class, and to have achieved a <u>perfect</u> attendance record for this year. Torrey is the <u>only</u> student in this school who has received As in <u>all</u> of her classes, but she has been absent three times this year.

Words like "some," "could," and "many" encompass many different possibilities and are broad scope indicators. Words like "only" and "none" indicate a narrow scope.

The scope of the stimulus is relatively narrow, and most of the modifiers are absolute.

Now, look at the rest of the problem and see how several of the answer choices attempt to prey upon those who did not read the stimulus closely. Here are the question stem and corresponding answer choices for the stimulus above:

2. To be considered for this year's Perfect Student Scholarship, a student needs to have received an A in every class, and to have achieved a perfect attendance record for this year. Torrey is the only student in this school who has received As in all of her classes, but she has been absent three times this year.

The claims above, if true, most strongly support which of the following conclusions?

(A) No student at this school has perfect attendance for the year.
(B) Some students at this school who did not earn all As also did not achieve perfect attendance this year.
(C) Torrey is the only student at this school who has some chance of being considered for the Perfect Student Scholarship this year.
(D) Every student at this school will be precluded from consideration for the Perfect Student Scholarship this year.
(E) Many students at this school have achieved perfect attendance for the year but have also received grades below an A.

With the previous discussion in mind, let us analyze the answer choices:

Answer choice (A): The very first word—"No"—should be a red flag. Although many absolute modifiers are used by the author, the stimulus does not support for the assertion that no student has perfect attendance this year. In fact, we are given information about the attendance record of only one student in the school—Torrey. Therefore the stimulus provides no basis for choosing this answer.

Answer choice (B): Although the language used here ("some") is not absolute, this choice is wrong for roughly the same reason that answer choice (A) is incorrect: The author provides no information about the attendance records of the other students at the school, so there is nothing in the stimulus to prove or disprove this answer choice. Do not forget the Fact Test—it will eliminate any answer choice without support.

Answer choice (C): Much like incorrect answer choice (B), this incorrect choice uses soft language ("some chance") in an effort to deceive. Based on the requirements discussed in the stimulus, Torrey meets one of two criteria. Although Torrey has earned all A's in her classes, her three absences mean that she has not achieved perfect attendance. Thus, sadly Torrey has no chance of being considered for the scholarship this year.
Answer choice (D): This is the correct answer choice. We can follow the chain of connections in the stimulus to prove this answer: To be considered

CHAPTER FOUR: MUST BE TRUE QUESTIONS

for the scholarship, students need all A's and perfect attendance. Torrey is the only student in the school with all A's, so we already know that everyone else in the school is now ineligible. But, Torrey does not have a perfect attendance record, so she cannot win this year either. From the two statements, we can thus conclude that no one in the school is eligible, which is essentially what answer choice (D) says.

Answer choice (E): Nothing in the passage proves this answer choice. Although the author provides that all other students earned less than perfect grades (since Torrey is the only student with all A's), the stimulus offers no information regarding the attendance records for the rest of the student body, so there is no way to determine whether many (or any) of the other students achieved perfect attendance.

The lesson from this question is simple: read closely and pay strict attention to the modifiers used by the author. Even though you must read quickly, the test makers expect you to know exactly what was said, and they will include answer choices specifically designed to test whether you understood the details.

There are other classic GMAT tricks that we will discuss in this and future chapters.

Language: Negatives and Double Negatives

One of the tools at the disposal of the test makers is the use of multiple negative terms within a sentence. While there are different types of negative words, let us start with simple negative indicators, such as "no," "not," and "never." When added to a sentence, these words produce a meaning that is opposite the meaning of the original sentence. For example, consider the following statement:

> Let's go to the store.

If a negative term is added to the sentence, then the meaning changes entirely:

> Let's *not* go to the store.

Both of the above example sentences are easy to understand, and would not be likely to cause problems during the GMAT. However, the test makers do not stop at just a single negative; some sentences use two or even three negative terms. The appearance of multiple negatives can make a basic sentence much more difficult to understand. For example, consider the following sentence:

Let's *never not* go to the store.

Now the sentence contains two negative terms. In English, two negatives *typically* equal a positive (much as in math where two negatives equal a positive). Thus, the sentence above, as stated, means:

Let's always go to the store.

Of course, negatives are not always conveyed using the classic negative words such as "no." For example:

Mary is *not un*happy.

Here, the first negative is "not," and the second negative is conveyed by the prefix "un-" which is attached to "happy." In this instance, the "not" then serves to negate "unhappy." As we will see in a later chapter, "not unhappy" is *not* the same as "happy" (because someone who is "not unhappy" could have a middle-ground emotion such as solemn or bored; the person does not have to necessarily be happy).

In addition to straight negative terms and prefixes that negate the terms they modify, there are other words that can connote negativity. For example, some adverbs carry a negative meaning. Examples include "barely," "hardly," and "merely," among others. And, some words relay a negative concept on their own, such as "ban," "miss," and "absent." When reading, you must pay close attention to the word choices made by the author, as these choices will often contain one or more negatives.

Correct Answers in Must Be True Questions Reviewed

Let us take a moment to review two types of answers that will always be correct in a Must Be True question.

> Paraphrased answers occur primarily in Must Be True and Main Point questions. Some students have said they missed paraphrased answer choices because they did not feel the test makers would simply change the language of the text. They will!

1. Paraphrased Answers

   Paraphrased Answers are answers that restate a portion of the stimulus in different terms. Because the language is not exactly the same as in the stimulus, Paraphrased Answers can be easy to miss. Paraphrased Answers are designed to test your ability to discern the author's exact meaning. Sometimes the answer can appear to be almost too obvious since it is drawn directly from the stimulus.

2. Answers that are the sum of two or more stimulus statements (Combination Answers)

   Any answer choice that would result from combining two or more statements in the stimulus will be correct.

Should you encounter either of the above as answer choices in a Must Be True question, go ahead and select the answer with confidence.

Incorrect Answers in Must Be True Questions

There are several types of answers that appear in Must Be True questions that are incorrect. These answers appear frequently enough that we have provided a review of the major types below. Each answer category below is designed to attract you to an incorrect answer choice, and after this brief review we will examine several GMAT questions and analyze actual instances of these types of answers.

1. Could Be True or Likely to Be True Answers

   Because the criteria in the question stem requires you to find an answer choice that Must Be True, answers that only could be true or are even likely to be true are incorrect. These answers are attractive because there is nothing demonstrably wrong with them (for example, they do not contain statements that are counter to the stimulus). Regardless, like all incorrect answers these answers fail the Fact Test. Remember, you must select an answer choice that must occur based on what you have read.

   This category of incorrect answer is very broad, and some of the types mentioned below will fall under this general idea but place an emphasis on a specific aspect of the answer.

2. Exaggerated Answers

Exaggerated Answers take information from the stimulus and then stretch that information to make a broader statement that is not supported by the stimulus. In that sense, this form of answer is a variation of a could be true answer since the exaggeration is possible, but not proven based on the information. Here is an example:

If the stimulus states, "*Some* software vendors recently implemented more rigorous licensing procedures."

An incorrect answer would exaggerate one or more of the elements: "*Most* software vendors recently implemented more rigorous licensing procedures." In this example, *some* is exaggerated to *most*. While it could be true that most software vendors made the change, the stimulus does not prove that it must be true. This type of answer is often paraphrased, creating a deadly combination where the language is similar enough to be attractive but different enough to be incorrect.

Here is another example:

If the stimulus states, "Recent advances in the field of molecular biology make it *likely* that many school textbooks will be rewritten."

The exaggerated and paraphrased version would be: "Many school textbooks about molecular biology will be re-written." In this example, *likely* has been dropped, and this omission exaggerates the certainty of the change. The paraphrase also is problematic because the stimulus referenced school textbooks whereas the paraphrased answer refers to school textbooks *about molecular biology.*

3. "New" Information Answers

Because correct Must Be True answers must be based on information in the stimulus or the direct result of combining statements in the stimulus, be wary of answers that present so-called new information—that is, information not mentioned explicitly in the stimulus. Although these answers can be correct when they fall under the umbrella of a statement made in the stimulus, they are often incorrect. For example, if a stimulus discusses the economic policies of Japan, be careful with an answer that mentions U.S. economic policy. Look closely at the stimulus—does the information about Japanese economic policy apply to the U.S., or are the test makers trying to get you to fall for an answer that sounds logical but is not directly supported? To avoid incorrectly eliminating a New Information answer, take the following two steps:

A. Examine the scope of the argument to make sure the "new" information does not fall within the sphere of a term or concept in the stimulus.

B. Examine the answer to make sure it is not the consequence of combining stimulus elements.

4. The Shell Game

The GMAT makers have a variety of psychological tricks they use to entice test takers to select an answer choice. One of their favorites is one we call the Shell Game: an idea or concept is raised in the stimulus, and then a very similar idea appears in the answer choice, but the idea is changed just enough to be incorrect but still attractive. This trick is called the Shell Game because it abstractly resembles those street corner gambling games where a person hides a small object underneath one of three shells, and then scrambles them on a flat surface while a bettor tries to guess which shell the object is under (similar to three-card Monte). The object of a Shell Game is to trick the bettor into guessing incorrectly by mixing up the shells so quickly and deceptively that the bettor mistakenly selects the wrong shell. The intent of the GMAT makers is the same.

Shell Game answers are exceedingly dangerous because, when selected, not only do you miss the question but you walk away thinking you got it right. This misperception makes it difficult to accurately assess your performance after the test.

Shell Game and Opposite answers occur in all GMAT question types, not just Must Be True.

5. The Opposite Answer

As the name suggests, the Opposite Answer provides an answer that is completely opposite of the stated facts of the stimulus. Opposite Answers are very attractive to students who are reading too quickly or carelessly. Because Opposite Answers appear quite frequently in Strengthen and Weaken questions, we will discuss them in more detail when we cover those question types.

6. The Reverse Answer

Reverse Answers can occur in any type of question.

Here is a simplified example of how a Reverse Answer works, using italics to indicate the reversed parts:

The stimulus might state, "*Many* people have *some* type of security system in their home."

An incorrect answer then reverses the elements: "*Some* people have *many* types of security systems in their home."

The Reverse Answer is attractive because it contains familiar elements from the stimulus, but the reversed statement is incorrect because it rearranges those elements to create a new, unsupported statement.

Reverse Answers are a specific type of Shell Game answer.

Stimulus Opinions versus Assertions

When you are reading a stimulus, keep a careful watch on the statements the author offers as fact, and those that the author offers as the opinion of others. In a Must Be True question, the difference between the two can sometimes be used to eliminate answer choices.

Authors use different language to indicate that accepted facts are being discussed than they use to indicate an opinion. For example, opinions will be introduced by phrases such as:

"Scientists believe..."

"I think..."

Facts, on the other hand, are introduced more plainly, often without any preamble, such as in the following case:

"It is..."

"There are..."

"It has been proven..."

"Scientists found..."

"In 1890, ..."

When a stimulus contains only the opinions of others, then in a Must Be True question you can eliminate any answer choice that makes a flat assertion without reference to those opinions. For example, if an answer choice makes a factual assertion ("It is..."), but only opinions were present, then no factual statement can be concluded, and that answer choice must be incorrect.

Similarly, if a stimulus contains only factual statements (just premises, no conclusion), then answers that present an opinion can also be eliminated.

In all cases, you must analyze the stimulus and determine which statements are fact, and which statements are opinion.

Conditional Reasoning

Conditional reasoning appears only occasionally on the GMAT, often in Must Be True questions.

Conditional reasoning is the broad name given to logical relationships composed of sufficient and necessary conditions. Any conditional statement consists of at least one sufficient condition and at least one necessary condition. Let us begin by defining each condition:

> A sufficient condition can be defined as an event or circumstance whose occurrence indicates that a necessary condition must also occur.

> A necessary condition can be defined as an event or circumstance whose occurrence is required in order for a sufficient condition to occur.

Now, let's try that in plainer language! In other words, if a sufficient condition occurs, you automatically know that the necessary condition also occurs. If a necessary condition occurs, then it is possible but not certain that the sufficient condition will occur. Thus, they always occur together (but they are not always introduced in the same sentence).

In everyday use, conditional statements are often brought up using the "if...then" construction (and any conditional relationship can always be reduced to an "if...then" form). Consider the following statement, which we will use for the majority of our initial discussion:

> If someone gets an A+ on a test, then they must have studied for the test.

If the above statement is true, then anyone who receives an A+ on a test *must* have studied for the test. Someone who studied might have received an A+, but it is not guaranteed. Since getting an A+ automatically indicates that studying must have occurred, the sufficient condition is "get an A+" and it follows that "must have studied" is the necessary condition.

In the real world, we know that a statement such as the above is usually true, but not always. There could be a variety of other ways to get an A+ without studying, including cheating on the test, bribing the teacher for a higher grade, or even breaking into the school computer system and changing the grade. However, in the GMAT world, when an author makes

Conditional reasoning can occur in any question type.

a conditional statement, he or she believes that statement to be true *without exception*. So, if the statement above is made in the GMAT world, then according to the author anyone who gets an A+ *must* have studied (they may have done other things, but studying had to occur).

To efficiently manage the information in conditional statements, we use arrow diagrams. For a basic conditional relationship, the arrow diagram has three parts: a representation of the sufficient condition, a representation of the necessary condition, and an arrow pointing from the sufficient condition to the necessary condition. Most often, this arrow points from left to right.

The diagram for the previously discussed statement would be as follows:

<u>Sufficient</u>   <u>Necessary</u>

A+ $\longrightarrow$ Study

Please note that during the GMAT, the need to diagram statements is rare. We use the diagramming here in order to help make the concept as clear as possible.

Three Logical Features of Conditional Reasoning

Conditional Reasoning statements have several unique features that you must know. When considering the diagram above, remember the following:

> In the diagram of a conditional statement, the sufficient condition always comes at the "beginning" of the arrow, and the necessary condition always comes at the "end" of the arrow. Thus, when a sufficient condition occurs, you can follow the arrow to the necessary condition.

1. The sufficient condition does not *make* the necessary condition occur. That is, the sufficient condition does not actively cause the necessary condition to happen. That form of reasoning is known as Causal Reasoning, which will be discussed in Chapter Seven. Instead, in a conditional statement the occurrence of the sufficient condition is a sign or indicator that the necessary condition will occur, is occurring, or has already occurred. In our discussion example, the occurrence of someone receiving an A+ is a sign that indicates that studying must also have occurred. The A+ does not *make* the studying occur.

2. Temporally speaking, either condition can occur first, or the two conditions can occur at the same time. In our discussion example, the necessary condition (studying) would most logically occur first. Depending on the example, the sufficient condition could occur first.

3. The conditional relationship stated by the author does not have to reflect reality. This point may help some students who thought that our diagram might be backwards. Some people read the statement and think, "studying would logically lead to an A+, so studying is the sufficient condition." As reasonable as that may sound, that way of thinking is incorrect because it does not reflect what the author said, but rather what you think of what the author said. *Your job is not to figure out what sounds reasonable, but rather to perfectly capture the meaning of the author's sentence.*

Valid and Invalid Statements

Although the discussion example may seem relatively easy, the makers of the GMAT can use conditional reasoning to ensnare unwary test takers, especially on 700-level questions. When analyzing a basic conditional statement, there are certain observations that can be inferred from the statement and there are observations that may appear true but are not certain.

Taking our discussion example *as undeniably true*, consider the following four statements:

1. John received an A+ on the test, so he must have studied for the test.

2. John studied for the test, so he must have received an A+ on the test.

3. John did not receive an A+ on the test, so he must not have studied for the test.

4. John did not study for the test, so he must not have received an A+ on the test.

Two of the four statements above are valid, and two of the four statements are invalid. Can you identify which two are valid? The answers are given below and on the next page.

Statement 1 is valid. According to the original statement, because John received an A+, he must have studied for the test. We call this type of inference the Repeat form because the statement basically repeats the parts of the original statement and applies them to the individual in question, John.

Conditional reasoning occurs when a statement containing sufficient and necessary conditions is used to draw a conclusion based on the statement.

The Repeat form simply restates the elements in the original order they appeared. This creates a valid inference.

We would use the following diagram for statement 1:

Sufficient   Necessary

A+$_J$ $\longrightarrow$ Study$_J$

Note how the A+ and Study elements are in the same position as our original statement, hence the "Repeat" form moniker. The "J" subscript represents "John." John is not a separate diagramming element because John is simply someone experiencing the conditions in the statement.

Statement 2 is invalid. Just because John studied for the test does not mean he actually received an A+. He may have only received a B, or perhaps he even failed. To take statement 2 as true is to make an error known as a Mistaken Reversal™. We use this name because the attempted inference looks like the reverse of the original statement:

Sufficient   Necessary

Study$_J$ $\longrightarrow$ A+$_J$

The form here reverses the Study and A+ elements, and although this statement *might* be true, it is not definitely true. Just because the necessary condition has been fulfilled does not mean that the sufficient condition must occur.

Statement 3 is also invalid. Just because John did not receive an A+ does not mean he did not study. He may have studied but did not happen to receive an A+. Perhaps he received a B instead. To take this statement as true is to make an error known as a Mistaken Negation™.

Sufficient   Necessary

A̸+$_J$ $\longrightarrow$ S̸tudy$_J$

The form here negates the A+ and Study elements (this is represented by the slash through each term), and although this statement *might* be true, it is not definitely true. Just because the sufficient condition has not been fulfilled does not mean that the necessary condition cannot occur.

Sidebar: A Mistaken Reversal switches the elements in the sufficient and necessary conditions, creating a statement that does not have to be true.

Sidebar: A Mistaken Negation negates both conditions, creating a statement that does not have to be true.

Sidebar	Main text
Because the contrapositive both reverses and negates, it is a combination of a Mistaken Reversal and Mistaken Negation. Since the contrapositive is valid, it is as if two wrongs do make a right.	**Statement 4 is valid.** If studying is the necessary condition for getting an A+, and John did not study, then according to the original statement there is no way John could have received an A+. This inference is known as the contrapositive, and you can see that when the necessary condition fails to occur, then the sufficient condition cannot occur.

$$\underline{\text{Sufficient}} \qquad\qquad \underline{\text{Necessary}}$$

$$\cancel{\text{Study}}_J \longrightarrow \cancel{\text{A+}}_J$$

The form here reverses *and* negates the Study and A+ elements. When you are looking to find the contrapositive, do not think about the elements and what they represent. Instead, simply reverse and negate the two terms.

There is a contrapositive for every conditional statement, and if the initial statement is true, then the contrapositive is also true. The contrapositive is simply a different way of expressing the initial statement. To analogize, it is like examining a penny: both sides look different but intrinsically the value is the same.

A contrapositive denies the necessary condition, thereby making it impossible for the sufficient condition to occur.

These four valid and invalid inferences are used by the test makers to test your knowledge of what follows from a given statement. Sometimes you will need to recognize that the contrapositive is present in order to identify a correct answer, other times you may need to recognize a Mistaken Reversal in order to avoid a wrong answer, or that an argument is using a Mistaken Negation, and so forth. When you analyze a conditional statement, you simply need to be aware that these types of statements exist. At first that will require you to actively think about the possibilities and this will slow you down, but as time goes by this recognition will become second nature and you will begin to solve certain questions extraordinarily fast.

One word of warning: many people read the analysis of valid and invalid statements and ignore the discussion of the form of the relationships (reversal of the terms, negation of the terms, etc.). This is very dangerous because it forces them to rely on their knowledge of the grading system to understand why each statement is valid or invalid, and if their perception differs from that of the author, they make mistakes. At first, it is difficult to avoid doing this, but as time goes on, focus more on the form of the relationship and less on the content. If you simply try to think through the content of the relationship, you will likely be at a loss when faced with a conditional relationship involving, for example, the hemolymph of arthropods.

Valid and Invalid Statement Recognition Mini-Drill

Each of the following problems presents a pair of arrow diagrams which feature a statement and then an attempted inference. The attempted inference is either a valid Repeat form or Contrapositive, or an invalid Mistaken Reversal or Mistaken Negation. Identify the form of the attempted inference in each problem. *Answers on page 112*

1. Original statement: A ⟶ B̸

   Attempted Inference: B̸ ⟶ A

2. Original statement: C ⟶ D̸

   Attempted Inference: D ⟶ C̸

3. Original statement: E̸ ⟶ F

   Attempted Inference: E ⟶ F̸

4. Original statement: G̸ ⟶ H

   Attempted Inference: H̸ ⟶ G

5. Original statement: I ⟶ J

   Attempted Inference: I ⟶ J

6. Original statement: K̸ ⟶ L̸

   Attempted Inference: L̸ ⟶ K̸

7. Original statement: M ⟶ N

   Attempted Inference: M̸ ⟶ N̸

8. Original statement: O̸ ⟶ P̸

   Attempted Inference: P ⟶ O

CHAPTER FOUR: MUST BE TRUE QUESTIONS

Valid and Invalid Statement Recognition Mini-Drill Answer Key

1. Mistaken Reversal

    Invalid. The A and B terms are reversed, but not negated. This is the classic Mistaken Reversal form.

2. Contrapositive

    Valid. The C and D terms are both reversed *and* negated, which is the mark of the contrapositive.

3. Mistaken Negation

    Invalid. The E and F terms are negated, but not reversed. This is the classic Mistaken Negation form.

4. Contrapositive

    Valid. The G and H terms are both reversed and negated. Compare this problem to #2. Although the "slashes" are in different places, each is a contrapositive because the terms are reversed and negated.

5. Repeat

    Valid. The terms are simply repeated.

6. Mistaken Reversal

    Invalid. Despite all the slashes, the only thing that occurs in this problem is that the K and L terms are reversed.

7. Mistaken Negation

    Invalid. The M and N terms are negated, but not reversed.

8. Contrapositive

    Valid. Although this may look "upside down," both terms are reversed and negated.

The Multiplicity of Indicator Words

So far we have discussed the nature of conditional relationships and what inferences can be made from a conditional statement. Now we turn to recognizing conditionality when it is present. One of the factors that makes identifying conditional statements difficult is that so many different words and phrases can be used to introduce a sufficient or necessary condition. The test makers have the advantage of variety in this regard, and so you must learn to recognize conditional reasoning when it is present in a stimulus. Take a moment to examine each of the following statements. Are they similar or different?

1. To get an A+ you must study.

2. Studying is necessary to get an A+.

3. When someone gets an A+, it shows they must have studied.

4. Only someone who studies can get an A+.

5. You will get an A+ only if you study.

You may be surprised to discover that each statement is diagrammed exactly the same way:

Sufficient		Necessary
A+	$\longrightarrow$	Study

In advanced Critical Reasoning problems it is essential that you be able to recognize the terms that identify and precede sufficient and necessary conditions. The following words or phrases are often to introduce conditional reasoning:

One of the challenges of the GMAT is that a single idea can be presented in so many different ways. Thus, part of your task is to determine exactly what the test makers are saying in each argument, and whether statements that appear different are in fact different in meaning.

CHAPTER FOUR: MUST BE TRUE QUESTIONS

To introduce a sufficient condition:	To introduce a necessary condition:
If	Then
When	Only
Whenever	Only if
Every	Must
All	Required
Any	Unless
Each	Except
In order to	Until
People who	Without

These lists are by no means comprehensive. Due to the vagaries of the English language many different terms can be used to introduce conditional statements. Since these lists can assist you in recognizing the types of situations where conditional statements arise, your first step should be to memorize the indicator words on each list. After you are comfortable with each word, focus on understanding the meaning of each conditional statement you encounter. Ultimately, your understanding of the relationship between sufficient and necessary conditions will allow you to easily manipulate any problem.

How to Recognize Conditionality

Using the words from the indicator lists, let's re-examine each of the five statements from page 113. In each sentence, the conditional indicator is in italics:

> Any synonym of the terms in the lists will also suffice.

1. To get an A+ you *must* study.

2. Studying is *necessary* to get an A+.

3. *When* someone gets an A+, it shows they *must* have studied.

4. *Only* someone who studies can get an A+.

5. You will get an A+ *only if* you study.

Comparing these five sentences reveals two critical rules about how conditional reasoning appears in a given sentence:

1. Either condition can appear first in the sentence.

   The order of presentation of the sufficient and necessary conditions is irrelevant. In statements 1, 3, and 5 the sufficient condition appears first in the sentence; in statements 2 and 4 the necessary condition appears first. Thus, when you are reading, you cannot rely on encountering the sufficient condition first and instead you must keep an eye out for conditional indicators.

2. A sentence can have one or two indicators.

   Sentences do not need both a sufficient condition indicator and a necessary condition indicator in order to have conditional reasoning present. As shown by statements 1, 2, 4, and 5, a single indicator is enough. Note that once you have established that one of the conditions is present, you can examine the remainder of the sentence to determine the nature of the other condition. For example, in statement 5, once the "only if" appears and you establish that "study" is the necessary condition, return to the first part of the sentence and establish that "A+" is the sufficient condition.

> Looking for conditionality is like being an air traffic controller: you must recognize and track the elements when they appear in a problem. If no conditional elements appear in a problem, then you do not have to worry about it.

CHAPTER FOUR: MUST BE TRUE QUESTIONS

Sufficient and Necessary Diagramming Drill

Each of the following statements contains a sufficient condition and a necessary condition; therefore, each of the following statements can be described as a "conditional statement." In the spaces provided write the proper arrow diagram for each of the following conditional statements. Then write the proper arrow diagram for the contrapositive of each of the following conditional statements. *Answers on page 118*

Example: If it is a bus, then it is yellow.   B = Bus   Y = Yellow

    __B__ ⟶ __Y__

    __B̸__ ⟶ __B̸__ (the contrapositive)

1. All of the State University professors lecture on Wednesdays.

2. People who drive fast are dangerous.

3. No electrician is an architect.

4. If you are not an electrician, then you must be an architect.

5. Sally will not attend the banquet unless Jan also attends the banquet.

Sufficient and Necessary Diagramming Drill

6. Maria will not speak during the meeting unless the chairman does not speak.

7. The children go to the park when the sun is shining.

8. Only the good die young.

9. I will be on time if I get the car by noon.

10. John will go to the meeting only if Paul goes to the meeting.

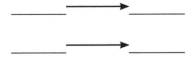

Sufficient and Necessary Diagramming Drill Answer Key

Note: Since a conditional statement and its contrapositive are identical in meaning, the order in which the two arrow diagrams appear is not important.

1. SUP = State University professor   LW = lecture on Wednesdays

    SUP ⟶ LW
    (If you are a State University professor, then you must lecture on Wednesdays.)

    L̶W̶ ⟶ S̶U̶P̶
    (If you do not lecture on Wednesdays, then you must not be a State University professor.)

2. DF = drive fast   D = dangerous

    DF ⟶ D
    (If you are a person who drives fast, then you must be dangerous.)

    D̶ ⟶ D̶F̶
    (If you are not dangerous, then you must not be a person who drives fast.)

    Note: The phrase "People who" generally introduces a sufficient condition.

3. E = electrician   A = architect

    E ⟶ A̶
    (If you are an electrician, then you cannot be an architect.)

    A ⟶ E̶
    (If you are an architect, then you cannot be an electrician.)

4. E = electrician   A = architect

    E̶ ⟶ A
    (If you are not an electrician, then you must be an architect.)

    A̶ ⟶ E
    (If you are not an architect, then you must be an electrician.)

5. SB = Sally attends the banquet   JB = Jan attends the banquet

    SB ⟶ JB
    (If Sally attends the banquet, then Jan must also attend the banquet.)

    J̶B̶ ⟶ S̶B̶
    (If Jan does not attend the banquet, then Sally will not attend the banquet.)

Sufficient and Necessary Diagramming Drill Answer Key

6. MS = Maria speaks   CS = chairman speaks

   MS $\longrightarrow$ C̶S̶
   (If Maria speaks during the meeting, then the chairman will not speak during the meeting.)

   CS $\longrightarrow$ M̶S̶
   (If the chairman speaks during the meeting, then Maria will not speak during the meeting.)

7. SS = the sun is shining   CGP = children go to the park

   SS $\longrightarrow$ CGP
   (If the sun is shining, then the children will go to the park.)

   C̶G̶P̶ $\longrightarrow$ S̶S̶
   (If the children do not go to the park, then the sun must not be shining.)

8. DY = die young   G = good

   DY $\longrightarrow$ G
   (If you die young, then you must be good.)

   G̶ $\longrightarrow$ D̶Y̶
   (If you are not good, then you cannot die young.)

   Note: "Only" generally introduces a necessary condition.

9. CN = get car by noon   OT = arrive on time

   CN $\longrightarrow$ OT
   (If I get the car by noon, then I will arrive on time.)

   O̶T̶ $\longrightarrow$ C̶N̶
   (If I do not arrive on time, then I will not have gotten the car by noon.)

10. JM = John goes to meeting   PM = Paul goes to meeting

    JM $\longrightarrow$ PM
    (If John goes to the meeting, then Paul must go to the meeting.)

    P̶M̶ $\longrightarrow$ J̶M̶
    (If Paul does not go to the meeting, then John cannot go to the meeting.)

    Note: The term "only if" generally introduces a necessary condition.

Final Note

This chapter is only the start of our question analysis, and the ideas discussed so far represent a fraction of what you will learn from this book. Future chapters will build on the ideas discussed herein, and present new concepts that will help you attack all types of questions.

On the following page is a review of some of the key points from this chapter. After the review, there is a short problem set of four questions to help you test your knowledge of some of the ideas. An answer key follows with explanations. Good luck!

Remember, this is a strategy guide, and thus the problem sets in this book are relatively short by design. If you are looking for a practice book or more Critical Reasoning questions, we strongly recommend the Official Guide for GMAT Review and the Official Guide for GMAT Verbal Review, both of which come directly from GMAC.

Must Be True Question Type Review

Must Be True questions require you to select an answer choice that is proven by the information presented in the stimulus. The question format can be reduced to, "What did you read in the stimulus, and what do you know on the basis of that reading?"

You cannot bring in information from outside the stimulus to answer the questions; all of the information necessary to answer the question resides in the stimulus.

All Must Be True answer choices must pass the Fact Test™:

> The correct answer to a Must Be True question can always be proven by referring to the facts stated in the stimulus.

If you find yourself having difficulty prephrasing an answer to a Must Be True question, do not be concerned.

The scope of the stimulus—especially if that scope is broad—often helps eliminate one or more of the answer choices.

You can often predict the occurrence of Must Be True questions because the stimulus of most Must Be True questions does not contain a conclusion.

Correct Answer Types:

> Paraphrased answers are answers that restate a portion of the stimulus in different terms. When these answers mirror the stimulus, they are correct.

> Combination answers result from combining two or more statements in the stimulus.

Incorrect Answer Types:

> Could Be True answers are attractive because they can possibly occur, but they are incorrect because they do not have to be true.

> Exaggerated answers take information from the stimulus and then stretch that information to make a broader statement that is not supported by the stimulus.

New Information answers include information not explicitly mentioned in the stimulus. Be careful with these answers: first examine the scope of the stimulus to make sure the "new" information does not fall under the umbrella of a term or concept in the stimulus. Second, examine the answer to make sure it is not the consequence of combining stimulus elements.

The Shell Game occurs when an idea or concept is raised in the stimulus, and then a very similar idea appears in the answer choice, but the idea is changed just enough to be incorrect while remaining attractive.

The Opposite answer is completely opposite of the facts of the stimulus.

The Reverse answer is attractive because it contains familiar elements from the stimulus, but the reversed statement is incorrect because it rearranges those elements to create a new, unsupported statement.

Must Be True Question Problem Set

Please complete the problem set and review the answer key and explanations. *Answers on page 125*

1. Headaches can often be effectively relieved by over-the-counter medication, without necessitating a physician's oversight. However, doctors warn against employment of this simple strategy for recurring or particularly long-lasting headaches, even if such medication can provide relief. Since such headaches are often symptomatic of more serious maladies, sufferers are strongly advised instead to consult their physicians.

    Which of the following conclusions is most strongly supported by the statements above?

    (A) The greater the pain associated with a particular headache, the more serious the underlying cause.
    (B) In some cases physicians advise against seeking immediate relief from pain.
    (C) Some headaches cannot be relieved with over-the-counter medications.
    (D) Physicians tend to focus less on pain relief rather than on other physical symptoms.
    (E) Over-the-counter medication cannot provide effective relief of a headache if the underlying cause is a serious malady.

2. Last year, the government of country A imposed large tariffs on steel imports in an effort to aid its domestic steel industry. Many domestic steel producers enjoyed record profits as a result, as foreign steel producers were in many cases unable to compete effectively under the burden of the newly imposed tariffs.

    Which of the following conclusions is best supported by the passage?

    (A) Not all steel producers were unaffected by country A's newly imposed tariffs.
    (B) Some foreign steel producers were able to compete effectively in country A even after the new tariffs were imposed.
    (C) After the new tariffs were imposed, most foreign steel producers were unable to compete effectively with country A's domestic steel producers.
    (D) Most domestic steel producers were able to increase their profits after the new tariffs were imposed.
    (E) If a government intends to protect a domestic industry, the imposition of tariffs on imports is generally an effective approach.

Must Be True Question Problem Set

3. For many years, alcohol producers followed a self-imposed industry ban on advertising on television. Eventually, some producers broke the ban and began advertising their products on television. The producers who advertised on television generally charged less for their products, and so if all producers began advertising in this fashion, overall costs to consumers would be lower than if they did not advertise.

   Which of the following must be true if the statements above are true?

   (A) More consumers will drink alcohol if there are more alcohol advertisements on television.
   (B) Alcohol producers who currently advertise their products on television will raise their prices if other producers decide to advertise on television.
   (C) When the self-imposed advertising ban was first broken, those alcohol producers who chose not to advertise on television generally charged more for their products than alcohol producers who had joined in breaking the ban.
   (D) If there had not been a self-imposed ban on television advertising, all alcohol producers would have advertised on television.
   (E) If additional alcohol producers decide to advertise and lower their prices, the alcohol producers who do not advertise on television will lower their prices.

4. Blood tests used to determine pregnancy can at times be inconclusive. This means that the test has been unable to determine if the woman is pregnant or not pregnant. Regardless, some doctors refuse to perform further surgeries because of an inconclusive pregnancy test result.

   If the statements above are true, which of the following conclusions is most strongly supported by them?

   (A) Pregnancy tests should always be given prior to surgery.
   (B) Most women with inconclusive pregnancy tests are actually pregnant.
   (C) Some surgical procedures are affected by whether or not a woman is pregnant.
   (D) Some doctors require a pregnancy test be given when evaluating female candidates for any surgery.
   (E) A pregnancy test that returns a negative result is sometimes incorrect.

Must Be True Problem Set Answer Key

All answer keys in this book indicate the question number, the question type classification, and the correct answer.

Question #1: Must Be True. The correct answer choice is (B)

The idea in this stimulus is that while headaches can often be relieved by certain types of medication, headaches that are recurring or long-lasting can indicate a more serious condition, and doctors recommend that the sufferer seek medical attention instead of relief from over-the-counter medicine. As we consider what would be proven true from these statements, it is important to not go beyond the information and facts presented, or make unwarranted assumptions beyond what the stimulus directly supports.

Answer choice (A): There is no information in the stimulus that correlates the severity of headache pain with the seriousness of the cause of the headache.

Answer choice (B): This is the correct answer. The stimulus indicates that while a person may be able to find relief from a recurring or long-lasting headache through the use of medication, physicians recommend that in these situations (hence the "in some cases") the sufferer should instead seek medical attention and not self-medicate (i.e. not seek immediate relief from the pain). Note that this answer can be easy to overlook because it goes against some commonly-held notions of physicians being obligated to attempt to quickly alleviate pain.

Answer choice (C): All that we know from the information presented is that "headaches can *often be relieved* by over-the-counter medication" (italics added for emphasis). There is nothing that suggests then that some headaches *cannot* be relieved by these same medications. Be careful not to assume that "some cannot" just because you are not explicitly told "all can."

Answer choice (D): This answer choice is simply much too broad to be completely supported by the information in the stimulus. In the specific instance of a recurring/long-lasting headache, physicians may be focused more on the underlying cause than on immediate pain relief, but that does not necessarily mean that physicians in general focus less on pain relief (in all instances) than on other physical symptoms.

Answer choice (E): This answer choice contradicts the information given, so it is an Opposite answer and is correct. The stimulus states that over-the-counter medications could potentially provide relief for a headache caused by something more serious ("even if such medication can provide relief"); the point is that physicians suggest sufferers forego immediate relief and seek to instead establish the underlying cause of the headache.

Must Be True Problem Set Answer Key

Question #2: Must Be True. The correct answer choice is (A)

This stimulus presents a fairly straightforward scenario: the tariffs imposed on steel imports by the government of country A have helped domestic steel producers become more competitive and make record profits, because in most cases foreign producers were unable to compete under the new tariffs. Note that there is no conclusion present, and so this is a fact set, not an argument.

Answer choice (A): This is the correct answer. Since we know that domestic steel producers benefited positively from the tariffs, and foreign steel producers were affected negatively, it must be true that not all steel producers were unaffected. Worded another way, answer choice A states "*some* steel producers *were affected* by...[the] tariffs."

As an aside, if, upon reading (A), you determined this was a strong answer, should you have simply selected it and skipped reading the remaining answers? No, because perhaps you misread (A), or perhaps there is a better answer among the remaining choices. The only reason not to read the remaining choices would be if you were just about out of time.

Answer choice (B): The stimulus tells us that "foreign steel producers were in many cases unable to compete effectively under the burden of the newly imposed tariffs." This does *not* imply that some foreign steel producers were able to compete effectively. Be careful not to assume that "some could compete" just because you are not explicitly told "all could not compete." Although this answer choice Could Be True, it does not have to be true.

Answer choice (C): Again, we know that in many cases foreign steel producers could not compete effectively, but we cannot know anything about the percentage of foreign steel producers that could not compete effectively. Again, this answer choice Could Be True, but it does not have to be true.

Answer choice (D): The stimulus states that "many" domestic steel producers enjoyed record profits, but "many" does not necessarily equal "most" (or "majority"). Logically speaking, "many" simply means "some," unless you have further information about the overall number under discussion (more on this in Chapter Twelve).

Answer choice (E): This answer choice is much too broad in scope to be completely supported by the information in the stimulus. We know that in country A these particular tariffs helped to aid the domestic steel industry, but that is not sufficient evidence to prove that tariffs are "generally an effective approach" to protecting any domestic industry in any country.

Must Be True Problem Set Answer Key

Question #3: Must Be True. The correct answer choice is (C)

The structure of the argument is as follows:

Premise:	For many years, alcohol producers followed a self-imposed industry ban on advertising on television.
Premise:	Eventually, some producers broke the ban and began advertising their products on television.
Premise:	The producers who advertised on television generally charged less for their products.
Conclusion:	so if all producers began advertising in this fashion, overall costs to consumers would be lower than if they did not advertise.

This stimulus is relatively easy to understand: a comparison is made between alcohol producers who began to advertise on television and alcohol producers who initially did not. We are told that the producers that first began to advertise on television generally charged less for their products and that, if all advertisers began to advertise this way (with lower prices), then the consumers' overall costs would be lower.

Answer choice (A): The information in the stimulus is about cost, not consumption. We cannot assume that increased advertising will automatically increase consumer consumption.

Answer choice (B): There is no way to know how alcohol producers who advertise on television will behave if other producers also begin to advertise. All we know is that if other producers begin to advertise similarly (i.e. charge less for their product), then overall consumer costs will decrease.

Answer choice (C): This is the correct answer. The stimulus tells us that when the first producers broke the ban and began to advertise, they generally charged less than non-advertising producers. So it must be true that those producers who did not initially advertise generally charged more for their products than the advertising producers.

Answer choice (D): The stimulus does not provide any information that would allow us to infer how alcohol producers might have behaved without the self-imposed advertising ban.

Answer choice (E): All that we can infer from the information provided is that if more producers begin to advertise and subsequently lower their prices, the overall cost to consumers will be lowered. We cannot know what effect that would have on the price of alcohol from producers who still choose not to advertise.

Must Be True Problem Set Answer Key

Question #4: Must Be True. The correct answer choice is (C)

This question presents a fact set that begins by telling us that blood tests are, at times, unable to conclusively determine if a woman is pregnant or not. Then we are told that some doctors refuse to perform certain surgeries due to an inconclusive pregnancy test result. These facts indicate that definitive knowledge of whether or not a patient is pregnant must have a potential impact on some surgical procedures. Hence, doctors will not operate on that patient without conclusive pregnancy tests results. Note too that we cannot know the number or type of surgical procedures that could potentially be affected by pregnancy; we simply know that some doctors will not perform further surgeries following an inconclusive test result.

Answer choice (A): This answer choice is far too broad in scope to be proven by the stimulus. Just because some surgical procedures may be potentially impacted by a patient's pregnancy does not mean that a pregnancy test should precede all surgeries. Further, by the logic presented in answer choice (A), all patients—men and women—should be given pregnancy tests prior to any surgery, and clearly the stimulus does not support that conclusion.

Answer choice (B): There is no information in the stimulus to indicate the frequency with which inconclusive tests turn out to ultimately be positive or negative.

Answer choice (C): This is the correct answer. As stated above, the facts of the stimulus support the notion that whether or not a patient is pregnant could potentially affect a surgical procedure to be performed on that patient.

Answer choice (D): This answer choice has very strong language, as it states that some doctors require a pregnancy test prior to "any surgery." However we cannot know that some doctors require a pregnancy test before *every* surgery they perform on a female candidate; we only know that some doctors refuse to perform certain surgeries following an inconclusive test result. Always be wary of extreme or absolute language in answer choice for Must Be True questions, since it takes similarly strong language in a stimulus to prove a strongly worded answer choice correct.

Answer choice (E): The stimulus is exclusively about inconclusive (non-result) pregnancy tests, so an answer choice that addresses tests producing a "negative result" goes beyond the facts provided in the stimulus.

Chapter Five:
Main Point Questions

Chapter Five: Main Point Questions

Main Point Questions 131

Two Incorrect Answer Types 132

Fill in the Blank Questions 136

Main Point—Fill in the Blank Questions 136

Final Chapter Note 137

Main Point Question Type Review 138

Fill in the Blank Question Type Review 138

Must Be True and Main Point Question Stem Mini-Drill 139

Main Point Question Problem Set 141

Main Point Questions

> **Important Note**: Main Point questions appear infrequently in GMAT Critical Reasoning. However, we have included this question type for two important reasons:
>
> 1. The process of identifying the main point is invaluable when you are attempting to perform other tasks with an argument, such as Weaken, Strengthen, etc.
>
> 2. Main Point questions appear frequently in GMAT Reading Comprehension, and therefore a discussion of this question type will benefit you when you face Reading Comprehension passages.

Main Point questions may be the question type most familiar to test takers. Many of the standardized tests you have already encountered, such as the SAT, contain questions that ask you to ascertain the Main Point. Even in daily conversation you will hear, "What's your point?" Main Point questions, as you might suspect from the name, ask you to summarize the author's point of view.

From a classification standpoint, Main Point questions are a subcategory of Must Be True questions and fall into the First Family type. As with all First Family questions, the answer you select must follow from the information in the stimulus. But be careful: even if an answer choice must be true according to the stimulus, if it fails to capture the main point it cannot be correct. This is the central truth of Main Point questions: like all Must Be True question variants the correct answer must pass the Fact Test, but with the additional criterion that the correct answer choice must capture the author's point.

Because every Main Point question stimulus contains an argument, if you apply the methods discussed in Chapters Two and Three you should already know the answer to a Main Point question by the time you read the question stem. Primary Objective #2 states that you should identify the conclusion of the argument, and the correct answer choice to these problems will be a rephrasing of the main conclusion of the argument. So, by simply taking the steps you would take to solve any question, you already have the answer to a Main Point question at your fingertips. Be careful, though: many Main Point problems feature a structure that places the conclusion either at the beginning or in the middle of the stimulus. Most students have an unstated expectation that the conclusion will appear in the last sentence, and the test makers are able to prey upon this

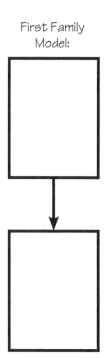

First Family Model:

expectation by creating wrong answers that paraphrase the last sentence of the stimulus. To avoid this trap, simply avoid assuming that the last sentence is the conclusion.

The Main Point question stem format is remarkably consistent, with the primary feature being a request for you to identify the conclusion or point of the argument, as in the following examples:

"Which of the following most accurately expresses the main conclusion of the argument?"

"Which of the following most accurately expresses the conclusion of the argument?"

"Which of the following most accurately restates the main point of the passage?"

"The main point of the argument is that"

Two Incorrect Answer Types

Two types of answers often appear in Main Point questions. Both are incorrect:

1. Answers that are true but do not encapsulate the author's point.

2. Answers that repeat premises of the argument.

Each answer type is attractive because they are true based on what you have read. However, neither summarizes the author's main point and therefore both are incorrect.

Because you have already learned the skills necessary to complete these questions, we will use just one question for discussion purposes. Please take a moment to complete the following problem:

1. Physician: Goliath Pharmaceutical Company has claimed that the recent increase in the number of diagnosed cases of Disease X shows that the disease is increasing in virulence. This is a questionable argument, just as it would be incorrect to claim that our increased success rate in treating patients with Disease X is due to the disease becoming less virulent. The real cause of both increases is a newly introduced screening process that reduces misdiagnoses of patients infected with the Disease X pathogen.

    The Physician's statements, if accurate, provide the most support for which of the following as a conclusion?

    (A) The new screening procedure is the reason that more people are requesting to be tested for Disease X.
    (B) It is not possible to determine that a patient has Disease X without using the new screening process.
    (C) The increase in diagnosed cases of Disease X is proportional to the increase in the number of clinics utilizing the new screening procedure.
    (D) The new screening process occasionally diagnoses patients with Disease X when they are actually suffering from another illness.
    (E) The increase in the number of diagnosed cases of Disease X is not due to an increase in the disease's virulence.

The argument can be broken into the following component parts:

Premise:	Goliath Pharmaceutical Company has claimed that the recent increase in the number of diagnosed cases of Disease X shows that the disease is increasing in virulence.
Conclusion:	This is a questionable argument,
Premise:	just as it would be incorrect to claim that our increased success rate in treating patients with Disease X is due to the disease becoming less virulent.
Premise:	The real cause of both increases is a newly introduced screening process that reduces misdiagnoses of patients infected with the Disease X pathogen.

Always identify the conclusion of any argument you read!

CHAPTER FIVE: MAIN POINT QUESTIONS

If an argument contains two conclusions, you will be forced to identify which one is the main conclusion and which one is the subsidiary conclusion.

From the breakdown above, you can see that the conclusion to this argument is the first clause of the second sentence, which begins with "This is..." By applying the Primary Objectives you should have identified this conclusion while reading, and then, upon classifying the question stem you should have looked for a paraphrase of this sentence. Answer choice (E) fits the bill, and is the correct answer.

Answer choice (A): The physician makes no statements about *requests* that people have made. Instead, the argument is about what has lead to the recent decrease in the number of misdiagnosed cases of Disease X. In short, the argument is about diagnoses whereas this answer choice is about patient requests.

Answer choice (B): The physician would not necessarily agree with this statement. The physician states that the newly introduced screening process has reduced misdiagnoses of patients infected with the Disease X pathogen, but that does not automatically lead to the conclusion that Disease X cannot be diagnosed without the screening process.

If you chose (B), you have made the error of believing that a process that is beneficial is also essential. Nowhere in the argument is the point made that the screening process is a necessary component for diagnosing the disease.

Answer choice (C): This answer is similar to answer choice (B) in some respects. Although the new screening process is stated as the cause of the decrease in misdiagnoses, there is no indication that an element of proportionality is in play. As this answer states that the increase in diagnosed cases is "proportional to the increase in the number of clinics utilizing the new screening procedure," this answer choice does not pass the Fact Test and is therefore incorrect.

Answer choice (D): This answer choice can be tricky. The argument is about reducing misdiagnoses of Disease X, meaning that there has been a reduction in two types of patients:

1. Those who did not have Disease X but were mistakenly diagnosed with the disease.

2. Those who had Disease X but were mistakenly diagnosed with another disease.

Now that these patients in the first group have been removed from the group of "Disease X" patients, the treatment of those patients is likely to be more successful. And, now that patients in group 2 have been added to the group, the disease appears to be increasing in virulence.

However, there is no indication that the new screening process occasionally misdiagnoses patients. Instead, it appears to be more accurate, and there is no prohibition on the possibility that the new screening process is 100% accurate. Consequently, this answer choice is incorrect.

Answer choice (E): This is the correct answer. Remember, any answer that is a paraphrase of the conclusion of the argument will be the correct answer to a Main Point question.

Paraphrased answers are always correct in Must Be True questions. Answers that paraphrase the conclusion are correct in Main Point questions.

The lesson learned from this particular problem is that you must isolate the conclusion and then look for a paraphrase of that conclusion.

Like the question above, many Main Point question stimuli avoid using traditional conclusion indicators and this lack of argument indicator "guideposts" makes your task more challenging. Remember, if you are struggling to identify the conclusion in an argument, you can always use the Conclusion Identification Method discussed in Chapter Two:

> Take the statements under consideration for the conclusion and place them in an arrangement that forces one to be the conclusion and the other(s) to be the premise(s). Use premise and conclusion indicators to achieve this end. Once the pieces are arranged, determine if the arrangement makes logical sense. If so, you have made the correct identification. If not, reverse the arrangement and examine the relationship again. Continue until you find an arrangement that is logical.

If you cannot identify the conclusion in a Main Point question, you must go back and apply this methodology. Otherwise, without the conclusion how can you answer the question?

Fill in the Blank Questions

Within the Critical Reasoning problems, you will occasionally encounter questions where the stimulus is *preceded by* the question stem, and then the stimulus that *ends with an underlined blank space*. The question stem in these problems directs you to fill in the blank with the answer that best completes the passage. While not one of the most common question types, a Fill in the Blank question can throw off test takers who are surprised by the unusual stimulus formation. No need to worry, though, these questions are always one of several main question types—Main Point, Must Be True, Strengthen, Assumption, etc.

The placement of the blank in the stimulus is not random—the blank is typically at the very end of the stimulus. There is often an argument indicator at the start of the last sentence or just before the blank to help you recognize what you must supply, and then the question stem specifies the exact nature of your task.

Because the focus of this chapter is Main Point questions, we will primarily address that question type here, then cover other fill in the Blank question types when those are discussed in detail. However, we will show how some of the other question types are presented for comparison purposes.

Main Point—Fill in the Blank Questions

Although relatively rare on the GMAT, the test makers can offer up Fill in the Blank questions that ask for a conclusion of the argument. In these instances, the blank is preceded by a conclusion indicator (as opposed to a premise indicator). You should then fill the blank with the answer choice that best represents the main point of the argument. In order to achieve this goal, you must read the stimulus for clues revealing the direction of the argument and the author's intent.

Here are some sample final stimulus sentences to give you an example of how a Main Point—Fill in the Blank question would appear:

"Therefore, _____."

"Hence, in the coming years, the rate of economic growth will likely _____."

"Thus, from the politician's statements, we can conclude _____."

Fill in the Blank questions should be approached in the same manner as any First Family question, but the emphasis is on using contextual clues provided in the stimulus to find the answer choice that best fits the blank.

As you can see, each sentence begins with a conclusion indicator that ultimately modifies the blank. This is the signal that you must supply the conclusion. Simply look for the answer that best summarizes the point of the author's argument.

The question stems that precede these stimuli typically ask you to complete the sentence or passage ("Which of the following most logically completes the passage?" or "Which of the following best completes the argument below?"), and, when combined with the indicators in the sentence containing the blank, indicate that the conclusion you are supplying is the main point of the argument.

By comparison, when other question types are presented, there are two significant differences:

1. The indicator modifying the blank is often a premise indicator (such as "because" or "since").

2. The question stem contains language indicating you are completing a different task, such as strengthening the argument.

Final Chapter Note

There are three elements remaining in this chapter: a review of Main Point questions; a brief Must Be True and Main Point Question Stem Mini-Drill; and two more Main Point questions with complete explanations. Please complete each element in the order presented and read the explanations carefully.

Main Point Question Type Review

From a classification standpoint, Main Point questions are a subcategory of Must Be True questions and thus fall into the First Family type.

The Main Point is the same as the conclusion of the argument. By applying the Primary Objectives you should already have the answer to a Main Point question by the time you read the question stem.

The correct answer choice must not only be true according to the stimulus, it must also summarize the author's point.

Two types of answers often appear in Main Point questions. Both are incorrect:

1. Answers that are true but do not encapsulate the author's point.

2. Answers that repeat premises of the argument.

Remember: Main Point questions are Must Be True questions with an additional criterion—you must also identify the author's point.

Fill in the Blank Question Type Review

Fill in the Blank questions can be one of several types of questions, including Main Point, Must Be True, Strengthen, and Assumption.

These questions are easily identifiable because the question stem precedes the stimulus, and then the stimulus ends with a blank space, which is typically preceded by an argument indicator. The argument indicator helps you better understand what type of answer you must supply.

In Main Point—Fill in the Blank questions, the sentence with the blank contains a conclusion indicator that ultimately modifies the blank. This is the signal that you must supply the conclusion of the argument. The question stems that precede these stimuli typically ask you to complete the sentence or passage ("Which one of the following most logically completes the argument below?"), and, when combined with the indicators in the sentence containing the blank, indicate that the conclusion you are supplying is the main point of the argument.

Main Point—Fill in the Blank questions are simply Main Point questions in disguise. They are approached in the same manner as any First Family question, but the emphasis is on using the contextual clues provided in the stimulus to find the choice that best fits the blank.

Must Be True and Main Point Question Stem Mini-Drill

Each of the following items contains a sample question stem. In the space provided, categorize each stem as either a Must Be True or Main Point question, and notate any Except (X) identifier you see.
Answers on page 140

1. Question Stem: "Which of the following statements is most strongly supported by the information above?"

    Question Type: _____

2. Question Stem: "The information above provides the LEAST support for which of the following?"

    Question Type: _____

3. Question Stem: "The author's reasoning provides basis for accepting which of the following assertions?"

    Question Type: _____

4. Question Stem: "Which of the following most accurately expresses the argument's conclusion?"

    Question Type: _____

5. Question Stem: "Which one of the following most logically completes the argument below?"

    Question Type: _____

6. Question Stem: "Which of the following can be drawn from the passage above?"

    Question Type: _____

Must Be True and Main Point Question Stem Mini-Drill Answer Key

1. Question Type: Must Be True

    In this case, the "most strongly supported" is used with the intent of proving one of the answers correct. Hence, this is a Must Be True question.

2. Question Type: Must Be True X

    The presence of "LEAST" makes this an Except question and the presence of the phrase "support for which one of the following" adds the Must Be True element. The four incorrect answer choices Must Be True; the correct answer choice is not necessarily true.

3. Question Type: Must Be True

    "Accepting which of the following assertions" is identical to asking you to find the answer that is proven by the information in the stimulus. Hence, this is a Must Be True question.

4. Question Type: Main Point

    In asking for the argument's conclusion, the stem asks you to identify the Main Point of the argument.

5. Question Type: Main Point—FIB

    This is the question stem for a Fill in the Blank (FIB) question (signified by the "most logically completes the argument below" portion in the stem), which asks you to identify the Main Point of the argument.

6. Question Type: Must Be True

    The words "drawn from" mean must be true. Hence, this is a Must Be True question.

Main Point Question Problem Set

Please complete the problem set and review the answer key and explanations. *Answers on page 142*

1. Many patients are hesitant to seek second opinions when making decisions about their health, even when considering major medical procedures. This hesitation is sometimes based on a lack of familiarity with a relatively new physician, but even where a strong relationship has been developed between doctor and patient, the person being treated often perceives the interest in a second opinion as an affront to the doctor who has provided the first opinion. This tendency is rather unfortunate, given the potential benefits, either of further confirmation that a particular path represents the proper course, or of contrary perspectives which can be considered for more fully informed decisions.

    Which of the following best represents the main point of the passage above?

    (A) Patients should seek second opinions only in cases of questionable intent on the part of the physician.
    (B) Some doctors consider the request for a second opinion offensive.
    (C) Doctors who tell patients not to seek second opinions are attempting to avoid competition with other physicians.
    (D) Many patients are hesitant to seek second opinions when making decisions about their health.
    (E) When considering major medical procedures, patients should not hesitate to seek a second opinion.

2. Which of the following best completes the passage below?

    When a market containing several competing products finds a single product offering beginning to dominate the competition in terms of consumer preference, most theories of economics predict that manufacturers of less-favored products will lower their prices to make their offerings more competitive. Thus, if these economic theories are correct, and a crowded market shows a trend of strong consumer preference towards a single product, one would expect that _____.

    (A) the most successful manufacturer in the market will begin to charge more for their product.
    (B) manufacturers of less successful products within the market will charge less for those products.
    (C) consumers will remain committed to the most popular product until new options are introduced.
    (D) the products with the lowest market share will be discontinued by manufacturers.
    (E) manufacturers will modify their products to more closely resemble the most preferred offering.

Main Point Problem Set Answer Key

Question #1: Main Point. The correct answer choice is (E)

Like the majority of Main Point stimuli, the argument in this case does not contain a traditional conclusion indicator. In the absence of a word such as "thus" or "therefore," you should look at the pieces of the argument in order to determine the point that the author is making. In this case, the conclusion is that "This tendency [the aversion to seeking a second opinion] is rather unfortunate." Use the Conclusion Identification Method to help establish that point if you are unsure. The author uses the various potential benefits associated with a second opinion to assert that many patients would be better off if they were to seek second opinions about major health decisions.

Answer choice (A): The word that immediately takes this answer choice out of contention is "only." The author of the stimulus believes that patients should be less hesitant *in general* to seek second opinions regarding major health decisions, and so seeking a second opinion would certainly not be limited to cases of questionable intent on the part of the physician.

Answer choice (B): This answer choice does not pass the Fact Test. Although the author points out that many patients avoid seeking second opinion out of concern that they *might* offend their doctor, the stimulus does not confirm that any doctors actually *are* offended by the practice.

Answer choice (C): The author does not discuss any examples of doctors who dissuade their patients from seeking a second opinion, so there is no way to confirm or deny this answer choice based on the information provided in the stimulus.

Answer choice (D): This answer is certainly true based on the stimulus, as it restates the first sentence of the stimulus and therefore passes the Fact Test. However, this choice does not reflect the author's main point, which is that many patients would be better off if they fought the aversion to seeking second opinions with regard to their health.

Answer choice (E): This is the correct answer, and this answer is a paraphrase of the author's conclusion.

Main Point Problem Set Answer Key

Question #2: Main Point—FIB. The correct answer choice is (B)

Because the stimulus is preceded by the question stem, and the stimulus ends with a blank, you know you are dealing with a Fill in the Blank (FIB) question.

Unlike question #1, this question provides a very recognizable conclusion indicator—"Thus"—so we should recognize this Fill in the Blank question as a Main Point question. The author states that if a single product offering dominates consumer preference, most economic theories would predict a decrease in the price of competing offerings. Thus, in cases of such a preference dominating product, one would expect what? This is an answer that can easily be prephrased: in the case of such market domination, we would expect the prices of competing products to drop as their manufacturers scramble to become more competitive.

Answer choice (A): Although we are told that economists would expect competing products' prices to drop, the author does not discuss what happens with the dominant product in such a case. Thus, this answer fails the Fact Test. In addition, this answer is somewhat of an Opposite answer as it trades on the dominant producer raising prices as opposed to the lesser producers lowering prices. Since it cannot be confirmed by the information provided in the stimulus, this choice does not reflect the author's main point.

Answer choice (B): This correct answer choice essentially restates our prephrase from the discussion above.

Answer choice (C): The author does not provide information regarding consumer trends going forward. Since this specific information is not discussed at all in the stimulus, this answer fails the Fact Test and cannot be the correct choice.

Answer choice (D): The stimulus provides that the response to a dominant offering will be a decrease in the prices of competing products. There is no reference to the question of whether the less popular offerings would be discontinued, so this choice cannot represent the main point of the passage.

Answer choice (E): This incorrect answer is a classic "could be true" answer, or perhaps even a "likely to be true" answer. That is, if we were to speculate as to the reactions of competing firms, this might be a tactic they would choose. However, since this idea was not referenced by the author, this choice cannot be confirmed by the information in the passage and cannot represent the author's main point.

Chapter Six:
Weaken Questions

Chapter Six: Weaken Questions

Weaken Questions 147

How to Weaken an Argument 149

Common Weakening Scenarios 151

Three Incorrect Answer Traps 152

Weaken Questions Analyzed 153

Final Note 157

Weaken Question Type Review 158

Weaken Question Problem Set 159

Weaken Questions

Weaken questions require you to select the answer choice that undermines the author's argument as decisively as possible. Overall, Weaken questions are the most frequently appearing Critical Reasoning question type on the GMAT.

Because Weaken questions are in the Third Family, these questions require a different approach than the Must Be True and Main Point questions we have covered so far. In addition to the Primary Objectives, keep the following rules in mind when approaching Weaken questions:

Third Family Information Model:

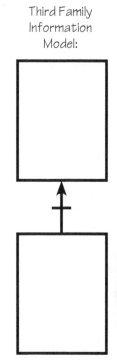

1. The stimulus will contain an argument. Because you are asked to weaken the author's reasoning, and reasoning requires a conclusion, an argument will always be present. In order to maximize your chances of success you must identify, isolate, and assess the premises and the conclusion of the argument. Only by understanding the structure of the argument can you gain the perspective necessary to attack the author's position.

2. Focus on the conclusion. Almost all correct Weaken answer choices impact the conclusion. The more you know about the specifics of the conclusion, the better armed you will be to differentiate between correct and incorrect answers.

3. The information in the stimulus is suspect. There are often reasoning errors present, and you must read the argument very carefully.

4. Weaken questions often yield strong prephrases. Be sure to actively consider the range of possible answers before proceeding to the answer choices.

5. The answer choices are accepted as given, even if they include "new" information. Unlike Must Be True questions, Weaken answer choices can bring into consideration information outside of or tangential to the stimulus. Just because a fact or idea is not mentioned in the stimulus is *not* grounds for dismissing an answer choice. Your task is to determine which answer choice best attacks the argument in the stimulus.

Remember, most Weaken question stems tell you to accept the answer choices as true.

By following the Primary Objectives and focusing on the points above, you will maximize your chances of success on Weaken questions.

CHAPTER SIX: WEAKEN QUESTIONS

Weaken question stems typically contain the following two features:

1. The stem uses the word "weaken" or a synonym. Following are some examples of words or phrases used to indicate that your task is to weaken the argument:

>   weaken
>   attack
>   undermine
>   refute
>   argue against
>   call into question
>   cast doubt
>   challenge
>   damage
>   counter

We discuss the Third Family before the Second Family because some of the skills required to complete Third Family questions are essential for Second Family questions.

2. The stem indicates that you should accept the answer choices as true, usually with the following phrase:

>   "Which of the following, if true, ..."

Here are several Weaken question stem examples:

"Which of the following, if true, most seriously weakens the argument above?"

"Which of the following, if true, casts the most doubt on the conclusion drawn above?"

"Which of the following, if true, most calls into question the claim above?"

"Which of the following, if true, is most damaging to the conclusion above?"

"Which of the following, if known, is evidence that contradicts the hypothesis above?"

"Which of the following, if discovered, would be evidence against the speculation above?"

How to Weaken an Argument

The key to weakening a GMAT argument is to attack the conclusion. But, keep in mind that to attack is not the same as to destroy. Although an answer that destroys the conclusion would be correct, this rarely occurs because of the minimal space allotted to answer choices. Instead, you are more likely to encounter an answer that hurts the argument but does not ultimately destroy the author's position. When evaluating an answer, ask yourself, "Would this answer choice make the author reconsider his or her position or force the author to respond?" If so, you have the correct answer.

You do not need to find an answer that destroys the author's position. Instead, simply find an answer that hurts the argument.

Because arguments are made up of premises and conclusions, you can safely assume that these are the parts you must attack in order to weaken an argument. Let us discuss each part, and the likelihood that each would be attacked by an answer choice.

1. The Premises

    One of the classic ways to attack an argument is to attack the premises on which the conclusion rests. Regrettably, this form of attack is rarely used on the GMAT because when a premise is attacked, the answer choice is easy to spot. Literally, the answer will contradict one of the premises, and most students are capable of reading an argument and then identifying an answer that simply negates a premise.

    In practice, almost all correct GMAT Weaken question answers leave the premises untouched.

    The one time you might see an answer choice attack a premise is when that "premise" is a sub-conclusion. That is, when a conclusion of one premise is used as a premise to support another conclusion.

2. The Conclusion

    The conclusion is the part of the argument that is most likely to be attacked, but the correct answer choice will not simply contradict the conclusion. Instead, the correct answer will undermine the conclusion by showing that the conclusion fails to account for some element or possibility. In this sense, the correct answer often shows that the conclusion does not necessarily follow from the premises even if the premises are true. Consider the following example:

    All my neighbors own blue cars. Therefore I own a blue car.

    Even though the statement that the neighbors have blue cars is entirely reasonable, the weakness in the argument is that this fact has no impact on the color of the car I own. In this overly simplified problem, the correct weakening answer would be

CHAPTER SIX: WEAKEN QUESTIONS

something along the lines of, "The cars of one's neighbors have no determinative effect on the car any individual owns." Would that conclusively disprove that I own a blue car? No. Does it show that perhaps I do not own a blue car? Yes. Does it disprove that my neighbors own blue cars? No.

Answers that weaken the argument's conclusion will attack assumptions made by the author. In the example above, the author assumes that the neighbors' ownership of blue cars has an impact on the color of the car that he owns. If this assumption were shown to be questionable, the argument would be undermined.

Assumptions will be discussed in more detail in Chapter Eight.

The stimuli for weaken questions contain errors of assumption. This makes sense, because the easiest argument to weaken is one that already has a flaw. Typically, the author will fail to consider other possibilities or leave out a key piece of information. In this sense the author assumes that these elements do not exist when he or she makes the conclusion, and if you see a gap or hole in the argument immediately consider that the correct answer might attack this hole.

As you consider possible answers, always look for the one that attacks the way the author arrived at the conclusion. Do not worry about the premises and instead focus on the effect the answer has on the conclusion.

So, we know that we must first focus on the conclusion and how the author arrived at the conclusion. The second key to weakening arguments is to personalize the argument. Most students perform considerably better when they see the argument from their perspective as opposed to trying to understand the issues abstractly. When analyzing the author's argument, imagine how you would respond if you were talking directly to the author. Would you use answer choice (A) or would you prefer answer choice (B)? Students who personalize the argument often properly dismiss answer choices that they would have otherwise wasted time considering.

Personalizing helps you see the argument from a very involved perspective, and that helps you assess the strength of each answer.

Common Weakening Scenarios

Although there are many classical logical fallacies, the most common of which we will discuss in the Flaw in the Reasoning section, several scenarios that occur in GMAT Weaken question stimuli are easy to recognize and attack:

1. Incomplete Information. The author fails to consider all of the possibilities, or relies upon evidence that is incomplete. This flaw can be attacked by bringing up new possibilities or information.

2. Improper Comparison. The author attempts to compare two or more items that are essentially different.

3. Overly Broad Conclusion. The author draws a conclusion that is broader or more expansive that the premises support.

While these three scenarios are not the only ways an argument can be weak, they encompass a large proportion of the errors that appear in GMAT stimuli.

Three Incorrect Answer Traps

There are certain incorrect answer choices that appear frequently in Weaken questions:

1. Opposite Answers. As discussed in the Must Be True question chapter, these answers do the exact opposite of what is needed. In this case, they strengthen the argument as opposed to weakening it. Although you might think answers of this type are easy to avoid, they can be very tricky. To analogize, have you ever gotten on a highway thinking you were going south when in fact you later discovered you were going north? It is easy to make a mistake when you head in the exact opposite direction. In the same way, Opposite answers lure the test taker by presenting information that relates perfectly to the argument, but just in the wrong manner.

2. Shell Game Answers. Like Opposite answers, the Shell Game is the same as in the Must Be True discussion. Remember, a Shell Game occurs when an idea or concept is raised in the stimulus and then a very similar idea appears in the answer choice, but the idea is changed just enough to be incorrect but still attractive. In Weaken questions, the Shell Game is usually used to attack a conclusion that is similar to, but slightly different from, the one presented in the stimulus. Later in this chapter you will see some excellent examples of this answer type.

3. Out of Scope Answers. These answers simply miss the point of the argument and raise issues that are either not related to the argument or tangential to the argument.

While these three answer types are not the only ways an answer choice can be attractively incorrect, they appear frequently enough that you should be familiar with each form.

Some of the wrong answer types from the Must Be True chapter do not apply to Weaken questions. For example, the New Information answer is usually wrong in a Must Be True question, but not in a Weaken question because new information is acceptable in Weaken answer choices.

Weaken Questions Analyzed

In the following questions we will discuss the form of the stimulus and answer choices against the background of our discussion so far. Please take a moment to complete the following problem:

1. Nurse: Dr. Roark's patients tend to require far more time for recuperation than the patients of any other surgeon at Oceanside Hospital. Although she is reputed to be quite talented, Dr. Roark is clearly not as skilled as the other surgeons at Oceanside.

    Which of the following, if true, most seriously weakens the nurse's argument?

    (A) Dr. Roark's patients tend to require fewer procedures than those of other doctors in the hospital.
    (B) The recuperation required after a given surgery can vary significantly based on the skill level of the doctor who performed the surgery.
    (C) Dr. Roark has been associated with Oceanside for three years longer than any other surgeon in the hospital.
    (D) Operations which require less skill tend to require shorter periods of post-operative recuperation.
    (E) Dr. Roark has operated on two other doctors at Oceanside.

This would be classified as an easy question, but as a starting point for our discussion that is helpful. The structure of the argument is simple, and it is easy to see why the premise does not undeniably prove the conclusion. The answers contain several predictable forms, and this is the type of question you should quickly destroy. You do not need to spend a great deal of time trying to find a specific prephrased answer because there are so many possibilities, and the answers can be eliminated without a great deal of time spent considering which are Losers and which are Contenders.

Prephrasing is often easier with Weaken questions than with some other question types. Simply put, many people are good at attacking a position and prephrasing puts that skill to use.

Let's look at the argument structure first:

Premise: Dr. Roark's patients tend to require far more time for recuperation than the patients of any other surgeon at Oceanside Hospital.

Counter-Premise: Although she is reputed to be quite talented,

Conclusion: Dr. Roark is clearly not as skilled as the other surgeons at Oceanside.

CHAPTER SIX: WEAKEN QUESTIONS

The stimulus uses a premise about recuperation time to form a conclusion about Dr. Roark's competency as a surgeon. Ask yourself—does the premise prove the conclusion? No, because there are many factors that could have affected the recuperation time of Dr. Roark's patients. In this sense, the stimulus has incomplete information, and we should try to discover a relevant piece of information in one of the answer choices that will shed more light on why Dr. Roark's patients need far more recuperation time. Use this knowledge to make a general prephrase that indicates that you are looking for a piece of information that shows Dr. Roark's skill is not as low as it seems or that other factors affected the recuperation time of Dr. Roark's patients.

Answer choice (A): This is an Opposite answer that strengthens the claim that Dr. Roark is not as skilled as other surgeons by showing that Dr. Roark's patients required fewer procedures than the patients of other doctors. In general, one would expect that a patient with fewer procedures would require less recuperation time than a patient that required a greater number of procedures.

Answer choice (B): This is another Opposite answer that is also incorrect. The answer seems to strengthen the claim that Dr. Roark is of lower skill by connecting recuperation time with surgical skill.

Answer choice (C): This answer is irrelevant. It tries to use Dr. Roark's tenure as an indicator of skill. Personalize the answer—is this the answer you would offer to weaken the argument against Dr. Roark if she were your friend?

Answer choice (D): This is the correct answer. The answer suggests that the longer recuperation times are linked to procedures that required greater skill, a proposition that hurts the contention that Dr. Roark is not as skilled as the other surgeons at Oceanside. Consider, for example, what the case would be if Dr. Roark were performing heart transplants. A procedure of that nature would likely only be done by a surgeon of superior skill, and the recovery time for such an operation would likely be significant.

Notice that this answer does not attack the premises. Even though the premises are still true, the conclusion is undermined by the new evidence. This is typical of most Weaken question answers—the premises are not addressed and the focus is on the conclusion.

Answer choice (E): This answer goes beyond the scope of the argument by discussing the fact that Dr. Roark operated on two other Oceanside doctors. That fact does not allow one to infer that Dr. Roark's skill is higher than the skill level of those two doctors.

Now we will move on to another example. Please take a moment to complete the following problem:

2. Consumer: The problem with bottled spring water is that it is no more healthy than well-filtered tap water, and many companies produce effective water filtration systems for home use. Further, the price of a 16 ounce bottle of water is, on average, over ten times that of the same amount of water run through a home filtration system. Thus, most bottled spring water producers will soon go out of business.

Which of the following, if true, most severely weakens the argument presented above?

(A) Several of the companies who bottle and sell spring water have gone out of business during the past five years.
(B) Because of the inherent costs associated with the bottling and transport, most bottled spring water suppliers are unable to reduce the wholesale prices they must charge for bottled spring water.
(C) Most consumers who regularly purchase bottled spring water base their beverage purchase decisions exclusively on preference for taste.
(D) Some people prefer the taste of tap water to that of bottled spring water.
(E) Because of technological advances and growing demand, home-based water filtration systems are more effective and more commonly available than they had been when bottled spring water was first widely distributed.

CHAPTER SIX: WEAKEN QUESTIONS

The conclusion of this argument is the final sentence, which begins with the indicator "thus," introducing the consumer's conclusion that "most bottled spring water producers will soon go out of business." Personalize this stimulus and ask yourself, "are there any holes in the consumer's argument?" In this case the consumer makes a fairly big leap to the conclusion, so there are several holes in his or her argument: First, without knowing the cost of the home filtration systems, the economic benefit of such systems is impossible to assess. Further, the consumer seems to believe that cost is the only consideration in bottled water purchase. Perhaps people enjoy the status of drinking French spring water, or the convenience of being able to pick up a cold bottle of water on the go.

Answer choice (A): This Opposite answer choice can be quickly ruled out, because if many such companies had gone out of business in recent years, this would not weaken the author's argument; instead this choice actually lends strength to the conclusion.

Answer choice (B): This choice would also strengthen the author's argument. If the bottled water companies are unable to lower their wholesale prices, this makes it more likely that the gap in price between bottled water and home-filtered water will remain. So this choice, which bolsters the conclusion from the stimulus, cannot be the correct answer.

Answer choice (C): This is the correct answer choice, and the one which points to a previously unreferenced basis for consumer preference—that of taste. If consumers base such purchases on taste alone, then the margin in cost is not likely to sway them toward home-filtration. Note also how the argument avoids a discussion of taste; the stimulus simply references the fact that bottled water is no more "healthy" than well-filtered tap water.

Answer choice (D): To begin with, the word "some" is very vague, and of no value in this instance. "Some" can be defined as one or more, so this choice basically provides that there is at least one person who prefers tap water. Further, this information plays no role in the author's argument, which deals with bottled water vs home-filtered tap water; plain tap water falls into neither category.

Answer choice (E): Like many (but not all) incorrect responses to Weaken questions, this choice actually strengthens the author's conclusion. The more effective and readily available the home-filtration systems are, the stronger the assertion that they will hurt the bottled water industry.

Answer choice (E) is a great place for the test makers to place an attractive wrong answer because (E) is the last answer that a student will read, and the contents of (E) "reverberate" in the test taker's mind and begin to sound reasonable.

In that same vein, answer choice (A) is a great place to put the correct answer if the stimulus is exceedingly difficult to understand or if the question stem is extremely unusual. Why? Because most test takers use the first answer choice in a difficult problem to get a handle on what they are reading and the type of answers they will see. If a problem is tough, it can be difficult to immediately identify answer choice (A) as correct. Then, by the time they have read all five answers, they are prone to have forgotten the details of the first answer choice.

Final Note

We will continue our discussion of Weaken questions in the next chapter, which addresses Cause and Effect Reasoning. We will also continue to discuss argumentation in more detail as we progress through the Second Family of questions and into Method of Reasoning and Parallel Reasoning.

The following page is a review of key points from this chapter. After the review, there is a short problem set to help test your knowledge of these ideas. The problem set is followed by an answer key with explanations. Good luck!

Weaken Question Type Review

Weaken questions require you to select an answer choice that undermines the author's argument as decisively as possible. Keep these fundamental rules in mind when you approach Weaken questions:

1. The stimulus will contain an argument.

2. Focus on the conclusion.

3. The information in the stimulus is suspect. There are often reasoning errors present, and you must read the argument very carefully.

4. Weaken questions often yield strong prephrases.

5. The answer choices are accepted as given, even if they include "new" information.

The conclusion is the part of the argument that is most likely to be attacked, but the correct answer choice will not simply contradict the conclusion. Instead, the correct answer will undermine the conclusion by showing that the conclusion fails to account for some element or possibility. In this sense, the correct answer often shows that the conclusion does not necessarily follow from the premises even if the premises are true.

Several scenarios that can occur in GMAT Weaken question stimuli are easy to recognize and attack:

1. Incomplete Information.

2. Improper Comparison.

3. Overly Broad Conclusion.

There are certain incorrect answer choices that appear frequently in Weaken questions:

1. Opposite Answers.

2. Shell Game Answers.

3. Out of Scope Answers.

Weaken Question Problem Set

Please complete the problem set and review the answer key and explanations. *Answers on page 161*

1. Cellular telephone towers are critical for their ability to allow wireless transmission of signals between cell phone users. Because many of the towers currently in use were built over a decade ago and rely on outdated circuitry, workers with specialized training are needed to repair them. Without repairs, a number of these older cell phone towers would soon fail. Thus, workers with the training required to repair older towers must continue to be utilized.

   Which of the following, if true, most seriously weakens the argument above?

   (A) Most people rely on cellular phones for email correspondence in addition to voice communication.
   (B) Programs that specialize in training technicians to repair older circuitry are extremely expensive.
   (C) Repairs attempted by unqualified technicians often result in further damage that requires subsequent and more extensive repairs.
   (D) Manufacturers of cellular tower circuitry all claim that the circuitry will function reliably for at least five years.
   (E) The high wages and scarcity of qualified repair technicians make repairing old cell phone towers more costly and time consuming than simply constructing new towers.

2. Scientists often study modern-day primates in an attempt to better understand the behavior and lifestyle of their now-extinct primate ancestors. This is a questionable technique, however, as primate groups have not always been exposed to the same types of external stimuli. Most primates now being observed have been seriously impacted by the loss of their former habitat due to deforestation.

   Which of the following, if true, most seriously undermines the argument above?

   (A) By studying the response of a primate group to any external factors, scientists can better predict how other primates would respond to different stimuli.
   (B) Primates from different regions tend to show more variation in behavior than do primates from the same geographical area.
   (C) Primate behavior is extremely complex and thus difficult to fully understand.
   (D) Many scientists who study modern-day primates are not concerned with the behavior of extinct primate groups.
   (E) Even those modern-day primate groups that have not been affected by habitat loss are still thought to be quite different from extinct primate groups.

CHAPTER SIX: WEAKEN QUESTIONS

Weaken Question Problem Set

3. The new Axis Starlight, Axis Auto's flagship electric-gas hybrid automobile, is considered so efficient by Axis that the company plans to sell the Starlight to consumers for no payment other than the difference between what the consumer paid for gasoline for the past three years of driving their previous vehicle and what they will pay for gasoline while driving the Starlight for the next three years. Consumers will make an initial downpayment, and then pay any remaining fees after fuel costs have been assessed at the end of the three year period.

   Which of the following, if true, would most significantly disadvantage Axis Auto based on their proposed payment system?

   (A) Most drivers own only one automobile.
   (B) Other car manufacturers are planning to introduce similar fuel-efficient vehicles.
   (C) Drivers interested in the Starlight tend to drive significantly more miles annually than the average driver.
   (D) The price of gasoline is expected to rise dramatically over the next three years.
   (E) The annual amount spent on gasoline by drivers can be accurately determined based on the number of miles driven in a specific make of automobile.

4. A new state-sponsored tax law aimed at increasing the state's college attendance rate gives local public universities tax incentives to encourage acceptance of a greater percentage of applicants from within the state. Legislators supporting the new law believe that it will not only allow more students from the state to obtain further education, but also provide a strong financial boost to in-state universities.

   Which of the following, if true, would provide the strongest critique of the legislators' proposal?

   (A) Public universities receive the majority of their funding through state-sponsored initiatives.
   (B) Public universities are generally less expensive than private universities.
   (C) Many college applicants find that relocating to a new state is the single largest obstacle to attending college.
   (D) Public universities feel that having a broader applicant pool is more financially beneficial than the incentives provided under the new law.
   (E) Applications to universities within the state reached an all-time high for the previous academic year.

Weaken Question Problem Set Answer Key

Question #1: Weaken. The correct answer choice is (E)

This is a nice straightforward question to start the problem set. The argument can be analyzed as follows:

> Premise: Cellular telephone towers are critical for their ability to allow wireless transmission of signals between cell phone users.
>
> Premise: Because many of the towers currently in use were built over a decade ago and rely on outdated circuitry,
>
> Subconclusion/ Premise: workers with specialized training are needed to repair them.
>
> Premise: Without repairs, a number of these older cell phone towers would soon fail.
>
> Conclusion: Thus, workers with the training required to repair older towers must continue to be utilized.

The main conclusion of the argument appears at the end of the stimulus: "workers with the training required to repair older towers must continue to be utilized." Note that there is a subconclusion present, but that subconclusion is used to support the main conclusion. To weaken the argument we must show that workers with the training do *not* have to be continued to be utilized.

Answer choice (A): This answer offers additional information that is not relevant to the workers under discussion. Email communications do not change the need for the cell phone towers, and so this answer has no effect on the argument.

Answer choice (B): While this answer provides information about the expense of training these workers, there is no comparative information provided that would allow us to determine that the workers are not necessary. Thus, while this answer could potentially be used as a starting point for an attack, there is no further avenue of attack, and the answer is incorrect.

Answer choice (C): This is an Opposite answer that supports the conclusion in the argument.

Answer choice (D): Regardless of manufacturer claims, when these towers fail they will need repairs, and thus there would be a need for workers with training (which is likely coming soon as "many" of the towers were built over a decade ago and the claim in this answer is only for at least five years of reliable operation). Thus, this is another Opposite answer that is incorrect.

Answer choice (E): This is the correct answer choice. If the statement in this answer is true, then the costs of the workers with training outweigh the costs of simply replacing the towers. Thus, instead of using qualified workers to repair old towers, the company can simply build a new tower as a replacement. Under this scenario, trained workers would not be necessary, and the conclusion is undermined.

Weaken Problem Set Answer Key

Question #2: Weaken. The correct answer choice is (A)

The author of this stimulus questions the practice of scientists studying modern-day primate behavior in order to gain insight into extinct primates. The author feels this technique is flawed due to the differences in external stimuli that primates have encountered over time, particularly the relatively recent effects of deforestation. Essentially the author is arguing that the scientists are making an invalid comparison: insights into today's primate's behavior aren't applicable to their primate ancestors because the two groups exist(ed) in such different environments.

To weaken this argument, we need to find an answer choice that provides a reason why the scientists' studies might have some value or produce some desirable results.

Answer choice (A): This is the correct answer. This answer choice tells us that the insights the scientists gain about today's primates are applicable to their primate ancestors, since a primate's response to *any* stimulus allows for more accurate predictions about other primates' (even extinct primates) responses to different stimuli. So even though the stimuli might be different, the insights gained by the scientists are universally applicable and their methods have merit.

Answer choice (B): The issue that the author raises in the stimulus is about comparing primates over a vast time difference, and has nothing to do with variations due to geography. This answer choice does not address the author's argument.

Answer choice (C): This answer is somewhat irrelevant, but if anything, this answer choice strengthens the author's argument. If primate behavior is extremely complex and hard to decipher, then it is even more likely that observations of today's primates would fail to yield valuable insights into long-extinct primates.

Answer choice (D): The group of scientists addressed in the stimulus *are* concerned about extinct primate groups, so an answer choice that references other scientists not concerned with extinct primate groups is not relevant to the information in this stimulus.

Answer choice (E): This is a tricky answer, but this answer also strengthens the author's argument. By suggesting that significant differences exist between modern primates and extinct primates, even among groups facing similar stimuli, this answer choice further undermines the comparison made by the scientists and calls into question their techniques. By undermining the scientists studying the modern primates, the answer strengthens the author's conclusion.

Weaken Problem Set Answer Key

Question #3: Weaken. The correct answer choice is (D)

This stimulus presents the somewhat unusual payment system proposed by Axis Auto: it plans to charge only the amount that drivers save in gas over the next three years of driving the new Axis Starlight, compared to what they paid driving their previous car for the past three years. So if a driver spent a total of $6000 on gas in the past three years of driving, and they will spend only $1000 on gas over the next three years in the more fuel-efficient Starlight, they owe Axis the $5000 difference. Obviously Axis feels that purchasers will save a significant amount on gasoline over the next three years, as the more the driver saves, the more he or she owes Axis.

The question stem asks us to attack this proposed payment system. To do so, we need an answer choice that would reduce the profitability of Axis' plan: we need to find a way to minimize the difference in gas costs from a driver's previous three years to the next three years with the Starlight. That is, we want to show that the cost of gas from the past several years will be as close as possible to the cost of gas over the next several years.

Answer choice (A): This answer choice has nothing to do with the amount of money drivers of the Starlight are likely to spend on gas versus what they spent in the previous three years, and so it is incorrect.

Answer choice (B): The question stem only asks us to attack the Axis Auto proposal, so what other car manufacturers plan to do in the coming years has nothing to do with Axis' proposal.

Answer choice (C): This answer choice actually benefits Axis: the more miles drivers travel in a very fuel-efficient car (the Starlight), the more they will ultimately save on gas compared to traveling that same distance in a less fuel-efficient car. The driver will spend more overall on gas, but the *difference* will be greater and that is how Axis will profit. So this answer does the opposite of what we want.

Answer choice (D): This is the correct answer. If the price of gasoline rises significantly over the next three years, then even in a more fuel-efficient car drivers will still spend more on gas and the difference in gas costs relative to the last three years will be reduced. Since this difference is what Axis gets paid, a smaller difference hurts Axis. So higher gas prices would hurt Axis by offsetting the Starlight's better fuel efficiency, and thus this answer is correct.

Weaken Problem Set Answer Key

To show how this answer works, consider the following example:

Three years prior to buying an Axis Starlight:

Gallons of gas bought	x	Price per gallon	=	Total gas cost
3000	x	$1	=	$3000

Don't laugh about that $1 cost—this is just an example! Now, compare those figures to the figures from the three years after buying an Axis Starlight, which feature fewer gallons purchased but a higher cost-per-gallon:

Three years after buying an Axis Starlight:

Gallons of gas bought	x	Price per gallon	=	Total gas cost
1000	x	$3	=	$3000

After buying an Axis Starlight, gas usage decreased, but the increase in the cost of gas offset that decrease, resulting in the same total gas cost before and after the purchase of an Axis Starlight. Under the proposed plan, in this scenario Axis would be paid the difference, which is $0. Not a great business model!

Answer choice (E): This answer choice has no real effect on Axis' proposal. All that an ability to accurately measure gas costs means is that Axis can accurately determine how much drivers spent in the past three years, and how much they will spend in the next three. But that has nothing to do with their profitability.

Weaken Problem Set Answer Key

Question #4: Weaken. The correct answer choice is (D)

This stimulus describes a new tax law that gives tax incentives to in-state universities that accept a greater percentage of applicants from their state compared to applicants from out-of-state. Legislators in favor of the law believe it will both allow more in-state students to obtain further education (since more will be accepted into local schools), and provide a financial incentive to in-state universities. Of course, for this to be appealing (and beneficial) to state schools, the legislators are assuming that the schools would in fact find a greater financial benefit in accepting a higher percentage of in-state applicants, as opposed to keeping the applicant pool as-is.

The components of the argument can be broken down as follows:

> Proposal: A new state-sponsored tax law aimed at increasing the state's college attendance rate gives local public universities tax incentives to encourage acceptance of a greater percentage of applicants from within the state.
>
> Premise: Legislators supporting the new law believe that it will not only allow more students from the state to obtain further education,
>
> Premise: but also provide a strong financial boost to in-state universities.

The "proposal" referenced in the question stem is in the first sentence, that local public universities will be given tax incentives in order to induce them to accept a greater percentage of applicants from within the state

To weaken this proposal, we need an answer choice that shows that schools would find it more financially beneficial to *not* accept this new tax law.

Answer choice (A): The fact that state schools receive the majority of their funding from state-sponsored initiatives does not attack the presumed benefits of this particular tax law, or show that some alternative would be preferable. Hence this answer choice cannot be thought to attack the legislators' belief that this particular law and its tax incentives would be beneficial to state schools.

Answer choice (B): This stimulus is only about public universities and the effect that this new law would have on them. So a comparison of public and private schools' tuition costs does not undermine the proposed benefits.

Weaken Problem Set Answer Key

Answer choice (C): This answer choice actually supports the legislators' beliefs by showing that many college applicants find it difficult to attend schools in states outside their own. If this is true, then those applicants would be best served by attending a school in their home state and, if in-state schools are accepting a greater percentage of in-state applicants per the tax law, then those applicants would indeed be better able to obtain further education. Put in slightly different terms: many applicants find themselves forced to apply to schools within their own states because relocating is quite challenging, so if there is a greater likelihood that in-state schools will accept them, then more of these applicants will be able to obtain further education and the proposal in the stimulus is strengthened.

Answer choice (D): This is the correct answer. The legislators argue that public universities will find the new tax law to be financially beneficial. However, according to this answer public universities actually find a broader applicant pool to be more financially beneficial than the tax law would be. Of course, if schools can accept more applicants from across the country (or around the world), then they would have a much broader applicant pool than if they were required to accept more students from within a single state (a much smaller, less diverse group of applicants). So this directly attacks the legislators' beliefs and therefore weakens their proposal.

Answer choice (E): This answer choice, like answer choice (C), would support the proposal. Clearly, from the information in (E), a larger number of in-state applicants are applying to local universities. So if those universities are compelled by the new law to accept a greater percentage of those applicants, then the tax law would certainly allow more in-state applicants to obtain higher education.

Chapter Seven: Cause and Effect Reasoning

Chapter Seven: Cause and Effect Reasoning

What is Causality? 169

How to Recognize Causality 169

Causality in the Conclusion versus Causality in the Premises 170

Situations That Can Lead to Errors of Causality 172

The Central Assumption of Causal Conclusions 173

How to Attack a Causal Conclusion 174

Diagramming Causality 175

Two Cause and Effect Problems Analyzed 176

Causal Reasoning Review 180

Final Note 181

Causal Reasoning Problem Set 182

What is Causality?

When examining events, people naturally seek to explain why things happened. This search often results in cause and effect reasoning, which asserts or denies that one thing causes another, or that one thing is caused by another. On the GMAT, cause and effect reasoning appears in many Critical Reasoning problems, often in the conclusion where the author mistakenly claims that one event causes another. For example:

> Last week Apple announced a quarterly deficit and the stock market dropped 10 points. Thus, Apple's announcement must have caused the drop.

Like the above conclusion, most causal conclusions are flawed because there can be alternate explanations for the stated relationship: another cause could account for the effect; a third event could have caused both the stated cause and effect; the situation may in fact be reversed; the events may be related but not causally; or the entire occurrence could be the result of chance.

In short, causality occurs when one event is said to make another occur. The *cause* is the event that makes the other occur; the *effect* is the event that follows from the cause. By definition, the cause must occur before the effect, and the cause is the "activator" or "ignitor" in the relationship. The effect always happens at some point in time after the cause.

How to Recognize Causality

A cause and effect relationship has a signature characteristic—a single cause *makes* the effect happen. Thus, there is an identifiable type of expression used to indicate that a causal relationship is present. The list on the following page contains a number of the phrases used by the makers of the GMAT to introduce causality, and you should be on the lookout for these phrases when reading Critical Reasoning stimuli.

Causality is the most-tested logical concept in GMAT Critical Reasoning stimuli. The second most tested concept is Numbers and Percentages, which will be addressed in Chapter Twelve.

As mentioned before, this is a book about GMAT logic, not general philosophy. Therefore, we will not go into an analysis of David Hume's Inquiry or Mill's Methods (both of which address causality) because although those discussions are interesting, they do not apply to the GMAT.

The following terms often introduce a cause and effect relationship:

> caused by
> because of
> responsible for
> reason for
> leads to
> induced by
> promoted by
> determined by
> produced by
> product of
> played a role in
> was a factor in
> is an effect of

Be sure to memorize this list!

Because of the variety of the English language, there are many alternate phrases that can introduce causality. However, those phrases would all have the similar characteristic of suggesting that one event *made* another occur.

Causality in the Conclusion versus Causality in the Premises

Causal statements can be found in the premise or conclusion of an argument. If the causal statement is the conclusion, then the reasoning is flawed. If the causal statement is the premise, then the argument may be flawed, but not because of the causal statement. Because of this difference, one of the critical issues in determining whether flawed causal reasoning is present is identifying where in the argument the causal assertion is made. The classic mistaken cause and effect reasoning we will refer to throughout this book occurs when a causal assertion is made in the *conclusion*, or the conclusion presumes a causal relationship. Let us examine the difference between an argument with a causal premise and one with a causal conclusion.

In the GMAT world, when a cause and effect statement appears as the conclusion, the conclusion is flawed. In the real world that may not be the case because a preponderance of evidence can be gathered or visual evidence can be used to prove a relationship.

This is an argument with a causal conclusion:

Premise:	In North America, people drink a lot of milk.
Premise:	There is a high frequency of cancer in North America.
Conclusion:	Therefore, drinking milk causes cancer.

In this case, the author takes two events that occur together and concludes that one causes the other. This conclusion is in error for the reasons discussed on the first page of this chapter.

If a causal claim is made in the premises, however, then no *causal* reasoning error exists in the argument (of course, the argument may be flawed in other ways). As mentioned previously, the makers of the GMAT tend to allow premises to go unchallenged (they are more concerned with the reasoning that follows from a premise) and it is considered acceptable for an author to begin his argument by stating a causal relationship and then continuing from there:

>Premise: Drinking milk causes cancer.
>
>Premise: The residents of North America drink a lot of milk.
>
>Conclusion: Therefore, in North America there is a high frequency of cancer among the residents.

The second example is considered valid reasoning because the author takes a causal principle and follows it to its logical conclusion. Generally, causal reasoning occurs in a format similar to the first example, but there are GMAT problems similar to the second example.

Situations That Can Lead to Errors of Causality

There are two scenarios that tend to lead to causal conclusions in Critical Reasoning questions:

1. One event occurs before another

    When one event occurs before another event, many people fall into the trap of assuming that the first event caused the second event. This does not have to be the case, as shown by the following famous example:

    > Every morning the rooster crows before the sun rises. Hence, the rooster must cause the sun to rise.

    The example contains a ludicrous conclusion, and shows why it is dangerous to simply assume that the first event must have caused the second event.

2. Two (or more) events occur at the same time

    When two events occur simultaneously, many people assume that one event caused the other. While one event could have caused the other, the two events could be the result of a third event, or the two events could simply be correlated without one causing the other.

    The following example shows how a third event can cause both events:

    > The consumption of ice cream has been found to correlate with the murder rate. Therefore, consuming ice cream must cause one to be more likely to commit murder.

    As you might imagine, the conclusion of the example does not have to be true (yes, go ahead and eat that Ben and Jerry's!), and the two events can be explained as the effects of a single cause: hot weather. When the weather is warmer, ice cream consumption and the murder rate tend to rise (this example is actually true, especially for large cities).

If you have taken a logic course, you will recognize the first scenario produces the Post Hoc, Ergo Propter Hoc fallacy.

In the second example, the two events could simply be correlated. A positive correlation is a relationship where the two values move together. A negative correlation is one where the two values move in opposite directions, such as with age and eyesight (the older you get, the worse your eyesight gets).

The Central Assumption of Causal Conclusions

Understanding the assumption that is at the heart of a causal conclusion is essential to knowing why certain answers will be correct or incorrect. Most students assume that the GMAT makes basic assumptions that are similar to the real world; this is untrue and is a dangerous mistake to make.

When we discuss causality in the real world, there is an inherent understanding that a given cause is just one possible cause of the effect, and that there are other causes that could also produce the same effect. This is reasonable because we have the ability to observe a variety of cause and effect scenarios, and experience shows us that different actions can have the same result. The makers of the GMAT do *not* think this way. When a GMAT speaker concludes that one occurrence caused another, that speaker also assumes that the stated cause is the *only* possible cause of the effect and that consequently the stated cause will *always* produce the effect. This assumption is incredibly extreme and far-reaching, and often leads to surprising answer choices that would appear incorrect unless you understand this assumption. Consider the following example:

Understanding this assumption is absolutely critical to your GMAT success. The makers of the test will closely examine your knowledge of this idea, especially in Strengthen and Weaken questions.

> Premise: Average temperatures are higher at the equator than in any other area.
>
> Premise: Individuals living at or near the equator tend to have lower per-capita incomes than individuals living elsewhere.
>
> Conclusion: Therefore, higher average temperatures cause lower per-capita incomes.

This argument is a classic flawed causal argument wherein two premises with a basic connection (living at the equator) are used as the basis of a conclusion that states that the connection is such that one of the elements actually makes the other occur. The conclusion is flawed because it is not necessary that one of the elements caused the other to occur: the two could simply be correlated in some way or the connection could be random.

In the real world, we would tend to look at an argument like the one above and think that while the conclusion is possible, there are also other things that could cause the lower per-capita income of individuals residing at or near the equator, such as a lack of natural resources. *This is not how speakers on the GMAT view the relationship.* When a GMAT speaker makes an argument like the one above, he or she believes that the *only* cause is the one stated in the conclusion and that there are *no other* causes that can create that particular effect. Why is this the case? Because for a GMAT speaker to come to that conclusion, he or she must have weighed and considered every possible alternative and then rejected each one. Otherwise, why would the speaker draw the given conclusion? In the final analysis, to say that higher average temperatures cause lower per-capita incomes the speaker must also believe that nothing else could be the cause of lower per-capita incomes.

Thus, in every argument with a causal conclusion that appears on the GMAT, the speaker believes that the stated cause is in fact the only cause and all other theoretically possible causes are not, in fact, actual causes. This is an incredibly powerful assumption, and the results of this assumption are most evident in Weaken, Strengthen, and Assumption questions. We will discuss this effect on Strengthen and Assumption questions in a later chapter. Following is a brief analysis of the effect of this assumption on Weaken questions.

How to Attack a Causal Conclusion

Whenever you identify a causal relationship in the conclusion of a GMAT problem, immediately prepare to either weaken or strengthen the argument. Attacking a cause and effect relationship in Weaken questions almost always consists of performing one of the following tasks:

A. Find an alternate cause for the stated effect

Because the author believes there is only one cause, identifying another cause weakens the conclusion.

B. Show that even when the cause occurs, the effect does not occur

This type of answer often appears in the form of a counterexample. Because the author believes that the cause always produces the effect, any scenario where the cause occurs and the effect does not weaken the conclusion.

C. Show that although the effect occurs, the cause did not occur

This type of answer often appears in the form of a counterexample. Because the author believes that the effect is always produced by the same cause, any scenario where the effect occurs and the cause does not weaken the conclusion.

Answer choices that otherwise appear irrelevant will suddenly be obviously correct when you understand the central causal assumption.

Stimuli containing causal arguments are often followed by Weaken, Strengthen, Assumption, or Flaw questions.

D. Show that the stated relationship is reversed

   Because the author believes that the cause and effect relationship is correctly stated, showing that the relationship is backwards (the claimed effect is actually the cause of the claimed cause) undermines the conclusion.

E. Show that a statistical problem exists with the data used to make the causal statement

   If the data used to make a causal statement are in error, then the validity of the causal claim is in question.

Diagramming Causality

Causal statements can be quickly and easily represented by an arrow diagram, and in this book we use designators ("C" for cause and "E" for effect) above the terms when diagramming. We use these designators to make the meaning of the diagram clear. During the GMAT, however, students should not write out the designators on a notebook (they should just use the arrow diagram) because they want to go as fast as possible.

Here is an example of a causal diagram:

Statement: "Smoking causes cancer."

S = smoking
C = cancer

<u>C</u>   <u>E</u>

S ⟶ C

These arrow representations have a different meaning than the arrows used for Conditional Reasoning in Chapter Four.

As you diagram a causal statement, you will face a decision about how to represent each element of the relationship. Because writing out the entire condition would be onerous, the best approach is to use a symbol to represent each condition. For example, we have already used "S" to represent the idea of "smoking." The choice of symbol is yours, and different students will choose different representations. For example, to represent a phrase such as "they must have studied for the test," you could choose "Study" or the more efficient "S." Whatever you decide to choose, the symbolization must make sense to you and it must be clear. Regardless of how you choose to diagram an element, once you use a certain representation within a problem, stick with that representation throughout the duration of the question.

During the GMAT, the choice to create an arrow diagram for a causal statement is yours.

Two Cause and Effect Problems Analyzed

Please take a moment to complete the following problem:

1. In the last five years there has been a significant increase in the consumption of red wine. During this same period, there have been several major news reports about the beneficial long-term effects on health that certain antioxidants in red wine can provide. Thus, the increase in red wine consumption can be directly attributed to consumers' recognition of the beneficial effects of antioxidants.

   Which of the following, if true, most seriously undermines the explanation above?

   (A) Sales of other alcoholic beverages have not increased in the last five years.
   (B) On average, people consume about 10 percent more red wine than they did five years ago.
   (C) The health benefits of red wine are usually not noticeable for several years.
   (D) The consumption of grape juice and other antioxidant-rich products has also increased in the last five years.
   (E) Red wine prices have decreased significantly in the last five years, while the prices of other alcoholic beverages have risen steadily.

Weaken questions were covered in Chapter Six.

This is a Weaken question. You should have identified the following argument structure in the question above:

> Premise: In the last five years there has been a significant increase in the consumption of red wine.
>
> Premise: During this same time, there have been several major news reports about the beneficial long-term effects on health that certain antioxidants in red wine can provide.
>
> Conclusion: Thus, the increase in red wine consumption can be directly attributed to consumers' recognition of the beneficial effects of antioxidants.

The premises indicate that red wine consumption has increased in the last five years, and that during this time there have been several major news reports about the benefits of certain components of red wine. From this information we cannot draw any conclusions, but the author makes the classic GMAT error of concluding that one of the conditions causes the other. Your job is to find the answer that weakens this flawed reasoning.

From the "Situations That Can Lead to Errors of Causality" discussion, the scenario in this stimulus falls under item 2—"Two (or more) events occur at the same time." As described in that section, "While one event could have caused the other, the two events could be the result of a third event, or the two events could simply be correlated without one causing the other." Thus, you should search either for an answer that identifies a third event that could have caused the two events or one that shows the author mistook a correlation for causation. Answer choice (E) presents the former.

Answer choice (A): This answer does not hurt the conclusion. The information in the answer choice suggests that the increase in red wine consumption is unusual, but this answer still allows the news coverage to be the cause of that increase.

Answer choice (B): This answer agrees with the first premise, and so it does not hurt the conclusion.

Answer choice (C): The delay between wine consumption and the benefits of that consumption is not an issue in the argument.

Answer choice (D): Similar to answer choice (A), this answer does not undermine the conclusion. Because the argument mentions antioxidants in red wine were covered by the news reports, it is not unreasonable to think that other antioxidant-rich products would also see increased consumption. Thus, this answer can be seen as an additional effect to the cause in the stimulus, and that additional effect does not weaken the suggested cause.

Answer choice (E): This is the correct answer. The conclusion can be diagrammed as:

NR = news reports
RWCI = red wine consumption increased

<u>C</u>   <u>E</u>

NR ⟶ RWCI

This answer presents an alternate cause for the increase in wine consumption, namely that prices dropped.

Remember, the classic error of causality appears when two events occurring simultaneously are mistakenly interpreted to be in a causal relationship. There can be many other possibilities for the arrangement: the two events could be caused by a third event (for example, a study touting the benefits of wine consumption could have caused both events), the events could be reversed (the increase in consumption could actually create the news coverage), or there may be other situations where the two do not occur together.

Please take a moment to complete the following problem:

2. The gill lining of lobsters in which the disease-causing parasite *An. haemophila* resides is completely regenerated every 30 days. The *An. haemophila* parasite typically produces moderate discoloration of the gills of infected lobsters, and can occasionally lead to more chronic symptoms. However, because these parasites cannot transfer directly from infected gill lining to newly generated gill lining in their host lobster, any discoloration appearing on the gills of lobsters more than 30 days after they have been moved to parasite-free water is not due to infection by *An. haemophila*.

   Which of the following, if true, would most weaken the argument above?

   (A) Other parasites are found more frequently in lobsters than *An. haemophila*.
   (B) Lobsters that remain in parasite-rich waters can be re-infected by new *An. haemophila* parasites once newly generated gill lining has been produced.
   (C) *An. haemophila* can also cause digestive and respiratory distress in infected lobsters.
   (D) In some cases *An. haemophila* migrates from the gill lining to the stomach, where it can then re-infect its original host.
   (E) Once infected by a particular parasite, lobsters frequently develop a strong immunity to that parasite allowing them to better resist re-infection.

This is a challenging Weaken question with a scientific undertone. As with any stimulus containing argumentation, it becomes imperative that you identify the conclusion as given by the author. Here, the author concludes that lobsters' gill discoloration appearing more than 30 days after begin removed from water with parasites *cannot* be due to *An. haemophila*. The reasoning given for this conclusion is that the gill-discoloring parasite *An. haemophila* resides in gill lining which is completely regenerated every 30 days and, since these parasites cannot go directly from infected gill lining to new, regenerated gill lining, then future gill discoloration must be the result of something else. Put more simply: *An. haemophila* cannot go directly from old to new gill lining, so it seems that continued gill infections must be caused by some other factor.

Since we want to weaken this causal argument, we are looking for an answer choice that shows how *An. haemophila* could possibly re-infect a lobster and cause further gill discoloration.

Answer choice (A): The argument in the stimulus is not about other parasites or how frequently various parasites are found in lobsters, so this answer choice has no effect on the author's conclusion.

Answer choice (B): For an answer choice to weaken a particular argument it is important that the scenario or situation described in the answer match the specific details of the situation in the argument itself. This answer is incorrect because the lobsters in the conclusion are said to be in parasite-free water, so information about lobsters in "parasite-rich" water is irrelevant.

Answer choice (C): The stimulus is only concerned with *An. haemophila*'s effect on the gill lining of lobsters, so information about other problems the parasite can cause has no bearing on the argument.

Answer choice (D): This is the correct answer. The author presumes that because the parasite cannot re-infect a host lobster by directly moving from the infected gill lining to the newly generated gill lining then *An. haemophila* cannot be the cause of future gill discoloration. However, if answer choice (D) is true, then *An. haemophila* can migrate from infected gill lining to the lobster's stomach, and then later re-infect that lobster's regenerated gill lining. This answer choice provides an alternative pathway for re-infection and thereby directly attacks the author's conclusion.

Answer choice (E): This answer choice actually strengthens the author's argument by showing that a previously infected lobster is more resistant to re-infection by the same parasite. Thus it would be even more difficult for *An. haemophila* to infect the same lobster a second time.

A good portion of the GMAT is about recognition of existing patterns. Recognizing these patterns in a stimulus will help you increase your speed and accuracy.

CHAPTER SEVEN: CAUSE AND EFFECT REASONING

Causal Reasoning Review

Causality occurs when one event is said to make another occur. The *cause* is the event that makes the other occur; the *effect* is the event that follows from the cause.

Most causal conclusions are flawed because there can be alternate explanations for the stated relationship: some other cause could account for the effect; some third event could have caused both the stated cause and effect; the situation may in fact be reversed; the events may be related but not causally; or the entire occurrence could be the result of chance.

Causal statements can be used in the premise or conclusion of an argument. If the causal statement is the conclusion, then the reasoning is flawed. If the causal statement is a premise, then the argument may be flawed, but not because of the causal statement.

There are two scenarios that tend to lead to causal conclusions in Critical Reasoning questions:

1. One event occurs before another

2. Two (or more) events occur at the same time

When a GMAT speaker concludes that one occurrence caused another, that speaker also assumes that the stated cause is the *only* possible cause of the effect and that the stated cause will *always* produce the effect.

In Weaken questions, attacking a cause and effect relationship almost always consists of performing one of the following tasks:

A. Find an alternate cause for the stated effect

B. Show that even when the cause occurs, the effect does not occur

C. Show that although the effect occurs, the cause did not occur

D. Show that the stated relationship is in fact reversed

E. Show a statistical problem exists with the data used to make the causal statement

Final Note

Causal reasoning occurs in many different question types, and the discussion in this chapter is designed to acquaint you with situations that produce causal statements, how to identify a causal statement, and some of the ways that causality appears in GMAT problems. We will revisit these concepts as we discuss other question types.

As you examine GMAT questions, remember that causal reasoning may or may not be present in the stimulus. Your job is to recognize causality when it appears and react accordingly. If causality is not present, you do not need to worry about it.

On the following page is a short problem set to help you work with some of the ideas. The problem set is followed by an answer key with explanations. Good luck!

Causal Reasoning Problem Set

Please complete the problem set and review the answer key and explanations. *Answers on page 184*

1. Many scientists of the 1940s predicted that, new, exceptionally potent antibiotics would soon revolutionize the entire medical field. Patients would be given large dosages of these antibiotics, which would attack and kill harmful bacteria in the body, making the patients stronger as a result.

    Which of the following, if true, best describes a reasoning error in the scientists' prediction?

    (A) To achieve the proper dosage requirements, several rounds of antibiotics would likely be necessary.
    (B) In the 1940s, antibiotics had only recently been discovered.
    (C) Some patients respond more quickly than others to strong antibiotics.
    (D) Strong antibiotics act on all bacteria in the body in the same manner, including beneficial bacteria critical to human health.
    (E) Some of the proposed antibiotic treatments would be quite expensive to develop.

2. Alpha Cola, the best selling soft drink nationally among soda drinkers aged 18 to 25, recently completed an expensive and successful ad campaign. The makers of Epsilon Cola, a less popular soft drink that has been on the market for many years, claim that without the recent ad campaign, Alpha Cola would be no more popular than Epsilon.

    Which of the following, if true, would cast the most serious doubt on the assertion of the makers of Epsilon Cola?

    (A) Alpha Cola's recent ad campaign was intended in part to increase sales of the soft drink to soda drinkers aged 18 to 25.
    (B) Beverage buying decisions can be significantly influenced with effective ad campaigns.
    (C) Alpha Cola's recent advertising campaign was one of the most expensive advertising campaigns in history.
    (D) Prior to the recent campaign, Alpha Cola had never advertised but had significantly outsold all other soft drinks on the market for several years.
    (E) Most people prefer the taste of Epsilon Cola to that of Alpha Cola.

Causal Reasoning Problem Set

3. Among consumers in this country who take cruises regularly, the percentage who chose High Seas' cruise lines has decreased by 5 percentage points over the past five years. Since High Seas obviously relies on consumers to earn profits, these declines must have had a measurably negative impact on High Seas' earnings.

   Which of the following, if true, most seriously weakens the argument above?

   (A) Some trips were cut from the cruise schedule, and they were trips during which ticket sales had historically been sufficient to achieve profitability.
   (B) There are many more cruise lines in existence today than there were five years ago.
   (C) The number of people who regularly take cruises has increased significantly over the past five years.
   (D) Five years ago, High Seas reduced the number of cruises on its annual schedule.
   (E) High Seas cruises travel to several different destinations.

4. Medical Student: Last week, a certain patient at this hospital weighed 150 lbs. Since the same patient weighs 160 lbs. today, and he appears to be much healthier than he was last week, he would be well advised to gain another ten pounds during the coming week.

   Which of the following, if true, undermines the argument above?

   (A) The same scale was used to measure the patient's weight in both instances.
   (B) The patient was notified by his physician of this week's weight gain.
   (C) During the past week, the patient has eaten less food than he would normally eat.
   (D) When the patient was weighed last week, an illness had caused the patient's weight to drop ten pounds below its normal level.
   (E) Quick weight loss can be hazardous to one's health.

CHAPTER SEVEN: CAUSE AND EFFECT REASONING

Causal Reasoning Problem Set Answer Key

Question #1: Weaken—CE. The correct answer choice is (D)

This is an interesting problem because the causality is presented entirely in the last sentence with the causal indicator at the end of the sentence. The phrase used to indicate that causality is present is "as a result."

> A = large dosages of antibiotics
> PS = kill harmful bacteria in the body and make the patient stronger as a result
>
> $\underline{C}$ $\qquad$ $\underline{E}$
>
> A $\longrightarrow$ PS

The question stem asks you to weaken the argument, and according to the "How to Attack a Causal Conclusion" section you should be on the lookout for one of several primary methods of attacking the argument.

Answer choice (A): This answer is consistent with the argument, and thus cannot undermine the argument. The stimulus clearly notes that "large doses" would be administered, and administering those antibiotics over several rounds is not ruled out by the author's statements.

Answer choice (B): This answer agrees with statements in the stimulus and has no effect on the argument. The fact that antibiotics had only recently been discovered plays no role in the further assertion that those antibiotics, when given to a patient, would have a positive effect.

Answer choice (C): This information has no effect on the argument. The wording in the stimulus is clear about making the patient "stronger as a result," which allows for a variety of time horizons for patient benefit.

Answer choice (D): This is the correct answer, and this answer falls into the second category for weakening a causal argument: "Show that even when the cause occurs, the effect does not occur." In this instance, because the antibiotics can kill helpful bacteria as well as harmful bacteria, the effect of the antibiotics is not necessarily a stronger patient, but one that may in fact be weakened. Because the antibiotics do not necessarily make the patient stronger as a result, the argument is undermined.

Answer choice (E): This answer choice has no impact on the argument. The expense of the proposed antibiotic treatments is not an issue in the argument.

Causal Reasoning Problem Set Answer Key

Question #2: Weaken—CE. The correct answer choice is (D)

In this stimulus the author discusses Alpha Cola, a popular soda that just spent a lot on a national advertising campaign. A less popular competitor, Epsilon Cola, claims that without the advertising campaign Alpha Cola would be no more popular than Epsilon Cola. The implication: Alpha's success is attributed to the company's advertising expenditures.

The Epsilon causal claim is as follows:

A$ = spending on successful and expensive advertising campaign
AC Pop = Alpha Cola's popularity

$$\underline{C} \qquad \underline{E}$$

$$A\$ \longrightarrow AC\ Pop$$

As discussed previously, there are five possible ways to attack the author's causal claim that greater spending on Epsilon's part would lead to popularity that equals Alpha's. The correct answer in this case, answer choice (D), uses the third method of attack discussed—showing that the effect has occurred even in the absence of the supposed cause.

Answer choice (A): The intention behind the successful ad campaign has no effect on the causal argument advanced in the stimulus; clearly, the intention behind an advertising campaign is often to increase sales, and this certainly doesn't hurt the Epsilon argument that Alpha's popularity gap was the result of the recent ad campaign.

Answer choice (B): Because this choice actually strengthens Epsilon's conclusion that Alpha's popularity resulted from a successful ad campaign, this choice cannot be the correct answer to this causal weaken question.

Answer choice (C): The stimulus provided the information that the campaign was costly, and if it was the most expensive in history this certainly wouldn't weaken the conclusion that Alpha's margin in popularity was the effect of that costly ad campaign.

Answer choice (D): This is the correct answer choice, providing information that significantly undermines the Epsilon assertion. If both colas have been available for years, and Alpha has enjoyed significantly more sales for years (even without advertising) then this hurts the claim that the Alpha advantage resulted from heavy advertising expenditures.

Answer choice (E): Since this answer rules out the alternative cause of taste preference, this choice actually strengthens the assertion that the ad campaign is the cause of the Alpha Cola sales advantage. As such, this choice cannot be the correct answer to this Weaken question.

Causal Reasoning Problem Set Answer Key

Question #3: Weaken—CE. The correct answer choice is (C)

This is a tricky problem. The premise contains information concerning a decrease in the percentage of consumers who chose High Seas' cruise lines in the past five years. This is where smart GMAT reading comes into play: does the argument say *fewer* people sailed on the line, or does it say there was a *lower percentage* of people making the choice of High Seas? Recognizing the difference is critical for successfully solving this problem, because the five percent decrease is among "consumers in this country," which, as a whole, could have grown dramatically over the past five years, and also does not include cruisers from other countries.

The conclusion about the negative earnings indicates the author believes the following causal relationship:

5% Down = decrease of 5 percentage points over the past five years
EN = negative impact on earnings

Literally, the author believes that the five percent decrease translated into fewer cruisers, which then lead to lower earnings. The question stem asks you to weaken the argument, and the correct answer falls into one of the five basic methods for weakening a causal argument.

Answer choice (A): The argument does not indicate or rely upon the assertion that trips were cut from the cruise schedule. Although cutting trips may be a cause of the five percent decrease (the cause of the cause), or, alternatively, an effect of lower earnings (the effect of the effect), it does not attack the causal relationship about whether the five percent decrease resulted in lower earnings. Literally, this answer can be seen to involve events either before or after the causal assertion, but that does not affect the causal relationship posited in the stimulus.

Answer choice (B): At best, this answer has no effect on the stimulus, and at worst, this answer would strengthen in the stimulus.

Answer choice (C): This is the correct answer. This answer shows that although five percent fewer people of the total may have chosen High Seas, that five percent reduction could have come against a much larger overall pool of people. Here's an example:

Causal Reasoning Problem Set Answer Key

	5 Years Ago	Now
% Choosing High Seas:	55%	50%
Total Cruise Consumers:	100	1000
Total High Seas Customers:	55	500

Thus, this answer choice undermines the causal relationship by showing that even though the cause is present, the effect does not occur.

Answer choice (D): This answer would possibly serve to support the idea that earnings are down, and so it cannot undermine the argument.

Answer choice (E): This information, while nice for consumers, is useless for attacking the conclusion.

Question #4: Weaken—CE. The correct answer choice is (D)

In this example, the medical student concludes that a particular patient should gain ten pounds in the coming week, based on the premise that the patient has gained ten pounds since last week and appears healthier. The presumption on the part of the medical student appears to be that the ten-pound weight weekly weight gain caused the healthier appearance, and so another weight gain would have a similar effect.

The stimulus is followed by a Weaken question, so the correct answer choice will provide some reason to question the medical student's conclusion that the patient would be well-advised to gain another ten pounds this week.

Answer choice (A): This answer choice supports the premise that the patient gained ten pounds, but this information would not weaken the medical student's conclusion in any way.

Answer choice (B): There is no way to assess what role patient notification might play (would this make the patient more or less likely to continue to gain weight at the same pace?), so this answer would not weaken the medical student's conclusion that last week's weight gain should be matched this week.

Answer choice (C): Some students are thrown off by this answer choice, because of the discrepancy between eating less and gaining weight. However, this choice does nothing to undermine the conclusion that the weight gain should be replicated during the coming week.

Causal Reasoning Problem Set Answer Key

Answer choice (D): This is the correct answer choice. If the patient was ten pounds below normal weight before gaining the ten pounds, this means that the patient is currently right at his or her normal weight. As such, it wasn't the ten pound weight increase that led to the patient's better health, it was a return to his or her normal weight. This answer choice provides an alternate cause for the healthier appearance, and undermines the medical student's conclusion that it was the mere gaining of weight that increased health.

Answer choice (E): Since the stimulus does not deal with the issue of weight loss, this choice does not undermine the medial student's conclusion.

Chapter Eight: Strengthen and Assumption Questions

Chapter Eight: Strengthen and Assumption Questions

The Second Family	191
The Difference Between Strengthen and Assumption Questions	192
Strengthen Questions	193
How to Strengthen an Argument	194
Three Incorrect Answer Traps	195
Strengthen Questions Analyzed	196
Causality and Strengthen Questions	198
Weaken vs Strengthen Questions	201
Strengthen Question Type Review	202
Strengthen Question Problem Set	203
Assumption Questions	206
The Supporter/Defender Assumption Model™	208
The Assumption Negation Technique™	215
Negating Statements	216
Logical Opposition	216
Statement Negation Drill	219
Three Quirks of Assumption Question Answer Choices	221
Assumptions and Causality	222
Assumption—Fill in the Blank Questions	224
Assumption Question Type Review	226
Assumption Question Problem Set	228

The Second Family

With this chapter, we begin our exposition of the Second Family of questions. Two of the question types within this family—Strengthen and Assumption—are considered to be among the hardest Critical Reasoning question types. These two question types are closely related and will be examined consecutively in this chapter. The remaining Second Family question type—Resolve the Paradox—will be examined in the next chapter.

Although all Second Family question types are related by their shared information model, there are distinct differences between each question type that ultimately determine the exact nature of the correct answer. Your performance on these questions will depend on your ability to distinguish each question type and understand the task you must fulfill.

Some students compare the Second Family information model diagram to the Third Family (Weaken) model and assume the two groups are exact opposites. While Strengthen and Weaken questions require you to perform opposite tasks, there are many similarities between the two types in terms of how information is used in each question. Assumption questions are variations on the Strengthen theme.

In addition to the Primary Objectives, keep these fundamental rules in mind when approaching Strengthen and Assumption questions:

1. The stimulus will contain an argument. Because you are being asked about the author's reasoning, and reasoning requires a conclusion, an argument will almost always be present. In order to maximize your chances of success you must identify, isolate, and assess the premises and the conclusion of the argument. Only by understanding the structure of the argument can you gain the perspective necessary to understand the author's position.

2. Focus on the conclusion. Almost all correct answer choices impact the conclusion. The more you know about the specifics of the conclusion, the better armed you will be to differentiate between correct and incorrect answers.

3. The information in the stimulus is suspect. There are often reasoning errors present, and you must read the argument very carefully in order to know how to shore up the argument.

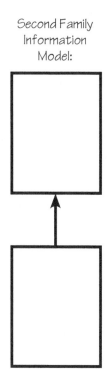

Second Family Information Model:

CHAPTER EIGHT: STRENGTHEN AND ASSUMPTION

4. These questions often yield strong prephrases. Make sure you actively consider the range of possible answers before proceeding to the answer choices.

5. The answer choices are accepted as given, even if they include "new" information. Like Weaken questions, the answer choices to the problems in this chapter can bring into consideration information outside of or tangential to the stimulus. Just because a fact or idea is not mentioned in the stimulus is *not* grounds for dismissing an answer choice.

By following the Primary Objectives and focusing on the points above, you will maximize your chances for success on these questions.

The Difference Between Strengthen and Assumption Questions

Chapter Three contained a basic definition of each question type. Now we will expand those definitions and compare and contrast each type:

> Strengthen questions ask you to support the argument in any way possible. This type of answer has great range, as the additional support provided by the answer choice could be relatively minor or major. Speaking in numerical terms, any answer choice that strengthens the argument, whether by 1% or by 100%, is correct.

> Assumption questions ask you to identify a statement that the argument assumes or supposes. An assumption is simply an unstated premise—what must be true in order for the argument to be true. An assumption can therefore be defined as something that is *necessary* for the argument to be true.

An assumption is simply an unstated premise of the argument.

Because the two question types are confusingly similar, let's use a simple example to clarify the difference among the correct answer choices that appear with each question type:

> An argument concludes that a teenager is an outstanding golfer.

> In an Assumption question, the correct answer could be: "The teenager almost always hits the ball" or "The teenager almost never swings and misses the ball." Either statement is an assumption of the argument; otherwise how could the teenager be an outstanding golfer?

In a Strengthen question, the correct answer could be: "The teenager won a local club tournament." This answer choice supports the idea that the teenager is an outstanding golfer, but does not undeniably prove the teenager to be outstanding (what if the tournament was composed primarily of pre-teen players?) nor is the answer an assumption of the conclusion.

Admittedly, this is a simple example, but take a moment to examine the different types of answers to each question.

Strengthen Questions

Strengthen questions ask you to identify the answer choice that best supports the argument. The correct answer choice does not necessarily justify the argument, nor is the correct answer choice necessarily an assumption of the argument. The correct answer choice simply helps the argument in some way.

Most Strengthen question stems typically contain the following two features:

1. The stem uses the word "strengthen" or a synonym. Following are some examples of words or phrases used to indicate that your task is to strengthen the argument:

    strengthen
    support
    helps
    most justifies

2. The stem indicates that you should accept the answer choices as true, usually with the following phrase:

    "Which of the following, if true, ..."

Following are several Strengthen question stem examples:

"Which of the following, if true, most strengthens the argument?"

"Which of the following, if true, most strongly supports the statement above?"

"Which of the following, if true, does most to justify the conclusion above?"

"Each of the following, if true, supports the claim above EXCEPT:"

Whether you are finding an assumption of the argument or strengthening the conclusion, you are doing something positive for the stimulus.

CHAPTER EIGHT: STRENGTHEN AND ASSUMPTION

How to Strengthen an Argument

Use the following points to effectively strengthen arguments:

1. Identify the conclusion—this is what you are trying to strengthen!

   Because Strengthen questions are the polar opposite of Weaken questions, the correct approach to supporting a GMAT argument is to help the author's conclusion. When evaluating an answer, ask yourself, "Would this answer choice assist the author in some way?" If so, you have the correct answer.

2. Personalize the argument.

   Personalizing allows you to see the argument from a very involved perspective and helps you assess the strength of each answer.

3. Look for weaknesses in the argument.

   This may seem like a strange recommendation since your task is to strengthen the argument, but a weak spot in an argument is tailor-made for an answer that eliminates that weakness. If you see a weakness or flaw in the argument, look for an answer that eliminates the weakness. In other words, close any gap or hole in the argument.

   Many Strengthen questions require students to find the missing link between a premise and the conclusion. These missing links are assumptions made by the author, and bringing an assumption to light strengthens the argument because it validates part of the author's thinking. This idea will be discussed further in the Assumption section of this chapter.

4. Arguments that contain analogies or use surveys rely upon the validity of those analogies and surveys. Answer choices that strengthen the analogy or survey, or establish their soundness, are usually correct.

5. Remember that the correct answer can strengthen the argument just a little or a lot. This variation is what makes these questions difficult.

Three Incorrect Answer Traps

The same type of wrong answer traps appear in Strengthen as in Weaken questions:

1. Opposite Answers. These answers do the exact opposite of what is needed—they weaken the argument. Because of their direct relation to the conclusion they are attractive answer choices, despite the fact that they result in consequences opposite of those intended.

2. Shell Game Answers. Remember, a Shell Game occurs when an idea or concept is raised in the stimulus and then a very similar idea appears in the answer choice, but the idea is changed just enough to be incorrect but still attractive. In Strengthen questions, the Shell Game is usually used to support a conclusion that is similar to, but slightly different from, the one presented in the stimulus.

3. Out of Scope Answers. These answers simply miss the point of the argument and support issues that are either unrelated to the argument or tangential to the argument.

These three answer types are not the only ways an answer choice can be attractively incorrect, but they appear frequently enough that you should be familiar with each form.

The stimuli for Strengthen and Weaken questions tend to be similar: both often contain faulty reasoning.

Strengthen Questions Analyzed

Please take a moment to complete the following problem:

1. Consumer advocate: Many household cleaners contain ingredients which are highly toxic when ingested by children or pets. Because of this significant risk, I propose a law prohibiting the use of such toxic ingredients in household cleaners.

    Which of the following, if true, provides the most support for the argument above?

    (A) Most toxic household cleaners have labels which clearly warn of their toxicity.
    (B) There are many different types of household cleaners, and some are more effective than others.
    (C) When the use of household cleaners is discontinued, harmful bacteria are more likely to propagate in areas where children and pets are commonly found.
    (D) The toxic ingredients in most household cleaners could be replaced by comparably priced, non-toxic ingredients of equal or better quality.
    (E) The amount of toxic ingredients found in most household cleaners is much less than the amount contained in most types of common gasoline.

The consumer advocate suggests a law which prohibits all household cleaners containing ingredients that are toxic when consumed by children or animals. The simple argument above is constructed as follows:

>   Premise: Many household cleaners contain ingredients that are toxic when ingested.
>
>   Conclusion: There should be law prohibiting the use of such toxic ingredients in household cleaners.

The stimulus in this case is followed by a Strengthen question, which means that the correct answer choice will bolster the advocate's argument in some way.

Answer choice (A): If most such cleaners have clear warning labels, this would reduce the need for an across-the-board prohibition of the cleaners. Since this choice does not strengthen the advocate's conclusion, but instead weakens it, this answer should be eliminated.

Answer choice (B): This choice basically provides that household cleaners are not all created equal. Since there is no reference whatsoever to the toxic ingredients, however, this choice does not strengthen or weaken the consumer advocate's argument.

Answer choice (C): The advocate does not suggest that the use of household cleaners be discontinued—just those with toxic ingredients—so this choice would not be entirely relevant to the argument (if it played any role, this answer would weaken the assertion that household cleaners should be discontinued, by pointing to a detrimental effect of their prohibition).

Answer choice (D): This is the correct answer choice because it provides information that shows that the advocate's plan is practicable. If the toxic ingredients could be removed with no increase in cost or decrease in effectiveness, then this preempts any cost-based or effectiveness-based objection to the proposed law. Literally, from the perspective of the test makers, by effectively protecting the argument from one or more avenues of attack, the answer strengthens the argument.

Answer choice (E): The comparison between the amount of toxic chemicals in household cleaners with the amount in gasoline is irrelevant to the question of whether such cleaners should be outlawed.

One thing that makes the GMAT difficult is that the test makers have so many options for testing you. In this question they could have chosen to strengthen a different part of the argument.

Causality and Strengthen Questions

Because Strengthen and Weaken questions require you to perform opposite tasks, to strengthen a causal conclusion you take the exact opposite approach that you would in a Weaken question.

In Strengthen questions, supporting a cause and effect relationship almost always consists of performing one of the following tasks:

A. Eliminate any alternate causes for the stated effect

Because the author believes there is only one cause (the stated cause in the argument), eliminating other possible causes strengthens the conclusion.

B. Show that when the cause occurs, the effect occurs

Because the author believes that the cause always produces the effect, any scenario where the cause occurs and the effect follows lends credibility to the conclusion. This type of answer can appear in the form of an example.

C. Show that when the cause does not occur, the effect does not occur

Using the reasoning in the previous point, any scenario where the cause does not occur and the effect does not occur supports the conclusion. This type of answer also can appear in the form of an example.

D. Eliminate the possibility that the stated relationship is reversed

Because the author believes that the cause and effect relationship is correctly stated, eliminating the possibility that the relationship is backwards (the claimed effect is actually the cause of the claimed cause) strengthens the conclusion.

E. Show that the data used to make the causal statement are accurate, or eliminate possible problems with the data

If the data used to make a causal statement are in error, then the validity of the causal claim is in question. Any information that eliminates error or reduces the possibility of error will support the argument.

Remember, to strengthen a causal argument you must perform tasks that are opposite those that weaken a causal argument.

Take a moment to consider each of these items, as they will reappear in the discussion of causality and Assumption questions—the approach will be identical for that combination.

Please take a moment to complete the following problem:

2. Among the three 24-hour pharmacies in the city, Sonny's Pharmacy is consistently the most profitable. Sonny's claims that since the three pharmacies carry the same products, the store's success is attributable to its superior customer service.

    Which of the following, if true, most strongly supports Sonny's claim?

    (A) The other two pharmacies in town advertise less than Sonny's.
    (B) The other two pharmacies' products are sold for approximately the same prices as similar products at Sonny's.
    (C) Sonny's is near the center of the city, a location that is convenient for most of the city's pharmacy customers.
    (D) Sonny's customer service was, according to a city-wide survey, comparable to that of the city's other two pharmacies.
    (E) The three pharmacies in town often require different wait times for the same prescription.

The conclusion of the argument is based on the causal assumption that the superior customer service caused Sonny's Pharmacy to be more profitable:

SCS = superior customer service
MP = Sonny's Pharmacy more profitable

<u>C</u>   <u>E</u>

SCS ⟶ MP

As you attack the answer choices, look for one of the five causal strengthening answer types discussed earlier.

Answer choice (A): This is an Opposite answer. As opposed to strengthening the argument, this answer hurts the argument by suggesting an alternate cause for why Sonny's Pharmacy was more profitable.

Answer choice (B): This is the correct answer. This answer strengthens the argument by eliminating an alternate cause for the effect (Type A). By stating that the pharmacies all have similar pricing, prices cannot be a factor in Sonny's greater profitability, and so the answer choice closes a hole in the argument.

Answer choice (C): Like answer choice (A), this is an Opposite answer. As opposed to strengthening the argument, this answer hurts the argument by suggesting an alternate cause for why Sonny's Pharmacy was more profitable.

Answer choice (D): Like answer choices (A) and (C), this is an Opposite answer. As opposed to strengthening the argument, this answer hurts the argument by the suggested cause for Sonny's Pharmacy profitability.

Answer choice (E): This answer has no effect on the argument. The information about wait times cannot be used to determine if Sonny's has better or worse wait times than its competitors, and thus this answer is incorrect.

Weaken vs Strengthen Questions

For individuals performing certain tasks, when they make mistakes they are most likely to make a mistake in the "opposite" direction from what is needed. For example, when a person drives on the freeway, it is easy to accidentally go north when one instead intended to go south. Although the direction is polar opposite from what you intended, that aspect is what makes it easier to fall into the error.

Applying this idea to Strengthen and Weaken questions, the two tasks required by those questions also force you to perform opposite tasks. As such, it is extremely easy to get confused when you are faced with one of these two question types. In each instance, you must isolate the elements present in the stimulus, and then constantly remind yourself during your review of the answer choices of the type of question you are facing.

However, this opposition has benefits for you as a test taker. As noted earlier, with certain reasoning types, the correct answers will also have opposite characteristics. For example, in causal reasoning, the correct answer to a Weaken question will be opposite of the correct answer in a Strengthen question. Thus, as you learn how to weaken an argument, you automatically learn how to strengthen it as well. This aspect makes remembering the various methods of solution easier, and also places you in the enviable position of having a "back door" to finding the correct answer should you find yourself forgetting the steps you should take while under the pressure of the test.

Overall, the goal is to know every element of the correct approach to each question, but if that fails, knowing how Strengthen and Weaken questions relate to each other can give you an advantage.

Strengthen Question Type Review

Strengthen questions ask you to identify the answer choice that best supports the argument.

Use the following points to effectively strengthen arguments:

1. Identify the conclusion—this is what you are trying to strengthen!

2. Personalize the argument.

3. Look for weaknesses or holes in the argument.

The same type of wrong answer traps appear in Strengthen as in Weaken questions:

1. Opposite Answers.

2. Shell Game Answers.

3. Out of Scope Answers.

Although you do not need to memorize the types of wrong answer choices that appear in Strengthen questions, you must memorize the ways to strengthen a causal argument.

In Strengthen questions, supporting a cause and effect relationship almost always consists of performing one of the following tasks:

A. Eliminate any alternate causes for the stated effect

B. Show that when the cause occurs, the effect occurs

C. Show that when the cause does not occur, the effect does not occur

D. Eliminate the possibility that the stated relationship is reversed

E. Show that the data used to make the causal statement is accurate, or eliminate possible problems with the data

Strengthen Question Problem Set

Please complete the problem set and review the answer key and explanations. *Answers on page 204*

1. Most managers in the financial industry work for several different companies over the course of their careers, seeking new employment in response to market pressures and changing corporate policies. Paxton Investment Group, however, is renowned in the financial sector for its exceptionally low managerial turnover. Paxton attributes its ability to retain managers to its extremely generous managerial salaries.

    Which of the following, if true, would provide the strongest support for Paxton Investment Group's statement regarding its managers' reluctance to change companies?

    (A) Many managers in the financial sector have spouses that also work in finance.
    (B) The majority of managers at Paxton Investment Group had previously worked at several other companies before working at Paxton.
    (C) Managers in the financial industry consistently list "income" as the greatest motivator for seeking employment with a new firm.
    (D) Investment firms with lower managerial salaries than those at Paxton often compensate by offering their managers performance-based bonuses.
    (E) Other investment firms provide their managers with salaries similar to those at Paxton Investment Group.

2. Last year, in an effort to decrease fossil fuel use, Suzanne traded in her late-model gas-powered car for a brand new gas/electric "hybrid" vehicle which uses significantly less gasoline for each mile driven. Because she has not changed her normal driving habits since then, it is obvious that Suzanne is now responsible for less fossil fuel use than she would have been if she had not switched to a hybrid vehicle.

    Which one of the following, if true, most strengthens the argument above?

    (A) Many drivers who have not switched to hybrid vehicles have nonetheless decreased their gasoline use by using various modes of public transportation.
    (B) Suzanne's old, gas-powered car is more fuel efficient than some hybrid vehicles.
    (C) Many drivers who switch to gas/electric hybrid vehicles do so in part to make a statement regarding the importance of the environment.
    (D) The original retail price of Suzanne's old car was significantly greater than the retail price of her new hybrid vehicle.
    (E) The total amount of fossil fuels used in the production and use of Suzanne's new hybrid vehicle was less than the amount that Suzanne would have used had she not switched to a hybrid vehicle.

CHAPTER EIGHT: STRENGTHEN AND ASSUMPTION

Strengthen Problem Set Answer Key

Question #1: Strengthen—CE. The correct answer choice is (C)

Paxton Investment Group's belief is that, despite a tendency of most managers in the financial industry to transition between several companies over the course of their careers, Paxton has such a low managerial turnover because they have such high managerial salaries. Essentially Paxton retains managers by paying them extremely well.

To strengthen this causal argument, a correct answer choice could either emphasize the significance of the suggested cause (money), or eliminate other, competing causes (something besides money that would cause managers to stay with one company).

Answer choice (A): The industry in which managers' spouses work has no effect on the motivating factor(s) that cause Paxton's managers to remain at Paxton, so this answer does not impact the argument in the stimulus.

Answer choice (B): The argument in the stimulus is about why Paxton Investment Group's managers tend to stay at Paxton. Since this answer never addresses the cause (money) and effect (low turnover) relationship given in the stimulus, it cannot strengthen the argument and is incorrect.

Answer choice (C): This is the correct answer. If managers in the financial industry list "income" as the most important factor in deciding where to work, then Paxton's high salaries would be more likely to be the reason that their managers do not seek employment elsewhere.

Answer choice (D): This answer choice actually weakens the statement made by Paxton: if other firms also compensate their managers well (via bonuses) then that undermines the significance of Paxton's high salaries. In other words, this answer shows that the money Paxton's managers make may not be as "generous" as Paxton states, suggesting some alternate cause could exist that motivates their managers to not leave. An answer choice that attacks a proposed cause weakens a causal argument.

Answer choice (E): This answer, like (D), minimizes the significance of the salaries offered by Paxton relative to other firms, thereby weakening the argument in the stimulus. Since the question stem asks for an answer that strengthens the stimulus, this answer is incorrect.

Strengthen Problem Set Answer Key

Question #2: Strengthen. The correct answer choice is (E)

The argument in this stimulus is that Suzanne is now responsible for less fossil fuel use than she would have been had she not switched to a hybrid car. The author bases this conclusion on the fact that Suzanne's hybrid uses significantly less gasoline than her previous vehicle, and that she has not changed her driving habits (that is, if she switched but then starting driving more miles, the additional driving could negate the improved fuel efficiency).

To strengthen the argument that she is responsible for less fossil fuel use with the purchase/use of her hybrid, we need an answer choice that eliminates the possibility that Suzanne's new hybrid could have somehow made her responsible for more fossil fuel use.

Answer choice (A): The fact that other, non-hybrid drivers have found alternative ways to reduce their fossil use has no effect on the argument about Suzanne's fossil fuel use.

Answer choice (B): The comparison in the stimulus is between her old, gas-powered car and her new hybrid car. Comparing her old car to "some" other hybrids is not relevant.

Answer choice (C): The argument in question is not about *why* Suzanne switched to a hybrid (motivation), but simply about whether that switch would reduce her overall fossil fuel use (net effect). Since answer choice (C) only addresses the motivation of some drivers and does not provide any evidence to suggest a quantifiable reduction in fossil fuel use, it does not affect the argument.

Answer choice (D): This answer choice only discusses the price of the two vehicles being compared in the stimulus. Since the argument is about fossil fuel use, not price, this answer choice is irrelevant and incorrect.

Answer choice (E): This is the correct answer. By stating that the total amount of fossil fuels used in the production and use of her hybrid was less than the amount she would have produced had she not switched, we reinforce the argument in the stimulus that her switch to a hybrid reduced her overall fossil fuel use.

Assumption Questions

An argument can be analogized to a house: the premises are like walls, the conclusion is like the roof, and the assumptions are like the foundation.

As with a house foundation, an assumption is a hidden part of the structure, but critical to the integrity of the structure—all the other elements rest upon it.

For many students, Assumption questions are the most difficult type of Critical Reasoning problem. An assumption is simply an unstated premise of the argument; that is, an integral component of the argument that the author takes for granted and leaves unsaid. In our daily lives we make thousands of assumptions, but they make sense because they have context and we have experience with the way the world works. Think for a moment about the many assumptions required during the simple act of ordering a meal at a restaurant. You assume that: the prices on the menu are correct; the items on the menu are available; the description of the food is reasonably accurate; the waiter will understand what you say when you order; the food will not sicken or kill you; the restaurant will accept your payment, et cetera. In a GMAT question, you are faced with the difficult task of figuring out the author's mindset and determining what assumption he or she made when formulating the argument. This task is unlike any other on the GMAT.

Because an assumption is an integral component of the author's argument, a piece that must be true in order for the conclusion to be true, assumptions are *necessary* for the conclusion. Hence, the answer you select as correct must contain a statement that the author relies upon and is fully committed to in the argument. Think of an assumption as the foundation of the argument, a statement that the premises and conclusion rest upon. If an answer choice contains a statement that the author might only think *could* be true, or if the statement contains additional information that the author is not committed to, then the answer is incorrect. In many respects, an assumption can be considered a minimalist answer. Because the statement must be something the author believed when forming the argument, assumption answer choices cannot contain extraneous information. For example, let us say that an argument requires the assumption "all dogs are intelligent." The correct answer could be that statement, or even a subset statement such as "all black dogs are intelligent" or "all large dogs are intelligent" (black dogs and large dogs being subsets of the overall group of dogs, of course). But, additional information would rule out the answer, as in the following case: "All dogs and cats are intelligent." The additional information about cats is not part of the author's assumption, and would make the answer choice incorrect.

The correct answer to an Assumption question is a statement the author must believe in order for the conclusion to be properly drawn.

Because assumptions are described as what must be true in order for the conclusion to be true, some students ask about the difference between Must Be True question answers and Assumption question answers. The difference is one that can be described as *before* versus *after*: Assumption answers contain statements that were *used to make* the conclusion; Must Be True answers contain statements that *follow from* the argument made in the stimulus. In both cases, however, there is a stringent requirement that must be met: Must Be True answers must be proven by the information in the stimulus; Assumption answers contain statements the author must believe in order for the conclusion to be valid.

Question stem examples:

"The argument in the passage depends on which of the following assumptions?"

"The argument above assumes that"

"The conclusion above is based on which of the following assumptions?"

"Which of the following is an assumption made in drawing the conclusion above?"

"The conclusion of the argument above cannot be true unless which of the following is true?"

The Supporter/Defender Assumption Model™

Most GMAT publications and courses present a limited description of assumptions. An assumption is described solely as a linking statement, one that links two premises or links a premise to the conclusion. If no other description of assumptions is given, this limited presentation cheats students of the possibility of fully understanding the way assumptions work within arguments and the way they are tested by the makers of the exam.

On the GMAT, assumptions play one of two roles—the Supporter or the Defender. The Supporter role is the traditional linking role, where an assumption connects the pieces of the argument. Consider the following example:

> All male citizens of Athens had the right to vote. Therefore, Socrates had the right to vote in Athens.

The linking assumption is that Socrates was a male citizen of Athens. This connects the premise element of male citizens having the right to vote and the conclusion element that Socrates had the right to vote (affiliated assumptions are "Socrates was male" and "Socrates was a citizen of Athens").

Supporters often connect "new" or "rogue" pieces of information in the argument, and we typically use the term "new" or "rogue" to refer to an element that appears only in the conclusion or only in a premise. Thus, the conclusion in a Supporter argument often contains a piece of information not previously seen in the argument. In the example above, for instance, "Socrates" is a new element in the conclusion. These "new" elements create gaps in the argument, and Supporter assumptions on the GMAT are often relatively easy for students to identify because they can see the gap in the argument. The Supporter assumption, by definition, closes the hole by linking the elements together. Should you ever see a gap or a new element in the conclusion, a Supporter assumption answer will almost certainly close the gap or link the new element back to the premises.

If you see a weakness in the argument, look for an answer that eliminates the weakness or assumes that it does not exist. In other words, close the gaps in the argument.

The Defender role is entirely different, and Defender assumptions protect the argument by eliminating ideas that could weaken the argument. Consider our discussion from Chapter Two:

> "When you read a GMAT argument from the perspective of the author, keep in mind that he or she believes that their argument is sound. In other words, they do not knowingly make errors of

reasoning. This is a fascinating point because it means that GMAT authors, as part of the GMAT world, function as if the points they raise and the conclusions they make have been well-considered and are airtight."

This fundamental truth of the GMAT has a dramatic impact when you consider the range of assumptions that must be made by a GMAT author. In order to believe the argument is "well-considered and airtight," an author must assume that every possible objection has been considered and rejected. Consider the following causal argument:

> People who read a lot are more intelligent than other people. Thus, reading must cause a person to be intelligent.

Although the conclusion is questionable (for example, the situation may be reversed: intelligence might be the cause of reading a lot), in the author's mind *all* other alternative explanations are assumed not to exist. Literally, the author assumes that any idea that would weaken the argument is impossible and cannot occur. Consider some of the statements that would attack the conclusion above:

> Sleeping more than eight hours causes a person to be intelligent.
>
> Regular exercise causes a person to be intelligent.
>
> A high-protein diet causes a person to be intelligent.
>
> Genetics cause a person to be intelligent.

Each of these ideas would undermine the conclusion, but they are assumed by the author *not* to be possible, and the author therefore makes the following assumptions in the original argument:

> Sleeping more than eight hours does not cause a person to be intelligent.
>
> Regular exercise does not cause a person to be intelligent.
>
> A high-protein diet does not cause a person to be intelligent.
>
> Genetics do not cause a person to be intelligent.

Supporter answer choices lend themselves well to prephrasing. Defender answers do not because there are too many possibilities to choose from.

By assuming that any threat to the argument does not exist, the author can present the argument and claim it is valid. If the author knew of imperfections and still presented the argument without a caveat, then the author would be hard-pressed to claim that this conclusion—especially an absolute one—was reasonable.

CHAPTER EIGHT: STRENGTHEN AND ASSUMPTION

These assumptions protect the argument against statements that would undermine the conclusion. In this sense, they "defend" the argument by showing that a possible avenue of attack has been eliminated (assumed not to exist). As you can see, this list could go on and on because the author assumes *every* alternate cause does not exist. This means that although the argument only discussed reading and intelligence, we suddenly find ourselves with assumptions addressing a wide variety of topics that were never discussed in the stimulus. In a typical argument, there are an infinite number of assumptions possible, with most of those coming on the Defender side. Books and courses that focus solely on the Supporter role miss these assumptions, and students who do not understand how Defenders work will often summarily dismiss answer choices that later prove to be correct.

Let's review the two roles played by assumptions:

If there is no obvious weakness in the argument and you are faced with an Assumption question, expect to see a Defender answer choice.

Supporter Assumption: These assumptions link together new or rogue elements in the stimulus or fill logical gaps in the argument.

Defender Assumption: These assumptions contain statements that eliminate ideas or assertions that would undermine the conclusion. In this sense, they "defend" the argument by showing that a possible source of attack has been eliminated.

Let us examine examples of each type. Please take a moment to complete the following question:

1. Despite the fact that many professional writers consider travel writing a lesser form of journalism, it is in fact a legitimate journalistic enterprise, since it employs classical journalism techniques such as detailed research into the history of a given locale and extensive interviews with local residents.

   The argument above depends on which one of the following assumptions?

   (A) If a literary work is crafted via extensive interviews of noteworthy subjects it should be viewed as legitimate.
   (B) Since travel writing follows the methods of traditional journalism, it will produce intriguing material for readers.
   (C) Any writing that does not employ classical techniques is a lesser form of journalism.
   (D) If a literary pursuit involves classical journalism techniques, then it should be considered a legitimate journalistic enterprise.
   (E) The interview process used by travel writers can provide further information about the history of a region.

Once you understand the way Supporters work, they can often be predicted after you read an argument.

This is a Supporter assumption, and about sixty percent of the test takers identify the correct answer.

Take a look at the argument structure:

   Counter-premise: Despite the fact that many professional writers consider travel writing a lesser form of journalism.

   Premise: since it employs classical journalism techniques such as detailed research into the history of the locale and extensive interviews with local residents.

   Conclusion: it is in fact a legitimate journalistic enterprise.

The first step is to properly identify the conclusion—"it is in fact a legitimate journalistic enterprise"—which is presented in the middle of the argument. Given our discussion about linking new elements that appear in the conclusion, you should have recognized that a new element was

CHAPTER EIGHT: STRENGTHEN AND ASSUMPTION   211

present ("legitimate journalistic enterprise") and responded accordingly by linking that information with the main premise of the argument, namely that travel writing employs classic techniques. Given that Supporters connect new elements, one would suspect that the correct answer would include these two elements and that answer choice (D) was likely to be correct.

Answer choice (A): The author does not discuss "noteworthy subjects," and hence this is not an assumption of the argument.

Answer choice (B): The first part of this answer is extremely attractive, but the second half of the answer addresses "intriguing material," another subject that was not discussed in the argument. Like (A), this is not an assumption of the argument.

Answer choice (C): This is the most popular wrong answer choice. The answer connects two pieces of the argument, but those pieces are from the premise and the counter-premise. The author only discusses the fact that travel writing uses classic techniques, but the author does makes not assumption about writing that does not use those techniques.

Answer choice (D): This is the correct answer. The answer acts as a Supporter and connects the elements in the conclusion to the elements in the final sentence.

Answer choice (E): This answer attempts to falsely commingle two of the methods used by the classical journalism: research and interviews. There is no indication that the interviews with the residents reveals the history of the locale.

Now let us look at a Defender assumption. Please take a moment to complete the following question:

2. During the production of orange juice, calcium is sometimes added as a nutritional supplement. Certain individuals are allergic to calcium, and drinking orange juice fortified with calcium can cause an allergic reaction. Fortunately, some types of orange juice do not have calcium added during production, so calcium-allergic individuals can drink these orange juices without inducing an allergic reaction to calcium.

   Which of the following is an assumption on which the argument depends?

   (A) There are no other substances besides calcium that are typically present in orange juice that cause allergic reactions.
   (B) Orange juice has the same nutritional value whether calcium is added or not.
   (C) Calcium-allergic individuals cannot ingest any calcium without having an allergic reaction.
   (D) Calcium is often added to other beverages besides orange juice.
   (E) In orange juice that does not have calcium added during production, calcium is not naturally present in quantities that cause an allergic reaction.

Unlike Supporter assumptions, Defender assumptions can be extremely hard to prephrase because there are so many possibilities for the test makers to choose from. The correct answer in this problem is a Defender, but you should not feel bad if you could not predict the answer. The previous problem (a Supporter Assumption question) is perhaps more conducive to prephrasing.

In this stimulus, the author points out that orange juice sometimes has calcium added as a nutritional supplement, but that calcium causes an allergic reaction in some people. Based on the fact that orange juice is also available with no calcium added, the author concluded that this type of juice can be safely consumed by those with a calcium allergy.

The stimulus is followed by an Assumption question. Since there is no "missing link" in this case, we can see that this is a Defender Assumption question. If we do not have a prephrased answer for this one, we should assess the choices until we find an assumption that the author's argument requires.

CHAPTER EIGHT: STRENGTHEN AND ASSUMPTION

Answer choice (A): The author does not conclude that orange juice is free of all allergens—the far more limited conclusion present in the stimulus is that people who are allergic to *calcium* could safely consume orange juice that has not had calcium added.

Answer choice (B): The nutritional value of orange juice is not at issue in this question, and the argument does not require this assumption.

Answer choice (C): This choice simply provides that people who are allergic to calcium are *very* allergic. That is, any amount will trigger an allergic reaction. Since the author's conclusion indicates that non-calcium-added orange juice is safe for such people to consume, this is not an assumption on which the argument relies.

Answer choice (D): This choice is outside the scope of the issue under discussion. The author's comments are limited to orange juice and its safety for people who are allergic to calcium. The existence of other calcium supplemented products is irrelevant, so this is not an assumption on which the author's argument relies.

Answer choice (E): This is the correct answer choice, and an assumption that is required of the author's argument. The author must be assuming that orange juice has no naturally present calcium—if it does have some calcium naturally that would cause an allergic reaction, then this would destroy the author's conclusion that, as long as calcium has not been added, calcium-allergic people could safely drink orange juice.

The Assumption Negation Technique™

Only a few types of GMAT questions allow you to double-check your answer. Assumption questions are one of those types, and you should use the Assumption Negation Technique to decide between Contenders or to confirm that the answer you have chosen is correct.

The purpose of this technique is to take an Assumption question, which is generally difficult for most students, and turn it into a Weaken question, which is easier for most students. *This technique can only be used on Assumption questions.* To apply the technique take the following steps:

1. Logically negate the answer choices under consideration.

   We will discuss negation later in this section, but negating a statement means to alter the sentence so the meaning is logically opposite of what was originally stated. Negation largely consists of taking a "not" out of a sentence when one is present, or putting a "not" in a sentence if one is not present. For example, "The congressman always votes for gun control" becomes "The congressman does not always vote for gun control" when properly negated.

2. The negated answer choice that attacks the argument will be the correct answer.

   When the correct answer choice is negated, the answer *must* weaken the argument. This will occur because of the *necessary* nature of an assumption.

   The consequence of negating an assumption is that the validity of the conclusion is called into question. In other words, when you take away (negate) an assumption—a building block of the argument—it calls into question the integrity of the entire reasoning structure. Accordingly, negating the answer choices turns an Assumption question into a Weaken question.

Do not use the Assumption Negation Technique on all five answer choices. The process is too time-consuming and you can usually knock out a few answer choices without working too hard. Only apply the technique once you have narrowed the field.

CHAPTER EIGHT: STRENGTHEN AND ASSUMPTION

Negating Statements

Negating a statement consists of creating the *logical* opposite of the statement. The logical opposite is the statement that denies the truth of the original statement, and a logical opposite is different than the *polar* opposite. For example, consider the following statement:

> I went to the beach every day last week.

The logical opposite is the statement requiring the least amount of "work" to negate the original statement:

> I did not go to the beach every day last week.

The polar opposite typically goes much further:

> I did not go to the beach *any* day last week.

For GMAT purposes, the logical opposite is the statement you should seek when negating, and in order to do this you must understand logical opposition.

Logical Opposition

The concept of logical opposition appears frequently on the GMAT in a variety of forms. A complete knowledge of the logical opposites that most often appear will provide you with a framework that eliminates uncertainties and ultimately leads to skilled GMAT performance. Consider the following question:

> What is the logical opposite of sweet?

Most people reply "sour" to the above question. While "sour" is an opposite of "sweet," it is considered the polar opposite of "sweet," not the logical opposite. A logical opposite will always completely divide the subject under consideration into two parts. Sweet and sour fail as logical opposites since tastes such as bland or bitter remain unclassified. The correct logical opposite of "sweet" is in fact "not sweet." "Sweet" and "not sweet" divide the taste spectrum into two complete parts, and tastes

---

The polar opposite negation often works effectively to solve Assumption questions, but there are cases where it would not work perfectly (because it goes farther than necessary).

The logical opposite negation is the correct negation to use for the Assumption Negation Technique, and it will never fail to work when applied properly.

such as bland and bitter now clearly fall into the "not sweet" category. This same type of oppositional reasoning also applies to other everyday subjects such as color (what is the logical opposite of white?) and temperature (what is the logical opposite of hot?).

To help visualize pairs of opposites within a subject, we use an Opposition Construct. An Opposition Construct efficiently summarizes subjects within a limited spectrum of possibilities, such as quantity:

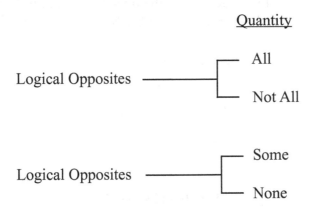

In this quantity construct, the range of possibilities extends from All to None. Thus, these two "ends" are polar opposites. There are also two pairs of logical opposites: All versus Not All and Some versus None. These logical opposites hold in both directions: for example, Some is the precise logical opposite of None, and None is the precise logical opposite of Some. The relationship between the four logical possibilities of quantity becomes more complex when we examine pairs such as Some and All. Imagine for a moment that we have between 0 and 100 marbles. According to the above construct, each logical possibility represents the following:

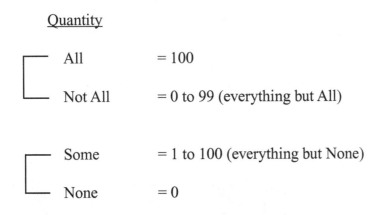

CHAPTER EIGHT: STRENGTHEN AND ASSUMPTION

By looking closely at the quantities each possibility represents, we can see that Some (1 to 100) actually includes All (100). This makes sense because Some, if it is to be the exact logical opposite of None, should include every other possibility besides None. The same relationship also holds true for Not All (0 to 99) and None (0).

The relationship between Some and Not All is also interesting. Some (1 to 100) and Not All (0 to 99) are largely the same, but they differ significantly at the extremes. Some actually includes All, the opposite of Not All, and Not All includes None, the opposite of Some. As a point of definition Not All is the same as Some Are Not.

The same line of reasoning applies to other subjects that often appear on the GMAT:

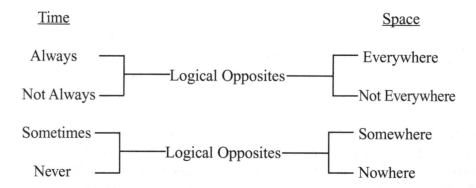

The Time and Space constructs are very similar to the Quantity construct. For example, Always is somewhat equivalent to "All of the time." Everywhere could be said to be "All of the space." Thus, learning one of these constructs makes it easy to learn the other two.

Statement Negation Drill

This drill will test your ability to use the Assumption Negation Technique™, which requires the conversion of Assumption question answer choices to Weaken answer choices. In the spaces provided write the proper logical negation of each of the following statements. *Answers on page 220*

1. The tax increase will result in more revenue for the government.

2. The councilmember could reverse her position.

3. The voting patterns in this precinct changed significantly in the past year.

4. The pattern of behavior in adolescents is not necessarily determined by the environment they are raised in.

5. Organic farming methods promote crop resistance to pest attack.

6. All of the missions succeeded.

7. The positive effects of the U.S. immigration policy are everywhere.

8. Exactly one police car will reach the scene in time.

CHAPTER EIGHT: STRENGTHEN AND ASSUMPTION

Statement Negation Drill Answer Key

The correct answer is listed below, with the negating elements italicized.

1. The tax increase *might not* result in more revenue for the government.

   The negation of "will" is "might not." In practice the polar opposite "will not" tends to be acceptable.

2. The councilmember *cannot* reverse her position.

   "Cannot" is the opposite of "could."

3. The voting patterns in this precinct *did not* change significantly in the past year.

4. The pattern of behavior in adolescents is *necessarily* determined by the environment they are raised in.

5. Organic farming methods *do not* promote crop resistance to pest attack.

6. *Not all* of the missions succeeded.

7. The positive effects of the U.S immigration policy are *not* everywhere.

   Note that "positive" in this sentence does not become "negative." To say "The negative effects of the U.S immigration policy are everywhere" would not negate the original.

8. *Not exactly one* police car will reach the scene in time.

   Typically, there are two ways to negate a phrase containing the words "only one" or "exactly one." One possibility is to use the term "none" and the other possibility is to use the phrase "more than once." Both are logical negations since you are attempting to negate a statement where something occurred a precise number of times. In this case, any statement that differs in number from the original statement will be a negation.

Three Quirks of Assumption Question Answer Choices

Over the years, certain recurring traits have appeared in Assumption answer choices. Recognizing these quirks may help you eliminate wrong answers or more quickly identify the correct answer at crunch time.

1. Watch for answers starting with the phrase "at least one" or "at least some."

    For some reason, when an Assumption answer choice starts with either of the above constructions the chances are unusually high that the answer will be correct. However, if you spot an answer with that construction, do not simply assume the answer is correct; instead, use the proper negation ("None") and check the answer with the Assumption Negation Technique.

2. Avoid answers that claim an idea was the most important consideration for the author.

    These answers typically use constructions such as "the primary purpose," "the top priority," or "the main factor." In every Assumption question these answers have been wrong. And, unless, the author specifically discusses the prioritization of ideas in the stimulus, these answers will continue to be wrong because an author can always claim that the idea under discussion was very important but not necessarily the most important idea.

3. Watch for the use of "not" or negatives in assumption answer choices.

    Because most students are conditioned to think of assumptions as positive connecting elements, the appearance of a negative in an Assumption answer choice often causes the answer to be classified a Loser. Do not rule out a negative answer choice just because you are used to seeing assumptions as a positive part of the argument. As we have seen with Defender answer choices, one role an assumption can play is to eliminate ideas that could attack the argument. To do so, Defender answer choices frequently contain negative terms such as "no," "not," and "never." One benefit of this negative language is that Defender answer choices can usually be negated quite easily.

In an Assumption question, there can be only one answer that will hurt the argument when negated. If you negate the answers and think that two or more hurt the argument, you have made a mistake.

Increasing your GMAT "speed" is a result of recognizing the patterns and elements that appear within GMAT questions, and then understanding exactly how to respond. The faster you are at recognition-response, the more questions you will complete.

Assumptions and Causality

The central assumption of causality was stated in the last chapter:

> "When a GMAT speaker concludes that one occurrence caused another, that speaker also assumes that the stated cause is the *only* possible cause of the effect and that the stated cause will *always* produce the effect."

Thus, because the author always assumes that the stated cause is the only cause, Assumption answer choices tend to work exactly like Strengthen answer choices in arguments with causal reasoning. The correct answer to an Assumption question will normally fit one of the following categories:

A. Eliminates an alternate cause for the stated effect

   Because the author believes there is only one cause (the stated cause in the argument), the author assumes no other cause exists.

B. Shows that when the cause occurs, the effect occurs

   Because the author believes that the cause always produces the effect, assumption answers will affirm this relationship.

C. Shows that when the cause does not occur, the effect does not occur

   Using the reasoning in the previous point, the author will always assume that when the cause does not occur, the effect will not occur.

D. Eliminates the possibility that the stated relationship is reversed

   Because the author believes that the cause-and-effect relationship is correctly stated, the author assumes that the relationship cannot be backwards (the claimed effect is actually the cause of the claimed cause).

E. Shows that the data used to make the causal statement are accurate, or eliminates possible problems with the data

   If the data used to make a causal statement are in error, then the validity of the causal claim is in question. The author assumes that this cannot be the case and that the data are accurate.

The above categories should be easy to identify because you should have already memorized them from the Strengthen question section. From now on, when you encounter Assumption questions containing causal reasoning, you will be amazed at how obvious the correct answer will seem. These types of patterns within questions are what make improvement on the GMAT possible, and when you become comfortable with the ideas, your speed will also increase.

Assumption—Fill in the Blank Questions

As first discussed in Chapter 5, a number of GMAT questions contain a stimulus that ends with a blank space. The question stem that precedes the stimulus asks you to fill in the blank with an appropriate answer. While not one of the most common question types, a Fill in the Blank question can throw off test takers who are surprised by the unusual stimulus formation. No need to worry; on the GMAT these are almost always Assumption questions in disguise (and when they are not Assumption questions they are often Must Be True/Main Point questions, as addressed in Chapter 5).

There are three notable features to these Assumption questions:

1. The stimulus is preceded by the question stem.

    For all Fill in the Blank questions, the question stem precedes the stimulus. And, the question stem simply directs you to complete the blank; it does not indicate that the question is an Assumption question. The following two examples are question stems that typically precede Fill in the Blank questions, and which give no indication of the task you must perform:

    "Which of the following most logically completes the passage?"

    "Which of the following best completes the argument below?"

2. The placement of the blank in the stimulus is not random—the blank is always at the very end of the stimulus, and appears at the very end of the last sentence.

3. There is a premise indicator at the start of the final sentence or just before the blank to help you recognize that you are being asked to fill in a missing premise, which is of course the same as an assumption.

    First, here are some sample final sentences to give you an example of how the sentence with the blank appears:

    "...because _____."

    "...is the fact that _____."

"...is that _____."

"...since _____."

"Thus, SafeCorp should hire Jones, because _____."

As you can see, just prior to the blank is a premise indicator; this is the signal that you must supply an assumption of the argument.

In order to achieve this goal, you must read the stimulus for clues revealing the direction of the argument and the author's beliefs.

Weaken—Fill in the Blank Questions

There is a trick that the GMAT makers will on occasion use to turn certain Fill in the Blank questions into Weaken-FIB questions. These questions have all the same features as an Assumption-FIB question, but then in the final sentence the test makers indicate that the plan under discussion in the stimulus is a bad or misguided idea, and ask you to supply the reason why in the blank.

Here are some sample final stimulus sentences to give you an example of how a Weaken—Fill in the Blank question would appear:

"However, this is a poor approach, because _____."

"Hence, the proposal should be discarded since _____."

As you can see, each sentence above begins by stating that the previously discussed idea is a not good or should not be followed, and then asks you to supply the reason why that is the case. The answer you select should weaken the argument.

CHAPTER EIGHT: STRENGTHEN AND ASSUMPTION

Assumption Question Type Review

An assumption is simply an unstated premise of the argument; that is, an integral component of the argument that the author takes for granted and leaves unsaid.

The answer you select as correct must contain a statement that the author relies upon and is fully committed to in the argument.

On the GMAT, assumptions play one of two roles: the Supporter or the Defender:

> Supporter Assumption: These assumptions link together new or rogue elements in the stimulus or fill logical gaps in the argument.
>
> Defender Assumption: These assumptions contain statements that eliminate ideas or assertions that would undermine the conclusion. In this sense, they "defend" the argument by showing that a possible avenue of attack has been eliminated (assumed not to exist).

Use the Assumption Negation Technique to decide between Contenders or to confirm that the answer you have chosen is correct. The purpose of this technique is to take an Assumption question, which is generally more difficult, and turn it into a Weaken question. *This technique can only be used on Assumption questions.* Take the following steps to apply this technique:

1. Logically negate the answer choices under consideration.

2. The negated answer choice that attacks the argument will be the correct answer.

Negating a statement consists of creating the *logical* opposite of the statement. The logical opposite is the statement that denies the truth of the original statement, and the logical opposite is different than the polar opposite.

Assumption answer choices tend to work exactly like Strengthen answer choices in arguments with causal reasoning. Because the author always assumes the stated cause is the only cause, the correct answer to an

Assumption question will normally fit one of the following categories:

A. Eliminates an alternate cause for the stated effect

B. Shows that when the cause occurs, the effect occurs

C. Shows that when the cause does not occur, the effect does not occur

D. Eliminates the possibility that the stated relationship is reversed

E. Shows that the data used to make the causal statement are accurate, or eliminates possible problems with the data

Fill in the Blank questions are almost always Assumption questions in disguise (and when they are not Assumption questions they are Must Be True/Main Point questions, or infrequently Weaken questions). The question stem always precedes the stimulus, and the placement of the blank is always at the very end of the stimulus. There is a premise indicator at the start of the sentence or near the blank to help you recognize that you are being asked to fill in a missing premise, which is of course the same as an assumption. In order to achieve this goal, you must read the stimulus for clues revealing the direction of the argument and the author's beliefs.

Assumption Question Problem Set

Please complete the problem set and review the answer key and explanations. *Answers on page 229*

1. Which of the following most logically completes the argument?

   The campus parking authority's claim that the university is losing substantial revenue each semester by allowing commuting students to park on campus for free is clearly false. Nearly all students who commute to campus live close enough to the university to easily walk there. Hence, the revenue generated by a pay-to-park system would actually be quite small, since _____.

   (A) only full-time students would be required to purchase parking permits.
   (B) most people who currently commute would rather walk to school than pay to park on campus.
   (C) enforcement of parking restrictions would require the hiring of many additional parking authority employees.
   (D) the university receives the majority of its revenue from charitable donations.
   (E) most of the free parking areas that are currently being used by students would be converted to paid parking areas.

2. Xani and Yata are the only two languages spoken in the country of Zorba, with Xani spoken by the majority of Zorba's residents. Thus, by learning Xani prior to visiting Zorba, tourists can feel confident that they have done the most that they can to assist in communicating with Zorba's locals.

   Which of the following is an assumption of the argument above?

   (A) Travelers to Zorba will not visit other countries in addition to Zorba.
   (B) Xani is easier to learn than Yata.
   (C) Most tourists are committed to effectively communicating with the residents of the countries that they visit.
   (D) Learning both Xani and Yata would not allow tourists to better communicate with the residents of Zorba than would only learning Xani.
   (E) Xani and Yata are both commonly spoken in countries other than Zorba.

Assumption Problem Set Answer Key

Question #1: Assumption—FIB. The correct answer choice is (B)

This is an unusual problem because the question stem appears before the stimulus. The stimulus then ends with a blank that is preceded by the premise indicator "since." Because an assumption is simply an unstated premise, and what fills the blank will be a premise of the argument, this is an Assumption question.

Re-ordered, the structure of the argument is as follows:

> Premise: Nearly all students who commute to campus live close enough to the university to easily walk there.
>
> Sub-Conclusion: Hence, the revenue generated by a pay-to-park system would actually be quite small.
>
> Conclusion: The campus parking authority's claim that the university is losing substantial revenue each semester by allowing commuting students to park on campus for free is clearly false.

The author notes that the campus parking authority claims to be losing substantial revenue due to free on-campus parking, but the author disagrees with that conclusion because nearly all the currently commuting students live close enough to campus to walk. Thus, to support the sub-conclusion that the revenue gained by a pay-to-park system would be small, the blank must be filled by an answer that connects the current commuters to the ability to walk to campus. This Supporter connection is perfectly stated in (B), the correct answer.

Answer choice (A): This answer does not address the fact that revenue would not increase, because no information is given about full-time students as they relate to the commuters. If every student is a full-time student, that might hurt the argument, but if there are hardly any full-time students, that would help the argument. In any event, the statement is not an assumption of the argument.

Answer choice (B): This is the correct answer, a Supporter.

Answer choice (C): The argument is about additional revenues, not about costs. Because this answer is about costs, it is not an assumption of the argument.

Answer choice (D): This answer is an immediate Loser. No discussion or assumption is made about the university's total revenue or overall revenue sources.

Answer choice (E): While this answer possibly supports the campus authority's argument, it neither assists nor damages the author's argument.

Assumption Problem Set Answer Key

Question #2: Assumption. The correct answer choice is (D)

The structure of the argument is as follows:

> Premise: Xani and Yata are the only two languages spoken in the country of Zorba.
>
> Premise: with Xani spoken by the majority of Zorba's residents.
>
> Conclusion: Thus, by learning Xani prior to visiting Zorba, tourists can feel confident that they have done the most that they can to assist in communicating with Zorba's locals.

At first glance the argument does not seem to have any gaping holes. This would suggest a Defender answer is coming, and indeed that is the case.

Answer choice (A): The author does not need to assume this statement because the stimulus is specifically about visitors visiting Zorba and communicating with Zorba's locals.

Answer choice (B): The ease of learning a particular language is not under examination in this question. This answer is thus irrelevant to the argument.

Answer choice (C): The author's argument concerns what tourists can do to assure themselves that they have done the most they can in order to assist in communicating with Zorba's locals. Whether tourists are committed to taking those steps is not part of the argument. When faced with the negation of the answer choice, the author would likely reply: "They may not be committed, but if they want to do the most they can, they should learn Xani prior to visiting Zorba." As you can see, the negation has not undermined the author's position, and so this answer is incorrect.

Answer choice (D): This is the correct answer. The key to this answer is the conclusion of the argument, where the author states that "tourists can feel confident that they have done *the most they can do* to assist in communicating with Zorba's locals" (italics added for emphasis). Because the author states that learning just the one language spoken by the majority of Zorbans is doing the "most they can do," this answer defends the conclusion by indicating that it would *not* be better to learn both Zorban languages. If this answer did not make sense at first glance, you should have noted the negative language and then negated the answer. Applying the Assumption Negation Technique produces a statement that would clearly attack the conclusion: "Learning both Xani and Yata *would* allow tourists to better communicate with the residents of Zorba than would only learning Xani." If learning both languages provides better communication, then learning just Xani would not be the most that a tourist could do to assist in communicating with Zorba's locals.

Answer choice (E): This answer is incorrect because the argument is about visiting Zorba and communicating with Zorba's locals. The fact that the two languages are spoken in other countries is not relevant.

Chapter Nine:
Resolve the Paradox Questions

Chapter Nine: Resolve the Paradox Questions

Resolve the Paradox Questions	233
Stimulus Peculiarities	233
Question Stem Features	234
Active Resolution	235
Address the Facts	237
Oppositional Circumstances and Cause	239
Resolve the Paradox Question Review	240
Resolve the Paradox Question Problem Set	241

Resolve the Paradox Questions

Resolve the Paradox questions are generally easy to spot because of their distinctive stimuli: each stimulus presents a situation where two ideas or occurrences appear to contradict each other. Because most people are very good at recognizing these paradox scenarios, they usually know after reading the stimulus that a Resolve the Paradox question is coming up.

Stimulus Peculiarities

Besides the discrepant or contradictory facts, most Resolve the Paradox stimuli contain the following features:

1. No conclusion

    One of the hallmarks of a Resolve the Paradox question is that the stimulus does not contain a conclusion. The author is not attempting to persuade you, he or she just presents two sets of contradictory facts. Thus, when you read a stimulus without a conclusion that contains a paradox, expect to see a Resolve question. If you read a fact set that does not contain a paradox, expect to see a Must Be True question or a Cannot Be True question (less likely).

2. Language of contradiction

    In order to present a paradox, the test makers use language that signals a contradiction is present, such as:

    > But
    > However
    > Yet
    > Although
    > Paradoxically
    > Surprisingly

If you can recognize the paradox present in the stimulus, you will have a head start on prephrasing the answer and completing the problem more quickly.

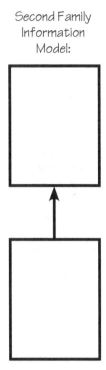

Second Family Information Model:

Question Stem Features

Resolve the Paradox question stems are easy to identify, and typically contain the following features:

1. An indication that the answer choices should be accepted as true

   Because Resolve the Paradox questions fall into the Second Question Family, you must accept the answer choices as true and then see if they resolve the paradox. Typically, the question stem will contain a phrase such as, "which of the *following*, if true, ..."

2. Key words that indicate your task is to resolve a problem

   To convey the nature of your task, Resolve the Paradox question stems usually use words from both of the lists below. The first list contains words used to describe the action you must take, the second list contains words used to describe the paradox present in the stimulus:

Action	Problem
Resolve	Paradox
Explain	Discrepancy
Reconcile	Contradiction
	Conflict
	Puzzle

Here are several Resolve the Paradox question stem examples:

"Which of the following, if true, most helps to resolve the apparent paradox?"

"Which of the following, if true, does the most to explain the result described above?"

"Which of the following, if true, best accounts for the seeming discrepancy described above?"

"Which of the following hypotheses best explains the contrast described above?"

You should attempt to prephrase an answer; many students are able to successfully predict a scenario that would explain the situation.

On the GMAT, the word "explain" is used more frequently than any other word to indicate the presence of a Resolve question.

A ResolveX question would present four incorrect answers that resolve or explain the situation. The one correct answer would either confuse the situation, or, more likely, have no impact on the situation.

Active Resolution

When first presented with a Resolve question, most students seek an answer choice that destroys or disproves one side of the situation. They follow the reasoning that if one side can be proven false, then the paradox will be eliminated. While this is true, the test makers know that such an answer would be obvious (it would simply contradict part of the facts given in the stimulus) and thus this type of answer does not appear in these questions. Instead, the correct answer will actively resolve the paradox, that is, it will allow both sides to be factually correct and it will either explain how the situation came into being or add a piece of information that shows how the two ideas or occurrences can coexist.

Because you are not seeking to disprove one side of the situation, you must select the answer choice that contains a *possible cause* of the situation. So, when examining answers, ask yourself if the answer choice could lead to the situation in the stimulus. If so, the answer is correct.

The correct answer will positively resolve the paradox so that both sides are true and the conditions in the stimulus have been met.

If an answer supports or proves only one side of the paradox, that answer will be incorrect. The correct answer must show how both sides coexist.

Please take a moment to complete the following problem:

1. After an earthquake several years ago in the country of Altrus—the first in over a century—many communication cables in the country were damaged. After another, more recent earthquake, very few communication cables were damaged.

    Which of the following, if true, most helps to explain why many communication cables were damaged in the first earthquake but few were damaged in the second earthquake?

    (A) In between the two earthquakes, the government of Altrus initiated a program emphasizing the use of cellular phones that do not rely on the use of communication cables.
    (B) The magnitude of the first earthquake was roughly the same as the magnitude of the second earthquake.
    (C) Many of the communication cables damaged in the first earthquake were in poor condition already, and they were subsequently replaced by newer, stronger cables.
    (D) Most of the cables damaged by the first earthquake were at least one foot in circumference.
    (E) The first earthquake was several magnitudes weaker than the second earthquake.

Like most Resolve questions, the stimulus contains just a fact set, and no conclusion is drawn. The paradox in the argument is fairly clear:

Fact 1: After an earthquake several years ago in the country of Altrus—the first in over a century—many communication cables in the country were damaged.

Fact 2: After another, more recent earthquake, very few communication cables were damaged.

In this instance, we need an answer that actively explains why many cables were damaged in the first earthquake but few were damaged in the second earthquake.

Answer choice (A): This answer may explain why usage rates of the cables have dropped over the years, but that was not the issue in the stimulus. The issue was about damage to those cables, not the actual use of the cables.

Answer choice (B): If a stimulus contains a paradox where two items are different (as in this stimulus), then an answer choice that explains why the two are similar cannot be correct. This answer, which states that the two earthquakes were of roughly the same magnitude, cannot thus explain the difference in the cable damage.

Answer choice (C): This is the correct answer, and this answer offers an explanation for the difference above. If many of the cables in the first earthquake were old, they would be more prone to damage. But, if those cables were then replaced by newer, stronger cables, in the second earthquake they would be less prone to damage. Since this scenario allows all sides of the situation to be correct and it explains how the situation could occur, this is the correct answer.

Answer choice (D): This answer addresses only one side of the paradox, and so is likely to be incorrect. Additionally, information about the circumference of the cables is not sufficient to explain the difference in damage caused by the two earthquakes.

Answer choice (E): This answer is similar to answer choice (B) in that it confuses the situation. If the second earthquake was stronger, then why would fewer cables have been damaged in that quake? As this answer offers no explanation for the difference, this answer is incorrect.

> If the stimulus contains a paradox where two items are similar, then an answer choice that explains a difference between the two cannot be correct.
>
> Conversely, if the stimulus contains a paradox where two items are different, then an answer choice that explains why the two are similar cannot be correct.
>
> In short, a similarity cannot explain a difference, and a difference cannot explain a similarity.

Address the Facts

When attempting to resolve the paradox in the stimulus, you must address the facts of the situation. Many incorrect answers will try to lure you with reasonable solutions that do not quite meet the stated facts. These answers are incorrect. The correct answer *must* conform to the specifics of the stimulus otherwise how could it resolve or explain the situation?

The importance of this point cannot be overstated, because many of the most attractive wrong answers in Resolve questions are based on ideas that are similar to the ones in the stimulus, but differ in some small, factual way. With this point in mind, let's take a look at another Resolve the Paradox question.

Please take a moment to complete the following problem:

2. Park Ranger: When snowfall levels are below average during the winter months, scattered patches of the forest floor often remain exposed and accessible to scavenging wildlife. Because squirrels are able to collect nuts only in snow-free areas of the forest, the squirrel population tends to increase when there is below average snowfall. However, after last year's unprecedented snow-free winter season, the squirrel population in this region was determined to be at a 20-year low.

   Which of the following, if true, most helps to explain the paradox above?

   (A) When snowfall is above average, squirrel populations tend to diminish, as squirrels are unable to forage for food in snow-covered areas.
   (B) The squirrels' spring breeding season does not begin until all of the snow in the forest has melted.
   (C) The red-tailed hawk, the squirrel's most common predator, does not migrate south out of the forest until the first snowfall of the winter season.
   (D) Forest squirrels rarely feed on fruits and berries, preferring nuts for their higher caloric content.
   (E) The current system of estimating squirrel population size is thought to be extremely accurate in its projections.

First, let's isolate the paradox in the argument:

> Fact 1: When snowfall levels are below average during the winter months, scattered patches of the forest floor often remain exposed and accessible to scavenging wildlife.
>
> Fact 2: Because squirrels are able to collect nuts only in snow-free areas of the forest, the squirrel population tends to increase when there is below average snowfall.
>
> Fact 3: However, after last year's unprecedented snow-free winter season, the squirrel population in this region was determined to be at a 20-year low.

In this stimulus, the first fact provides context, and the second and third facts reveal the paradox. Here, a snow-free winter has occurred (and obviously the ground would be bare) but instead of the squirrel population increasing as expected, it appears to be at a 20-year low.

Answer choice (A): Read closely! The stimulus discusses conditions that occur when snowfall is below average. This answer discusses what occurs when snowfall is above average. Because this information about a different situation than the one in the stimulus, this answer is incorrect.

Answer choice (B): This answer addresses spring breeding season, but the stimulus is about the winter months. Information about what occurs after the winter ends is extremely unlikely to produce an explanation for the situation in the stimulus.

Answer choice (C): This is the correct answer, and it can be a difficult one to correctly identify. At first glance, information on the red-tailed hawk's migration pattern would seem to be irrelevant to the problem at hand. But, because the red-tailed hawk is a predator of the squirrel, this does ultimately provide an explanation for the paradox. If the red-tailed hawk does not migrate until the first snowfall, and this year there was no snowfall, then the red-tailed hawk would have remained in the area. As the squirrel's most common predator, the hawk could have diminished the squirrel's numbers through hunting, providing an explanation for the 20-year low in squirrel population.

Answer choice (D): Squirrel food preferences are not likely to resolve the paradox, and in any event we know that the snow-free winter allowed squirrels access to more nuts.

Answer choice (E): Although this answer provides initial hope for an explanation of the situation, by stating that the projections are accurate, this answer does not provide any further insight into the paradox, and is thus incorrect.

Oppositional Circumstances and Cause

Resolve the Paradox problems are typically built around oppositional circumstances, wherein two elements with naturally opposing features are found to co-exist. One great example was presented earlier in this book, on page 153, in the problem about Dr. Roark's patient recuperation time. This same type of "surprisingly low/high rate of success" scenario has appeared in a number of Resolve the Paradox questions, including the following:

> An anti-theft device is known to reduce theft, but cars using the anti-theft device are stolen at a higher rate than cars without the device.
>
> Explanation: The device is placed on highly desirable cars that are prone to being stolen, and the device actually lessens the rate at which they are stolen.
>
> A surgeon has a low success rate while operating, but the director of the hospital claims the surgeon is the best on the staff.
>
> Explanation: The surgeon operates on the most complex and challenging cases.
>
> A bill collector has the lowest rate of success in collecting bills, but his manager claims he is the best in the field.
>
> Explanation: The bill collector is assigned the toughest cases to handle.

These scenarios underscore the issue present in the question: other factors in the situation make it more difficult to be successful, despite the high ability of the person at the center of the situation.

In all cases, the lesson to be learned is that whatever the paradox, there will always be a cause that can explain both sides actively. Search for the answer that explains both sides of the opposition, and ignore answers that address neither side of the cause or just one side of the cause.

Resolve the Paradox Question Review

Each Resolve the Paradox stimulus presents a situation where two ideas or occurrences contradict each other.

Besides the discrepant or contradictory facts, most Resolve the Paradox stimuli contain the following features:

1. No conclusion

2. Language of contradiction

The correct answer will actively resolve the paradox—it will allow both sides to be factually correct and it will either explain how the situation came into being or add a piece of information that shows how the two ideas or occurrences can coexist.

Because you are not seeking to disprove one side of the situation, you must select the answer choice that contains a *possible cause* of the situation. So, when examining answers, ask yourself if the answer choice could lead to the situation in the stimulus. If so, the answer is correct. The following types of answers are incorrect:

1. Explains only one side of the paradox

    If an answer supports or proves only one side of the paradox, that answer will be incorrect. The correct answer must show how both sides coexist.

2. Similarities and differences

    If the stimulus contains a paradox where two items are similar, then an answer choice that explains a difference between the two cannot be correct.

    Conversely, if the stimulus contains a paradox where two items are different, then an answer choice that explains why the two are similar cannot be correct.

    In short, a similarity cannot explain a difference, and a difference cannot explain a similarity.

When attempting to resolve the problem in the stimulus, you must address the facts of the situation. Many answers will try to lure you with reasonable solutions that do not quite meet the stated facts. These answers are incorrect.

All Resolve the Paradox questions require you to seek a cause of the scenario in the stimulus. However, we do not classify these questions as "CE" questions because the causality does not appear in the stimulus. The CE designator is reserved solely for indicating when causality is featured as the form of reasoning in an argument.

Resolve the Paradox Question Problem Set

Please complete the problem set and review the answer key and explanations. *Answers on page 242*

1. Omnifilm, a large film production studio, will release its next new major movie, *FastCar*, six months from now. Although OmniFilm generally begins advertising six months prior to the release of a major film, the studio plans to initiate the *FastCar* ad campaign three months from now.

   Which of the following, if true, best explains OmniFilm's decision to wait three months before beginning the ad campaign?

   (A) Many studies show that the benefits of advertising a film are maximized when the ad campaign is initiated no more than six months before a film's release.
   (B) Initiating the ad campaign for *FastCar* in six months would unquestionably be less effective than initiating the campaign in three months.
   (C) Commencing the ad campaign for *FastCar* would attract public attention away from another OmniFilm movie currently showing in theaters.
   (D) Early reviews predict that *FastCar* will be one of the highest-grossing films in OmniFilm's history.
   (E) *FastCar*'s advertising budget is at least 50% greater than that of any other movie ever released by OmniFilm.

2. Last year, David tested a product called Mega-Grow in his garden by applying the product to several different plants, all of which thrived as a result. When he applied Mega-Grow to the very same plants this year, however, several withered immediately.

   Which of the following, if true, most helps to explain the reason for the results described above?

   (A) Last year, David applied significantly more Mega-Grow than the product's directions advised.
   (B) Mega-Grow was recently taken off the market.
   (C) Mega-Grow's ingredients were modified significantly two years ago.
   (D) Mega-Grow contains insecticides which can be applied without risk of toxicity to plants no more than once in any fifteen-month period.
   (E) Mega-Grow is generally more effective when used in dry climates.

Resolve the Paradox Problem Set Answer Key

Question #1: Resolve the Paradox. The correct answer choice is (C)

This stimulus presents a rather interesting paradox: although OmniFilm generally begins advertising major movies six months prior to release, the studio does not plan to begin advertising for the major movie *FastCar* until three months prior to its release. As with any Resolve the Paradox question, the correct answer choice must provide an active resolution/explanation for why the apparent contradiction exists. In this case, the correct answer will provide a reason why OmniFilm would choose to delay the advertising of *FastCar* for three months.

Answer choice (A): The issue in the stimulus does not concern advertising initiated *more* than six months before a film's release. The paradox is about why *FastCar* is being advertised only three months before release, as opposed to the standard six months.

Answer choice (B): This answer choice could be tempting for test takers who do not read closely. Remember, the stimulus states that the ad campaign for *FastCar* will be released in six months, but advertising will not begin for another three months (only three months prior to the film's release). This answer choice states that an ad campaign that begins in three months, as *FastCar*'s will, will be more effective than one that begins in six months (which is when the film opens). However, the oddity of this stimulus is not about what would happen if the ads start in six months; the paradox concerns why the ad campaign doesn't begin *now*, six months prior to the film's release. So this answer choice has nothing to do with the facts in the stimulus.

Answer choice (C): This is the correct answer. This answer tells us that if the ad campaign were to begin now, six months prior to the film's release, it would distract people from another one of the studio's movies that is currently showing. Since the studio obviously doesn't want to attract attention away from its current movie, we now have a reason for the apparent delay in the advertising campaign for *FastCar*.

Answer choice (D): This answer seems to contribute even further to the paradox in the stimulus. If *FastCar* is expected to be hugely successful, then the studio should be even more willing to begin advertising it as soon as possible. So the three month delay becomes even more counterintuitive.

Answer choice (E): Like answer choice (D), this answer also makes the situation described in the stimulus seem even more puzzling. If the advertising budget for *FastCar* is at least 50% greater than any other film ever released by OmniFilm, then the delay in beginning the ad campaign becomes even more strange. Clearly this answer does nothing to help resolve the apparent discrepancy presented in the stimulus.

Resolve the Paradox Problem Set Answer Key

Question #2: Resolve the Paradox. The correct answer choice is (D)

The paradox in this stimulus concerns the vastly different results that David obtained when he applied Mega-Grow to the plants in his garden in two successive years. The first year the plants thrived following the application of Mega-Grow, while the next year some of the same plants withered immediately when Mega-Grow was applied. To resolve this discrepancy we need to select an answer choice that provides a reason why Mega-Grow could be successful on plants one year, and then harmful to those same plants the next year.

Answer choice (A): Since this answer choice does not provide a reason why last year's application of Mega-Grow was successful while this year's application was not, it does not help to resolve the paradox in the stimulus.

Answer choice (B): This answer is incorrect because, like answer choice (A), it does not explain the different reactions that the plants had to the successive applications of Mega-Grow. The fact that Mega-Grow was taken off the market may mean that other people also experienced adverse effects (it has fallen out of favor with consumers), but that doesn't explain *why* the different effects occurred.

Answer choice (C): If Mega-Grow's ingredients were modified two years ago, then they were modified before David's first application ever took place, and both applications used the same formulation of the product. Because a similarity cannot explain a differences, this answer choice is incorrect.

Answer choice (D): This is the correct answer. We are told in (D) that if Mega-Grow is applied to the same plants more than once in a fifteen-month period, its ingredients can be toxic to those plants. Since David applied Mega-Grow to the same plants only twelve months apart, this increased toxicity could explain why the plants withered after the second application.

Answer choice (E): Because we have no idea what kind of climate David's plants are in, this answer choice is completely irrelevant to the facts of the stimulus.

9

Chapter Ten: Method of Reasoning and Flaw in the Reasoning Questions

Chapter Ten: Method of Reasoning and Flaw in the Reasoning Questions

Method of Reasoning Questions 247
Flaw in the Reasoning Questions 248
Prephrasing in Method and Flaw Questions 249
The Fact Test in Method and Flaw Questions 250
Stimulus Notes 250
Incorrect Answers in Method and Flaw Questions 251
The Value of Knowing Common Errors of Reasoning 252
Common Errors of Reasoning Explained 254
Errors in the Use of Evidence 254
Source Argument 258
Circular Reasoning 259
Errors of Conditional Reasoning 260
Mistaken Cause and Effect 261
Straw Man 262
Appeal Fallacies 263
Survey Errors 265
Errors of Composition and Division 267
Uncertain Use of a Term or Concept 268
False Analogy 268
False Dilemma 269
Time Shift Errors 270
Numbers and Percentages Errors 270
Idea Application: Correct and Incorrect Answers Analyzed 271
Method of Reasoning—Bolded Argument Part Questions 273
Method—AP Stimulus Structure 273
A Common Wrong Answer 276
Final Note 276
Method of Reasoning and Flaw in the Reasoning Question Type Review 277
Identify the Flaw in the Argument Drill 279
Method of Reasoning and Flaw in the Reasoning Problem Set 288

Method of Reasoning Questions

Method of Reasoning questions require you to select the answer choice that best describes the method used by the author to make the argument. Structurally, Method of Reasoning questions are simply abstract Must Be True questions: instead of identifying the facts of the argument, you must identify the logical organization of the argument.

As part of the First Family of Questions, Method of Reasoning questions feature the following information structure, modified slightly for the abstract nature of these questions:

1. You can use only the information in the stimulus to prove the correct answer choice.

2. Any answer choice that describes an element or a situation that does not occur in the stimulus is incorrect.

The stimulus in a Method question can contain valid or flawed reasoning.

Method of Reasoning question stems use a variety of formats, but in each case the stem refers to the method, technique, strategy, or process used by the author while making the argument. Here are several question stem examples:

"The method of the argument is to"

"The argument proceeds by"

"The argument derives its conclusion by"

"Which of the following describes the technique of reasoning used above?"

"Which of the following is an argumentative strategy employed in the argument?"

"The argument employs which one of the following reasoning techniques?"

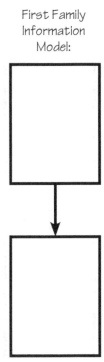

First Family Information Model:

As you attack each question, keep in mind that Method of Reasoning questions are simply abstract Must Be True questions. Use the information in the stimulus to prove or disprove each answer choice.

CHAPTER TEN: METHOD AND FLAW QUESTIONS

First Family
Information
Model:

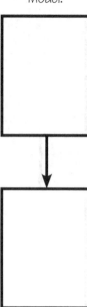

Flaw in the Reasoning Questions

Flaw in the Reasoning questions are exactly the same as Method of Reasoning questions with the important exception that the question stem indicates that the reasoning in the stimulus is flawed. Because the question stem reveals that a flaw is present, you need not make a determination of the validity of the stimulus; the question stem makes the determination for you. This information provides you with a tremendous advantage because you can identify the error of reasoning in the stimulus *before* proceeding to the answer choices. And, if you did not realize there was an error of reasoning in the stimulus, the question stem gives you the opportunity to re-evaluate the argument and find the error of reasoning.

When indicating that a flaw is present in the argument, the test makers will use phrases such as "the reasoning is flawed" and "the argument is vulnerable," or synonymous phrases. Here are several example question stems:

"Which of the following most accurately describes a flaw in the argument's reasoning?"

"The reasoning in the argument is most vulnerable to criticism on the grounds that the argument"

"The reasoning above is flawed because it fails to recognize that"

"A questionable aspect of the reasoning above is that it"

To identify the right answer choice, carefully consider the reasoning used in the stimulus. The correct answer will identify the error in the author's reasoning and then describe that error in general terms. Beware of answers that describe a portion of the stimulus but fail to identify the error in the reasoning.

Because Flaw in the Reasoning questions are so similar to Method of Reasoning questions, we will discuss the two in tandem throughout this chapter.

> **Important Note**: Method and Flaw questions appear infrequently in GMAT Critical Reasoning. However, we have included these question types for two important reasons:
>
> 1. Method and Flaw questions are more likely to show up when a test taker is doing very well on the GMAT.
>
> 2. The process of identifying and understanding the method of reasoning in the argument is invaluable when you are attempting to perform other tasks with an argument, such as Weaken, Strengthen, etc.

Prephrasing in Method and Flaw Questions

Method of Reasoning and Flaw in the Reasoning questions are challenging because they involve abstract thinking, which focuses on the *form* of the argument instead of the concrete facts of the argument. The answer choices will therefore describe the argument in abstract terms, and many students have difficulty because the test makers are experts at manipulating those terms to describe the argument in unexpected and deceptive ways. Often, students will have a firm grasp of the structure of the argument only to struggle when none of the answers match their prephrase. This situation occurs because the test makers can use one or two words to describe entire sections of the stimulus, and you are rigorously tested on your knowledge of the mechanics of the argument and your ability to discern the references in the answer choice.

When prephrasing in Method and Flaw questions, you may understand the details of the stimulus but not understand the structure of the argument. Thus, each answer may sound implausible since they are related primarily to the logical organization of the argument. Therefore, you must think about the structure of the argument *before* examining the answer choices. However, do not expect to see your exact prephrase as the answer; there are simply too many variations on the way an argument can be described. Instead, make a general, abstract prephrase of what occurred in the argument and then rigorously examine each answer choice to see if the test makers have created an answer that paraphrases your prephrase. Many students are deceived by the description used by the test makers, and the only way to overcome this problem is to compare the description given in the answer choice to the stimulus.

You may not have noticed, but this book began with the most concrete questions and slowly moved towards the most abstract questions. For example, we began with Must Be True questions, which require you to identify the details of an argument. Later we discussed Weaken and Strengthen questions, which require you identify both the structure and details of an argument. Now we have arrived at Method questions, which focus much more on structure. Because abstract thinking requires more work than concrete thinking, most students find abstract questions difficult.

The Fact Test in Method and Flaw Questions

Because Method of Reasoning and Flaw in the Reasoning questions are similar to Must Be True questions, you can use the principle behind the Fact Test to destroy incorrect answers. In Method and Flaw question, the Fact Test works as follows:

> If an answer choice describes an event that did not occur in the stimulus, then that answer is incorrect.

The test makers will try to entice you by creating incorrect answer choices that contain elements that did not occur, and you must avoid those answers and select the answer choice that describes what occurred in the stimulus. For example, if an answer choice states, "The argument accepts a claim on the basis of public opinion of the claim," *all* parts of the answer must be identifiable in the stimulus. First you must be able to identify where the author "accepts a claim," and then you must be able to identify where that is done "on the basis of public opinion of the claim." If you cannot identify part of an answer as having occurred in the stimulus, that answer is incorrect.

Watch out for answers that are partially true—that is, answers that contain a description of something that happened in the argument but that also contain additional things that did not occur. For example, an answer choice states that, "The author disagrees with the analogy used by the critic." When examining this answer, you must find both the "disagreement" and the "analogy"; if you can only find one, or neither, the answer is wrong. But let us say you know the author disagrees with the critic. That is a good start, but you will still have to find disagreement with the analogy for the answer to be correct.

Stimulus Notes

The stimuli for both Method and Flaw questions will contain an argument, and in the case of a Method question the argument can contain either valid or invalid reasoning; in the case of a flaw question the argument must contain invalid reasoning.

Because recognizing argument structure is such an important part of attacking Method and Flaw questions, you must watch for the presence of the premise and conclusion indicators discussed in Chapter Two. These indicators will help you identify the structure of the argument and help you better understand the answer choices.

Incorrect Answers in Method and Flaw Questions

In Chapter Four we discussed several types of incorrect answers that appear in Must Be True questions. In this section we will review selected answer types from that chapter that apply to Method and Flaw questions and add an additional wrong answer type.

1. "New" Element Answers

   Because correct Method of Reasoning answers must be based on elements of the stimulus, an answer that describes something that did not occur or describes an element new to the argument cannot be correct. All of the wrong answer choices described below are simply very specific variations on this theme.

2. Half Right, Half Wrong Answers

   The makers of the GMAT love to present answers that start out by describing something that in fact occurred in the stimulus. Unfortunately, they often end by describing something that did *not* occur in the stimulus. The rule for these answers is that half wrong equals all wrong, and these answers are always incorrect.

3. Exaggerated Answers

   Exaggerated Answers take a situation from the stimulus and stretch that situation to make an extreme statement that is not supported by the stimulus. Be careful, though! Just because an answer choice contains extreme language does not mean that the answer is incorrect.

4. The Opposite Answer

   As the name suggests, the Opposite Answer provides an answer that is exactly opposite of correct.

5. The Reverse Answer

   The Reverse Answer is attractive because it contains familiar elements from the stimulus, but reverses them in the answer. Since the reversed statement does not describe what occurred in the stimulus, it must be incorrect.

Interestingly, the incorrect answer choices in any Method or Flaw question can be a helpful study aid in preparing for future questions. Since

> Some Method of Reasoning answer choices can be difficult to understand because they are written in a way that is obviously designed to be confusing. The test makers excel at using deceptive language to make wrong answers attractive and to hide the correct answer.

CHAPTER TEN: METHOD AND FLAW QUESTIONS

As part of the First Family, Method and Flaw questions are grouped with Must Be True, Main Point, etc. Each type of question shares similar characteristics, but the exact execution of each is different. For example, one way to compare Must Be True questions to Method and Flaw questions is to use an analogy about trees in a forest. A Must Be True question is like examining a single tree and looking at the details: the bark, the branches, the leaves, etc. A Method or a Flaw question requires you to look at that same tree, but from a different perspective, one that is farther away and places that tree in the context of the forest. You are no longer looking at the individual branches and leaves, but rather at the general structure of the tree.

the makers of the GMAT tend to reuse certain methods of reasoning, familiarizing yourself with those methods and the language used to describe them helps you prepare for when you encounter them again. You should carefully study all Method of Reasoning and Flaw in the Reasoning answers—correct and incorrect—and it would not be unreasonable to keep a list of the different types of methods you encounter. Remember, the wrong answer choice on one question could be the right answer choice on another question. After you complete the problem and are reviewing each wrong answer choice, try to imagine what type of argument would be needed to fit that answer. This exercise will strengthen your ability to recognize any type of argument structure.

The Value of Knowing Common Errors of Reasoning

In logic there are many more recognized forms of invalid argumentation than there are forms of valid argumentation. The test makers, being human (yes, it's true), tend to repeat certain forms when creating stimuli and answer choices, and you can gain a demonstrable advantage by learning the forms most often used by the test makers. Applying the knowledge you acquire in this section will take two avenues:

1. Identifying errors of reasoning made in the stimulus

   If you learn the mistakes that are often made by authors, then you will be able to quickly identify the error in the argument and accelerate through the answer choices to find the correct answer. Students without this knowledge will be forced to work more slowly and with less confidence.

2. Identifying answer choices that describe a common error of reasoning

   In Flaw in the Reasoning questions, the test makers tend to use certain types of answers again and again. Depending on the reasoning used in the stimulus, these answers can describe the correct answer, but more often than not they are used as "stock" wrong answers. Familiarizing yourself with these answer choices will give you an advantage when you encounter similar answer choices in the future. For example, "attacking the source of an argument, not the argument itself" has appeared as the correct answer in several questions. But, it has appeared in many more questions as a wrong answer choice. If you are familiar with a "source" argument, you can then make an immediate determination as to whether that answer is correct or incorrect.

The paragraphs above help explain why test preparation works: the more you know about the exam before you walk in to take the test, the less time you have to waste during the exam thinking about these issues. Given the immense advantage you get by knowing the flawed reasoning that appears most frequently on the GMAT, the following section will detail a variety of errors of reasoning and provide examples of answer choices that describe the error under discussion. We strongly recommend that you spend a considerable amount of time learning these forms of flawed argumentation. It will definitely help you on the GMAT!

Please note that this discussion is not designed to include every possible error of reasoning, only those used most frequently by the makers of the GMAT.

Common Errors of Reasoning Explained

The following classic errors of reasoning appear with some frequency. The review is given in layman's, not philosophical, terms:

Errors in the Use of Evidence

In a certain sense, all flawed arguments contain errors of evidence. That is, they fail to use information correctly. However, in this section, we will examine several very specific errors of this type.

<u>General Lack of Relevant Evidence for the Conclusion</u>

Some GMAT authors misuse information to such a degree that they fail to provide any information to support their conclusion or they provide information that is irrelevant to their conclusion. Here is an example:

> "Some critics claim that scientific progress has increased the polarization of society and alienated large segments of the population. But these critics are wrong because even a cursory glance at the past shows that society is always somewhat polarized and some groups are inevitably alienated."

Note the use of the construction "some critics claim..." As usual, the author's main point is that the claim that the critics are making is wrong.

The author provides irrelevant evidence in an attempt to refute the claim that "scientific progress has increased the polarization of society and alienated large segments of the population." Citing facts that such a situation has always existed does not help disprove that scientific progress has *increased* the severity of the situation.

Here are examples of how this error of reasoning can be described in the answer choices:

> "The author cites irrelevant data."

> "It fails to give any reason for the judgment it reaches."

Internal Contradiction

An internal contradiction (also known as a self-contradiction) occurs when an author makes conflicting statements. An example is:

> "Everyone should join our country club. After all, it's an exclusive group that links many of the influential members of the community."

The self-contradiction occurs when the speaker says "Everyone should join" and then follows that by saying that it is "an exclusive group." *Exclusive*, by definition, means that some people are excluded.

The following show how this error of reasoning can be described in the answer choices:

> "bases a conclusion on claims that are inconsistent with each other"

> "introduces information that actually contradicts the conclusion"

Exceptional Case/Overgeneralization

This error takes a small number of instances and treats those instances as if they support a broad, sweeping conclusion. Here is an example:

> "Two of my friends were shortchanged at that store. Therefore, everyone gets shortchanged at that store."

This answer appears most frequently as an incorrect answer in Flaw questions, but as with any of the errors described in this chapter, occasionally it appears as a correct answer. Here are examples of how this error of reasoning is described in answer choices:

> "supports a general claim on the basis of a single example"

> "The argument draws a broad conclusion from a small a sample of instances"

Errors in Assessing the Force of Evidence

Mis-assessing the force of evidence is a frequent error committed by GMAT authors. Each of the following describes an error of reasoning involving the force of evidence:

1. Lack of evidence for a position is taken to prove that position is false.

   Just because no evidence proving a position has been introduced does not mean that the position is false. Here is an example:

   > "The White House has failed to offer any evidence that they have reached a trade agreement with China. Therefore no such agreement has been reached."

   In the example above, the White House may have valid reasons for withholding information about the trade agreement. The lack of confirming evidence does not undeniably prove that a trade agreement has *not* been reached.

   Here are two examples of how this error of reasoning can be described in the answer choices:

   > "treats failure to prove a claim as constituting denial of that claim"

   > "taking a lack of evidence for a claim as evidence undermining the claim"

2. Lack of evidence against a position is taken to prove that position is true.

   This error is the opposite of the previous error. Just because no evidence disproving a position has been introduced does not mean that the position is true. Here is a famous example:

   > "There has been no evidence given against the existence of God, so God must exist."

   The lack of evidence against a position does not undeniably prove a position. Here is an example of how this error of reasoning can be described in the answer choices:

> "treating the failure to prove a claim to be false as if it is a demonstration of the truth of that claim"

3. Some evidence against a position is taken to prove that the position is false.

    The introduction of evidence against a position only weakens the position; it does not necessarily prove the position false. Here is an example:

    > "Some historians claim that a lengthy drought preceded the fall of the Aztec empire. But we know from Aztec writings that in at least one year during the supposed drought there was minor flooding. Thus, the claim that there was a lengthy drought prior to the fall of the Aztec empire is false."

    The evidence offered in the example above weakens the claim that there was a lengthy drought, but it does not disprove it. A drought by definition is a prolonged period of unusually low rainfall, and thus it would be possible for flooding to occur on occasion, but not enough flooding to overcome the general drought conditions.

    Here is an example of how this error of reasoning can be described in an answer choice:

    > "it confuses weakening an argument in support of a given conclusion with proving the conclusion itself to be false"

4. Some evidence for a position is taken to prove that position is true.

    The introduction of evidence for a position only provides support for the position; it does not prove the position to be undeniably true. Here is an example:

    > "We know that the defendant was in the vicinity of the robbery when the robbery occurred. Therefore, the

defendant is guilty of the robbery."

As the above example proves, partial support for a position does not make the position invincible (especially in GMAT arguments, which are relatively short). As you might expect, partial evidence for a position can be outweighed by evidence against that position.

Here is an example of how this error of reasoning can be described in an answer choice:

> "the argument takes facts showing that its conclusion could be true as proof that the conclusion is indeed true"

Source Argument

Also known as an ad hominem, this type of flawed argument attacks the person (or source) instead of the argument they advance. Because the GMAT is concerned solely with argument forms, a speaker can never validly attack the character or motives of a person; instead, a speaker must always attack the *argument* advanced by a person. Here is an example:

> "The anti-smoking views expressed by Senator Smith should be ignored. After all, Smith himself is a smoker!"

A source argument can take different forms, including the following:

1. Focusing on the motives of the source.

2. Focusing on the actions of the source (as in the above example).

In the real world, you will often hear source arguments used by children and politicians (the two being alike in a number of ways, of course).

Here are examples of how this error of reasoning can be described in answer choices:

> "it is directed against the proponent of a claim rather than against the claim itself"

> "The attack is directed against the person making the argument rather than directing it against the argument itself"

Like Method of Reasoning questions, Flaw in the Reasoning questions are part of the First Family.

Circular Reasoning

In circular reasoning the author assumes as true what is supposed to be proved. Consider the following example:

"This essay is the best because it is better than all the others."

In this example the premise and the conclusion are identical in meaning. As we know, the conclusion should always follow from the premise. In the example above, the premise supports the conclusion, but the conclusion equally supports the premise, creating a "circular" situation where you can move from premise to conclusion, and then back again to the premise, and so on. Here is another example: "I must be telling the truth because I'm not lying."

Here are examples of how this error of reasoning can be described in answer choices:

"it assumes what it seeks to establish"

"presupposes the truth of what it sets out to prove"

"the argument assumes what it is attempting to demonstrate"

Unlike a college-level logic class, we will not waste time on classification distinctions, such as Formal versus Informal Fallacies.

Errors of Conditional Reasoning

In Chapter Four we discussed several mistakes GMAT authors make when using conditional reasoning, including Mistaken Negation and Mistaken Reversal. While you should now be comfortable recognizing those errors, Flaw in the Reasoning questions will ask you to describe those mistakes in logical terms. This often proves to be a more difficult task.

When describing a Mistaken Negation or a Mistaken Reversal, the test makers must focus on the error common to both: confusing the sufficient condition with the necessary condition. As such, here are examples of how these errors of reasoning can be described in the answer choices:

> "taking the absence of an occurrence as evidence that a necessary condition for that occurrence also did not take place" (Mistaken Negation)

> "mistakes being sufficient to achieve a particular outcome for being required to achieve it" (Mistaken Reversal)

Remember, a Mistaken Negation and a Mistaken Reversal are contrapositives of each other, so the error behind both is identical.

Note that the authors can either mistake a necessary condition for a sufficient condition, or mistake a sufficient condition for a necessary condition:

<u>Confuses a necessary condition for a sufficient condition</u>

> "From the assertion that something is necessary to a given goal, the argument concludes that that thing is sufficient for its achievement."

> "It acts as if something that is necessary for a good leader is something that is sufficient to create a good leader."

<u>Confuses a sufficient condition for a necessary condition</u>

> "confuses a sufficient condition with a required condition"

This discussion is not designed to include every possible error of reasoning, only those used most frequently by the makers of the GMAT.

It is interesting to note the frequency with which the words "sufficient" (or its synonym "assured") or "necessary" (or its synonym "required") are used when analyzing the answer choices used to describe conditional reasoning. This occurs because those words perfectly capture the idea and it is difficult to avoid using at least one of those words when describing conditionality. This is a huge advantage for you: if you identify a stimulus with conditional reasoning and are asked a Flaw question, you can quickly scan the answers for the one answer that contains "sufficient," "necessary," or both.

Mistaken Cause and Effect

As discussed in Chapter Seven, arguments that draw causal conclusions are inherently flawed because there may be another explanation for the stated relationship. Because of the extreme causal assumption made by GMAT authors (that there is only one cause), any of the following answer choice forms could be used to describe an error of causality. Underneath each item are examples of how the error of reasoning can be described in answer choices.

1. Assuming a causal relationship on the basis of the sequence of events.

    "falsely concludes from the fact that one thing happens after another for confirmation that the second thing is the result of the first"

2. Assuming a causal relationship when only a correlation exists.

    "confusing the coincidence of two events with a causal relation between the two"

3. Failure to consider an alternate cause for the effect, or an alternate cause for both the cause and the effect.

    "fails to exclude an alternative explanation for the observed effect"

4. Failure to consider that the events may be reversed.

    "the author mistakes an effect for a cause"

Note the frequency with which the words "cause" or "effect" are used. This occurs because there are few substitutes for those two words, and thus the test makers are often forced to use those words to describe an argument containing causality. If you identify a stimulus with causal reasoning and are asked a Flaw question, quickly scan the answers for one that contains "cause," "effect," or both.

To determine the error of reasoning, focus on the connection between the premises and the conclusion. Remember, GMAT authors are allowed to put forth virtually any premise when making an argument; the key is how those premises are used, not whether they are factually true.

Straw Man

Just a note: we did not make up the name "straw man." The term is the proper name used in logic.

This error occurs when an author attempts to attack an opponent's position by ignoring the actual statements made by the opposing speaker and instead distorts and refashions the argument, making it weaker in the process. In figurative terms, a "straw" argument is built up which is then easier for the author to knock down.

Often this error is accompanied by the phrase "what you're saying is" or "if I understand you correctly," which are used to preface the refashioned and weakened argument. Here is an example:

Politician A: "The platform proposed by my party calls for a moderate increase in taxes on those individuals making over $20,000 per year, and then taking that money and using it to rebuild the educational system."

Politician B: "But what you're saying is that everyone should pay higher taxes, and so your proposal is unfair."

In the example above, Politician B recasts Politician A's argument unfairly. Politician A indicated the tax increase would apply to those with incomes over $20,000 where Politician B distorts that to "everyone should pay higher taxes."

Here are examples of how this error of reasoning can be described in answer choices:

"refutes a distorted version of an opposing position"

"portrays the politician's views as more extreme than they really are"

Just a note: we did not make up the name "straw man." The term is the proper name used in logic.

Appeal Fallacies

While there are a number of "appeal" fallacies that appear in traditional logic (Appeal to Fear, Appeal to Force, Appeal to Tradition, etc.), the following three are the most applicable to the GMAT:

1. Appeal to Authority

An Appeal to Authority uses the opinion of an authority in an attempt to persuade the reader. The flaw in this form of reasoning is that the authority may not have relevant knowledge or all the information regarding a situation, or there may a difference of opinion among experts as to what is true in the case. Here is an example:

> "World-renowned neurologist Dr. Samuel Langhorne says that EZBrite Tooth Strips are the best for whitening your teeth. So, you know if you buy EZBrite you will soon have the whitest teeth possible!"

The primary defect in this argument is its use of a neurologist as an authority figure in an area of dentistry. While Dr. Langhorne can reasonably be appealed to in matters of the brain, dental care would be considered outside the scope of his expertise.

Here are examples of how this error of reasoning can be described in answer choices:

> "the judgment of scientists is applied to a matter in which their knowledge is irrelevant"

> "accepts a claim based on the authority of others, without requiring proof of said authority"

2. Appeal to Popular Opinion/Appeal to Numbers

This error states that a position is true because the majority believe it to be true. As you know, arguments are created by providing premises that support a conclusion. An appeal to popular opinion does not present a logical reason for accepting a position, just an appeal based on numbers. Here is an example:

CHAPTER TEN: METHOD AND FLAW QUESTIONS

> "A recent poll states that 75% of Americans believe that Google is a monopoly. Antitrust law states that monopolies have a deleterious effect on the marketplace (with the exception of utilities), and therefore Google should be controlled or broken into smaller pieces."

The author uses the results of a poll that indicate many people think Google is a monopoly to conclude that Google is in fact a monopoly. This type of persuasion is often used in the arguments made by advertisements ("All the trend setters use EZBrite Tooth Strips"), politicians ("Everyone loves the environment. Vote for the Green Party!"), and children ("C'mon, try this. Everyone does it.").

This type of reasoning most often appears as an incorrect answer. Here are examples of how this error of reasoning can be described in answer choices:

> "the author treats popular opinion as if it is reliable evidence supporting the claim in question"

> "the argument makes an appeal to popular opinion instead of using facts"

Remember, the correct answer choice must describe a flaw in the reasoning of the argument, not just something that occurred in the argument.

3. Appeal to Emotion

An Appeal to Emotion occurs when emotions or emotionally-charged language is used in an attempt to persuade the reader. Here is an example:

> "Officer, please do not give me a ticket for speeding. In the last month I've been fired from my job, kicked out of my apartment, and my car broke down. I don't deserve this!"

Here are examples of how this error of reasoning can be described in answer choices:

> "attempts to persuade by making an emotional appeal"

> "the argument appeals to emotion rather than reason"

Survey Errors

The makers of the GMAT believe that surveys, when conducted properly, produce reliable results. However, surveys can be invalidated when any of the following three scenarios arise:

1. The survey uses a biased sample.

   Perhaps the most famous example of a biased survey occurred in 1936. The Literary Digest weekly magazine sent out ballots to some 10 million voters (2.3 million were returned), and returns indicated that a solid majority would vote for Republican candidate Alf Landon in the upcoming presidential election. On the basis of these results (and the size of the sample), the Literary Digest predicted that Landon would win easily. Of course, when the election was held Franklin Roosevelt won in a landslide. The Literary Digest erred by sending the ballots to groups such as telephone owners and automobile owners, groups that in that era (late Depression) tended to be among the wealthiest individuals and overwhelmingly Republican. The Literary Digest ended up polling a large number of Republicans and on that basis declared that the Republican candidate would win.

   Note that a secondary error with the polling done by the Literary Digest is that the sample is self-selected; that is, the individuals being polled decided whether or not to respond. That opportunity introduces bias into the survey process because certain types of individuals tend to respond to surveys more often than others.

   A similar type of sampling error occurred in 1948 when the Chicago Daily Tribune predicted Thomas Dewey would prevail over Harry Truman. The Tribune even went so far as to print the morning edition of the newspaper with that headline.

2. The survey questions are improperly constructed.

   If a survey question is confusing or misleading, the results of the poll can be inaccurate.

   Questions can be confusing, such as "Do you feel it is possible that none of the candidates would not vote to increase taxes?" (The question actually asks, "Do you feel it is possible that all of the candidates would vote to increase taxes?"). If a respondent cannot understand the question, how can they accurately answer the question?

Questions can also be misleading, such as "How soon should the U.S. government withdraw from the United Nations?" The question presumes that the United States should withdraw from the United Nations—a course of action that the respondent may not agree with.

3. Respondents to the survey give inaccurate responses.

    People do not always tell the truth when responding to surveys. Two classic questions that often elicit false answers are "What is your age" and "how much money do you make each year?"

    If respondents give false answers to survey questions, the results of the survey are skewed and inaccurate.

Here are examples of how the errors of reasoning above can be described in answer choices:

"uses evidence drawn from a small sample that may well be unrepresentative"

"generalizes from an unrepresentative sample"

Errors of Composition and Division

Composition and division errors involve judgments made about groups and parts of a group.

An error of composition occurs when the author attributes a characteristic of part of the group to the group as a whole or to each member of the group. Here is an example:

> "Every party I attend is fun and exciting. Therefore, my life is fun and exciting."

Here are examples of how this error of reasoning can be described in answer choices:

> "assuming that because something is true of each of the parts of a whole it is true of the whole itself"

> "takes the opinion of one student to represent the opinions of all students"

An error of division occurs when the author attributes a characteristic of the whole (or each member of the whole) to a part of the group. Here is an example:

> "The United States is the wealthiest country in the world. Thus, every American is wealthy."

Here is an example of how this error of reasoning is described in GMAT answer choices:

> "presumes that what is true of a whole must also be true of each of its parts"

Uncertain Use of a Term or Concept

As an argument progresses, the author must use each term in a constant, coherent fashion. Using a term in different ways is inherently confusing and undermines the integrity of the argument. Here is an example:

> "Some people claim that the values that this country was built on are now being ignored by modern-day corporations. But this is incorrect. Corporations are purely profit-driven enterprises, beholden only to their shareholders, and as such they can only assess objects based on their value."

The term "value" is used in the example above in two different senses: first in a moral or ethical sense and then in a monetary sense. This shift in meaning undermines the author's position.

This type of answer choice appears more frequently as an incorrect answer than any other type. Here are examples of how this error of reasoning can be described in answer choices:

> "depending on the ambiguous use of a key term"

> "relies on interpreting a key term in two different ways"

> "allows a key term to shift in meaning"

False Analogy

An analogy is a comparison between two items. A False Analogy occurs when the author uses an analogy that is too dissimilar to the original situation to be applicable. Here is an example:

> "Just as a heavy rainfall can be cleansing, the best approach to maintain a healthy relationship is to store up all your petty grievances and then unload them all at one time on your partner."

The comparison in the example fails to consider that a heavy rainfall and an emotionally charged situation are fundamentally different.

Here are two examples of how a False Analogy can be described in answer choices:

> "treats as similar two cases that are different in a major respect"

> "treats two kinds of events that differ in critical respects as if they do not differ"

False Dilemma

A False Dilemma assumes that only two courses of action are available when there may be others. Here is an example:

> "Recent accidents within the oil industry have made safety of operation a critical public safety issue. Because the industry cannot be expected to police itself, the government must step in and take action."

The argument above falsely assumes that only two courses of action exist: industry self-policing or government action. But this ignores other courses of action, such as consumer watchdog groups.

Do not confuse a False Dilemma with a situation where the author legitimately establishes that only two possibilities exist. Phrases such as "either A or B will occur, but not both" can establish a limited set of possibilities, and certain real-world situations yield only two possibilities, such as "you are either dead or alive."

Here is an example of how a False Dilemma can be described in answer choices:

> "fails to consider that there are more than two choices in the matter at hand"

Time Shift Errors

Although this error has a rather futuristic name, the mistake involves assuming that conditions will remain constant over time, and that what was the case in the past will be the case in the present or future.

> "The company has always reimbursed me for meals when I'm on a business trip, so they will certainly reimburse me for meals on this business trip."

Clearly, what has occurred in the past is no guarantee that the future will be the same. Yet, many GMAT authors make this assumption, especially when hundreds or thousands of years are involved. Here are examples of how this error of reasoning can be described in answer choices:

> "treats a claim about what is currently the case as if it were a claim about what has been the case for an extended period"

> "uncritically draws an inference from what has been true in the past to what will be true in the future"

Numbers and Percentages Errors

In Chapter Twelve we will discuss numbers and percentages problems in detail. Meanwhile, consider that many errors in this category are committed when an author improperly equates a percentage with a definite quantity, or when an author uses quantity information to make a judgment about the percentage represented by that quantity.

Here is an example of how this error of reasoning can be described in an answer choice:

> "the argument confuses an increase in market share with an increase in overall revenue."

Idea Application: Correct and Incorrect Answers Analyzed

In this section we present and analyze two Critical Reasoning questions. We will use the two examples to discuss the various answer types presented in the previous section and to discuss the language used by the test makers in the answer choices.

Please take a moment to complete the following problem:

1. Proponents of the theory of social utilitarianism hold that the value of human capital should bear an inherent relation to its social utility. Although maximizing the value of human capital is both morally defensible and economically praiseworthy, the theory of social utilitarianism has severe practical limitations. If the price of labor were to become a measure of social utility and not of scarcity, the labor market would suffer significant distortions that may well reduce, and not increase, the current level of human capital.

   The argument proceeds by

   (A) Questioning a proposed strategy by showing that, if implemented, such a strategy could compromise the very objectives it is trying to achieve.
   (B) Criticizing a course of action by showing that, even if morally defensible, the end result does not always justify the means necessary to achieve it.
   (C) Criticizing a strategy by suggesting that there is an alternative way of achieving its proposed advantages without risking a number of serious disadvantages.
   (D) Conceding that a social policy may have certain ethical advantages that are ultimately outweighed by the impossibility of putting such a policy into effect.
   (E) Establishing that undesirable consequences result from the adoption of a social policy whose goal is antithetical to the central tenets of a free market economy.

Students who are good at Method and Flaw questions tend to be good at other question types as well. Why? Because question types such as Weaken and Strengthen require a knowledge of how the argument is structured. Thus, studying Method and Flaw questions will improve your ability to solve other question types.

As usual, we begin by analyzing the structure of the problem:

> Premise: Proponents of the theory of social utilitarianism hold that the value of human capital should bear an inherent relation to its social utility.

CHAPTER TEN: METHOD AND FLAW QUESTIONS

Counterpremise: Although maximizing the value of human capital is both morally defensible and economically praiseworthy,

Premise: If the price of labor were to become a measure of social utility and not of scarcity, the labor market would suffer significant distortions that may well reduce, and not increase, the current level of human capital.

Conclusion: The theory of social utilitarianism has severe practical limitations.

The argument begins with the classic device, "Proponents...hold that..." As expected, the author argues that the beliefs of these individuals are incorrect, although not before first offering up a counter-premise that does not undermine his argument. The last half of the argument is an example that supports the conclusion. Although the argument is challenging to understand, the conclusion seems reasonable.

Answer choice (A): This is the correct answer. Social utilitarianism is a theory (or strategy), and the author uses an example to show that if it were implemented, there could be adverse results.

Answer choice (B): This is a Half Right, Half Wrong answer. The argument does criticize a course of action. But, the argument does not use an "ends do not justify the means" approach in doing so.

Answer choice (C): The author does not suggest any alternatives, and thus this answer can be ruled out immediately.

Answer choice (D): The author makes no concessions, just criticisms, and so this answer is incorrect.

Answer choice (E): There is no indication that the author believes that social utilitarianism is antithetical to the central tenets of the free market, just that if implemented, social utilitarianism could result in negative consequences.

Note that this stimulus difficult to read, but eliminating answers is actually not that challenging because each incorrect answer contains an element that almost immediately takes the answer out of consideration.

Method of Reasoning—Bolded Argument Part Questions

Argument Part (AP) questions are a very rare subset of Method of Reasoning questions. In Method—AP questions, the question stem cites a specific portion or portions of the stimulus and then asks you to identify the role the cited portion plays in the structure of the argument or about the role the two portions play in relation to each other. Here are several example question stems:

> "The claim that politicians sometimes cater to special interests plays which one of the following roles in the argument?"
>
> "The statement 'no economic consequences could be observed' serves which one of the following roles in the argument?"
>
> "In the argument above, the two **boldface** portions play which of the following roles?"

The answer choices in each problem then describe the structural role of the citation, often using terms you are already familiar with such as "premise," "assumption," and "conclusion." At this point in the book, you are uniquely positioned to answer these questions because the Primary Objectives have directed you from the start to isolate the structure of each argument and to identify each piece of the argument. Method—AP questions reward the knowledge you naturally gain from this process.

Method—AP Stimulus Structure

The stimuli that accompany Method—AP questions tend to be more complex than the average GMAT stimulus. Some problems feature two conclusions (one is the main conclusion, the other is a subsidiary conclusion), and often the stimulus includes two different viewpoints or the use of counterpremises. Thus, the ability to identify argument parts using indicator words is important.

As you know from the discussion in Chapter Two, the order in which the conclusion and premises are presented is not relevant to the logical validity of the argument. Still, many people have difficulty becoming accustomed to arguments where the conclusion appears first, and we will discuss those arguments in a moment. Regardless, a large number of Method—AP problems feature the traditional formation with the conclusion at the end of the argument. If you do see the main conclusion at the end of a Method—AP problem, be prepared to answer a question about a part of the argument *other than* the conclusion. The test makers do this because they know students are very good at identifying the conclusion when it appears in the last sentence.

For more information on argument indicators, please review Chapter Two.

Please take a moment to complete the following problem:

2. Mayor: Some of my critics claim that the city's current budget deficit has been caused by my policies, and that I am responsible for the deficit. Although I admit that **the city has run a budget deficit during my tenure**, I do not agree that I am at fault for this problem. The economic policies of the prior administration caused the current deficit, and **were it not for the economic policies of my administration, the current deficit would be even worse**.

In the mayor's argument, the two boldface portions play which of the following roles?

(A) The first is a premise that has been used against the mayor; the second supports the critics of the mayor.

(B) The first is a statement accepted by the mayor; the second is a consequence of the critics' claims.

(C) The first is a fact that the mayor believes does not contradict his conclusion; the second offers support in consideration of that conclusion.

(D) The first is evidence of unlawful activity by the mayor; the second is evidence offered by the mayor to explain that activity.

(E) The first is evidence that undermines the mayor's main position; the second is a statement that follows from that position.

The presence of Method−AP questions signals that the makers of the GMAT expect you to understand argument structure. At the same time, the presence of this question type indicates that many students are unable to do so. Amazingly, you can gain time and points on the GMAT simply by doing the very things you have already learned in order to succeed on the test.

This argument begins with the classic "some of my critics claim" construction discussed in Chapter Two. As we know from that discussion, the conclusion of the argument will typically be the opposite of the claim. In this case, the conclusion comes in the second sentence when the mayor states the following:

Conclusion: I do not agree that I am at fault for this problem [the budget deficit].

Because neither bolded portion overlaps the conclusion, the bolded portions must be premises or counterpremises. Take a moment to go back and look at some of the indicator words—see the "although" just before the first bolded portion? The presence of that word means that the first bolded portion is given as a counterpremise to the author's conclusion. That is, the mayor admits that there was a budget deficit, and this fact possibly undermines his or her argument in some way, but the mayor still believes that the conclusion is true despite this fact.

The second bolded portion comes after the conclusion and is used as a premise to support the conclusion. Thus, one bolded portion is a counterpremise, and the other is a premise, and the correct answer must reflect that fact.

In summary, the pertinent portions of the argument appear as follows:

Critics claim: The critics claim that the mayor is responsible for the current budget deficit.

Bolded portion: In this counterpremise the mayor admits that there is a budget deficit.

Conclusion: The conclusion indicates that even though there is a budget deficit, the mayor is not responsible for the deficit, contrary to the claim of the critics.

Bolded portion: This is a premise that indicates that the mayor's economic policies have actually benefitted the city, not hurt the city.

A quick scan of the answer choices reveals that each will be broken into two parts: the first part will describe the first bolded section and the second part will describe the second bolded section.

If the use of premise/conclusion identifier words fails to identify the main conclusion, then use the Conclusion Identification Method described in Chapter Two: use one statement as a conclusion and the other as a premise and see if the arrangement makes sense.

CHAPTER TEN: METHOD AND FLAW QUESTIONS

Answer choice (A): The first half of this answer is a classic Contender. It may very well be that the counterpremise has been used against the mayor. Setting that aside, however, the description of the second bolded portion is inaccurate, and so this answer choice is incorrect.

Answer choice (B): This is classic Half-Right, Half-Wrong answer choice. The first bolded portion is a statement accepted by the mayor; however, it is not the case that the second bolded portion is a "consequence of the critics' claims."

Answer choice (C): This is the correct answer. In this case, although the mayor admits that the first bolded portion is true, he or she does not believe that fact has a negative impact on the conclusion.

Answer choice (D): This answer begins poorly because we do not know that the first boldface portion is evidence of unlawful activity by the mayor.

Answer choice (E): This is another answer where the first bolded portion causes many people to leave the answer as a Contender. However, the description of the second bolded portion is inaccurate because the second portion is not a consequence of the mayor's main position but rather supports the mayor's position (this is a direct test of your ability to discern a premise from a conclusion).

A Common Wrong Answer

One trick used by the test makers in Method—AP questions is to create wrong answers that describe parts of the argument other than the part named in the question stem. These answers are particularly attractive because they do describe a part of the argument, just not the part referenced in the question stem. Before proceeding to the answer choices, make sure you know exactly what part of the argument you are being asked about.

Final Note

This chapter is the first of two chapters that focus on questions that are primarily structural in nature. In the next chapter we will discuss Parallel Reasoning, which is very structurally oriented.

Method of Reasoning and Flaw in the Reasoning Question Type Review

Method of Reasoning questions require you to select the answer choice that best describes the method used by the author to make the argument. Structurally, Method of Reasoning questions are simply abstract Must Be True questions: instead of identifying the facts of the argument, you must identify the logical organization of the argument. The stimulus for a Method Reasoning question will contain an argument, and the argument can contain either valid or invalid reasoning.

Flaw in the Reasoning questions are exactly the same as Method of Reasoning questions with the important exception that the question stem indicates that the reasoning in the stimulus is flawed. Because the question stem reveals that a flaw is present, you need not make a determination of the validity of the stimulus.

As part of the First Family of Questions, Method and Flaw questions feature the following information structure:

1. You can use only the information in the stimulus to prove the correct answer choice.

2. Any answer choice that describes information or a situation that does not occur in the stimulus is incorrect.

You must watch for the presence of the premise and conclusion indicators discussed in Chapter Two.

Use the Fact Test to eliminate answers in Method and Flaw questions:

If an answer choice describes an event that did not occur in the stimulus, then that answer is incorrect.

Method of Reasoning and Flaw in the Reasoning Question Type Review

Several types of incorrect answers regularly appear in Method and Flaw questions:

1. "New" Element Answers

2. Half Right, Half Wrong Answers

3. Exaggerated Answers

4. The Opposite Answer

5. The Reverse Answer

Argument Part (AP) questions are a specific subset of Method of Reasoning questions. In Method—AP questions, the question stem cites a specific portion of the stimulus and then asks you to identify the role that the cited portion plays in the structure of the argument, or alternately the stem cites two portions of the stimulus and about the role the two portions play in relation to each other.

The stimuli that accompany Method—AP questions tend to be more complex than the average GMAT stimulus.

One trick used by the test makers in Method—AP questions is to create wrong answers that describe parts of the argument other than the part named in the question stem.

Identify the Flaw in the Argument Drill

Each of the following problems contains an error of reasoning. Based on the discussion in this chapter, identify the error of reasoning. *Answers on page 285*

1. "After several periods of record sales increases, the Janacek Group relocated their offices to the new Industrial Pointe complex and chose one of the most expensive office suites in the city. Despite the significant financial investment required, Janacek executives defended the move by noting the benefits to Janacek's image that would come with a location in a complex which, they concluded, must house all of the city's most expensive office space."

2. "Supporters of the theory of global warming claim that carbon emissions are causing our environment to slowly warm, which will eventually produce catastrophic results. However, this past winter was one of the coldest on record. Therefore, the claim that global warming is accelerating is false."

CHAPTER TEN: METHOD AND FLAW QUESTIONS

Identify the Flaw in the Argument Drill

3. "When temperatures drop just below freezing, the plant pathogen *Pseudomonas syringae* produces certain proteins that force ice to form on the surface of a plant. The damage caused by the freezing process releases plant nutrients that are then available to the *Pseudomonas syringae* bacteria. Although this fruit grove contains *Pseudomonas syringae* bacteria, temperatures have not dropped below freezing at any point during the last 30 days, so there should be no concern over *Pseudomonas syringae*-related damage during that period."

4. "Will executor: The maker of this will left a number of antiques as gifts to her descendents. I recently attempted to have each antique evaluated for value by a local university professor who is an international expert in the valuation and authentication of antiques. This month, however, she will be too busy to examine all of the pieces. Therefore, I must take all of the antiques to the local appraising firm for valuation."

Identify the Flaw in the Argument Drill

5. "Each member of Dr. Martin's research team is now well-known among the particle physics scientific community. We know this because the team recently published a ground breaking physics paper on baryon asymmetry. The paper created great excitement among those who study particle physics, and there has been intense debate on what the results of the paper mean for the science of particle physics. Consequently, the work of Dr. Martin's team of researchers has become world-renowned."

6. "Thompson has rightly been lauded for his academic achievements at this school, but Thompson is also an excellent overall athlete and he is obviously the school's best runner. This claim is decisively proven in those instances when Thompson does lose a race, because Thompson obviously would not lose unless the other runners cheated."

Identify the Flaw in the Argument Drill

7. "New restaurant manager: Several employees complained about the firing of a recently trained waiter after his very first erroneous order. They claim that the previous manager had been quite lenient with regard to the first few mistakes made by any recent trainee, but this claim is clearly false. I know the previous manager, and she would not have tolerated countless errors without any repercussions, even if those errors were made by recent trainees."

8. "Within certain library departments, established practice dictates that seniority be used as the main criterion for job advancement. Thereby, the employee who has worked the most years has priority in the promotion process. However, this process is patently unfair. Janet Watson, the local mayor, recently spoke out against this process and strongly criticized the library administration for adhering to what she called "a completely obsolete system.""

Identify the Flaw in the Argument Drill

9. "Veterinarian: There is serious cause for concern with the cattle herds in this state. Yesterday I treated two cows for listeriosis, a disease of the central nervous system, and the day before that I treated two different cows for the very same malady. We need to immediately begin testing all cows in the state for this disease, and take curative action on any cow exhibiting signs of illness."

_____
_____
_____
_____
_____
_____

10. "Board member: The protesters who recently criticized the Board for taking advantage of a loophole in the city charter are falsely informed. Although the Board agreed to provide further financing to the city transit system, the Board did not use the bank owned by one of the Board members. Thus, as the protesters have failed to show that any board member gained any benefit from the action we took, their claim is false."

_____
_____
_____
_____
_____
_____

CHAPTER TEN: METHOD AND FLAW QUESTIONS

Identify the Flaw in the Argument Drill

11. "Richardson recently claimed that we must do something in response to the university's current economic crisis. I have repeatedly proposed that we layoff a percentage of all workers and simultaneously reduce all budgets to last year's levels. If we are to follow Richardson's advice, and actually do something, we must implement my program of action immediately."

12. "Company travel manager: Although we had originally planned for the eight marketing department employees to drive the 250 miles to this week's advertising meeting, our car rental firm informed us today that no van will be available for rent until next week. Thus, we have no choice but to postpone the meeting."

Identify the Flaw in the Argument Drill Answer Key

1. Error of Composition

    An error of composition occurs when a person attributes a characteristic of part of the group or entity to the group or entity as a whole or to each member of the group. In this instance, the Janacek executives make the mistake of thinking that because their office suite is among the most expensive in the city, that the office building must contain all of the city's most expensive office space.

2. Error in the Use of Evidence

    Some evidence against a position is taken to prove that the position is false or invalid. Note that this argument does not contain a causal error although causal language is used. There is no causal error because the author simply describes a position involving causal reasoning held by another group (the supporters of the global warming theory); the author does not draw a causal conclusion in this argument.

3. Error of Conditional Reasoning—Mistaken Negation

    In the first sentence, the argument establishes a conditional relationship between below freezing temperatures and *Pseudomonas syringae* frost damage:

    Temperatures below freezing ⟶ *Pseudomonas syringae* cause plant damage

    The last sentence indicates that the sufficient condition about temperatures has not been met during the last 30 days, and then concludes that the necessary condition about bacteria damage also has not been met. This error is a Mistaken Negation, which arises when the lack of occurrence of a sufficient condition is used to conclude that a necessary condition will not occur.

4. False Dilemma

    The will executor indicates that one option for the appraisal of the antiques—a local university expert—is unavailable, and on that basis concludes that the antiques must be taken to a local appraisal firm. Thus, by eliminating one choice and then concluding that another choice must be made, the argument assumes there are only two choices. This error is known as a False Dilemma because other options for appraisal may exist.

Identify the Flaw in the Argument Drill Answer Key

5. Error of Division

   An error of division occurs when the author attributes a characteristic of the whole of a group to each member of the group. In this case, the first sentence is the main conclusion of the argument, namely that "Each member of Dr. Martin's research team is now well-known among the particle physics scientific community." This is supported by the premise/subconclusion in the final sentence that "the work of Dr. Martin's team of researchers has become world-renowned." Note as always the critical importance of understanding that a conclusion in an argument can be the main conclusion, or just a subsidiary conclusion.

6. Circular Reasoning

   The latter part of the conclusion of the argument is that Thompson is the school's best runner. The author attempts to support this conclusion by saying that if Thompson loses, someone must have cheated (*since Thompson, the school's best runner, would not lose!*) As this premise assumes the conclusion that the author is attempting to establish, the argument is circular and therefore flawed.

7. Straw Man

   In a Straw Man argument, the author distorts the opposition argument, thereby making it easier to attack. In this argument, several employees claimed that the previous manager "had been quite lenient with regard to the first few mistakes made by any recent trainee." The author recasts this position later, stating that the previous manager "would not have tolerated countless errors without any repercussions." This is a different position than the one made by the employees, and one that makes their position seem less defensible.

8. Appeal Fallacy—Appeal to Authority

   In this case, the authors' evidence for the conclusion that "this process is patently unfair" are the statements of the local mayor. This is a classic Appeal fallacy because the opinion of an authority is used to attempt to persuade the reader.

9. Exceptional Case/Overgeneralization

   The conclusion that all cows in the state need to be tested is based on just four examples. Given that the claim is made regarding the testing of "all cows in the state," more cases would be needed to justify a program that broad, or, alternatively, a testing program using sampling could be implemented.

Identify the Flaw in the Argument Drill Answer Key

10. Error in the Use of Evidence

    Lack of evidence for a position is taken to prove that the position is false. In this instance, the Board member states that there is no proof that "any board member gained any benefit from the action we took," and on the basis of this lack of evidence, concludes that the protesters claim is false.

11. Uncertain Use of a Term

    This is a tricky argument that may at first appear to be an Appeal to Authority. But Richardson is not cited as an authority, so that is unlikely to be the flaw. Instead, the author's conclusion is based on a shift in meaning within the argument of the word "something." Richardson's initial comment takes "something" to mean "some action or solution," which would typically refer to the best solution; at the least, Richardson takes "something" to mean that a minimal action must occur. The author shifts the meaning of "something" to refer to his proposal specifically, as in "something" means "this thing."

12. False Dilemma

    The Company Travel Manager states that because one option for travel is unavailable (driving a rented van), the conclusion is that the meeting must be postponed. This is a False Dilemma because other options most likely exist (e.g., an employee could drive his or her car, or the employees could take a bus or train, etc.).

Method of Reasoning and Flaw in the Reasoning Problem Set

Please complete the problem set and review the answer key and explanations. *Answers on page 290*

1. Car Advertisement: The new Electra Argive is among the best-driving cars on the road today. This fact is reflected in a recent poll at our dealerships of interested drivers who had test-driven the Argive, who rated it among the top cars they had driven; over 80% of those drivers indicated they would be buying an Argive in the near future.

   The argument is most vulnerable to criticism on which of the following grounds?

   (A) It assumes what it seeks to establish
   (B) It fails to consider the possibility that the survey respondents discussed may base their purchase decisions on a wide variety of factors.
   (C) It appeals to the judgment of experts in a matter to which their field of expertise is irrelevant.
   (D) It treats the failure to disprove a claim as if it constitutes conclusive evidence of that claim.
   (E) It generalizes from a sample that there is reason to believe is unrepresentative of the general population.

2. Manager: Last year, within the sales division of the company, the salespeople with highest average number of miles driven each week had the highest sales figures. Thus, we should immediately implement a policy requiring all salespeople to begin driving more miles each week.

   The reasoning in the manager's argument is flawed because the argument

   (A) relies on information about responses from the general public rather than on the opinions of experts.
   (B) fails to exclude an alternative explanation for the observed correlation.
   (C) bases a conclusion on two pieces of contradictory evidence.
   (D) responds to a distorted version of an opposing position.
   (E) attempts to persuade by making an emotional appeal.

Method of Reasoning and Flaw in the Reasoning Problem Set

3. Because few consumers are content without toilet paper, bread, or shampoo, such basic consumer goods have long been assumed to be "recession-proof," which is to say that the sales of such goods would be unaffected by economic recession. Many consumers, however, either choose to buy smaller quantities in order to reduce waste, or purchase items in bulk, which offers better value.

   Which of the following most accurately describes the role played by the claim that many consumers either choose to buy smaller quantities or purchase in bulk during times of economic recession?

   (A) It is a rationale behind a commonly adopted position whose validity the author challenges by giving specific counterexamples.
   (B) It is cited to refute a long-standing presumption.
   (C) It is a fact the author tries to refute by offering evidence concerning consumer behavior during a recession.
   (D) It is a claim that the author concedes to be correct, but only to the extent specified by the examples it cites.
   (E) It is cited to provide support for the assertion that some items are entirely recession-proof.

Method of Reasoning and Flaw in the Reasoning Problems Answer Key

Question #1: Flaw in the Reasoning. The correct answer choice is (E)

The advertisement in this stimulus claims that the Argive is one of the best-driving cars on the road today. This claim is based on a recent poll of people who test drove the Argive and then went on to rate it highly. Further, a significant percentage of test drivers (80%) indicated their intention to purchase an Argive in the future.

Since we are asked to identify a flaw in this argument, let's consider the relationship between the conclusion and the survey respondents upon whose statements the conclusion is based. The conclusion is that the Argive is among the best-driving cars available, a very broad and far-reaching statement that compares the Argive to all other cars and claims it is among the best for any/all consumers. But this claim is based solely upon the statements made by a group of people already interested in the Argive (or at least intrigued enough to test drive it), and that is where the advertisement becomes vulnerable to criticism.

This is a fairly common survey error, where the group of people being surveyed can be considered self-selecting: the reason they are in the survey is that they share a characteristic that may not be shared by the group the author uses the survey results to discuss. Here, the fact that the group being surveyed was already interested enough in the Argive to take it for a test drive means that they are also more likely to speak favorably about it; hence, their responses cannot be considered to apply to the average consumer who may no interest/knowledge in the Argive.

Answer choice (A): This answer choice reflects a circular reasoning argument, where the conclusion is simply restated, or given as evidence of itself. That does not happen in this stimulus.

Answer choice (B): The flaw in the argument is that the survey respondents may not be representative of the average car buyer. So, whether the survey respondents based their responses on a very wide, or very narrow variety of factors, this answer choice does not represent the flaw in the stimulus.

Answer choice (C): The argument is based on the responses of people who test drove the Argive, and makes no appeal to "experts" in establishing its conclusion.

Answer choice (D): This answer choice, which describes an error in the use of evidence, can be summed up as: no evidence disproving a claim is taken to mean the claim is true. However, the advertisement never references a lack of evidence against anything, so this answer choice cannot be correct.

Answer choice (E): This is the correct answer. As mentioned above, the error here is that the sample of people surveyed are already interested in the Argive (at least interested enough to test drive it), so their favorable review/opinion cannot be thought to be perfectly representative of auto buyers as a whole.

Method of Reasoning and Flaw in the Reasoning Problems Answer Key

Question #2: Flaw in the Reasoning—CE. The correct answer choice is (B)

The manager's argument in this stimulus is that, since the salespeople with the highest average miles driven weekly had the highest sales figures, the company should require salespeople to begin driving more. This is a causal argument, where the observed "effect" of higher sales figures is attributed to the presumed "cause" of high mileage:

HM = higher average number of miles driven each week
HS = higher sales

$\underline{C} \qquad \underline{E}$

$HM \longrightarrow HS$

As with any causal flaw argument, the correct answer choice will generally use causal language, with words such as "cause" and "effect" (or synonymous terms). In this case, the specific causal flaw is that the author overlooks the possibility that other, alternate causes (besides driving greater distances) could have produced the observed effect of higher sales. In fact, it seems entirely possible that the cause and effect could be reversed: a greater number of existing sales opportunities caused certain salespeople to drive a higher number of miles weekly.

Answer choice (A): There is no reference to responses from the general public or from experts, so this cannot be the correct answer.

Answer choice (B): This is the correct answer choice. As mentioned above, the flaw in the manager's argument is the presumption that the higher number of miles driven is what caused the higher sales figures, when instead there could be an alternate cause for the higher sales or the cause and effect could even be reversed. Note too the language used: "alternative explanation" and "observed effect" are both classic causal reasoning terms and clear indicators that this answer choice is a strong contender.

Answer choice (C): This answer choice describes an internal contradiction error, where the conclusion is based on evidence that actually supports an opposite conclusion. That does not occur in this stimulus.

Answer choice (D): This type of argument, often referred to as "Straw Man," is where a speaker rephrases/distorts an opposing speaker's argument to make it easier to argue against. Since the manager is not responding to an opposing position, much less distorting it, this cannot be the correct answer.

Answer choice (E): There is no appeal to the reader's emotions or sympathy, so this answer choice is also incorrect.

Method of Reasoning and Flaw in the Reasoning Problems Answer Key

Question #3: Method of Reasoning—AP. The correct answer choice is (B)

The author begins this stimulus by pointing out a long standing presumption: Since few consumers are content without such goods as toilet paper, bread, and shampoo, such goods have been thought of as recession-proof. In the following sentence, however, the author refutes this presumption by pointing to different strategies that consumers might take with regard to such goods during recession times.

The stimulus is followed by a Method—Argument Part question which requires us to define the role played by the claim about consumers during recession times. We should certainly attempt to prephrase the answer when we see this type of question: In this case, the author asserts that claim to undermine the long-standing presumption that sales of such staple products are recession proof.

Answer choice (A): The claim about recession purchase strategies is not a rationale behind a commonly adopted position; rather, it is evidence presented to undermine the commonly held belief that items such as toilet paper, bread and shampoo are not completely recession proof.

Answer choice (B): This is the correct answer choice. The author points to the referenced consumer goods in an effort to refute the long standing presumption that items such as the ones mentioned are recession-proof.

Answer choice (C): The author is not attempting to undermine the claim that many consumers change their buying habits during times of recession. On the contrary, the author provides this fact to support the assertion that such goods are not entirely recession proof.

Answer choice (D): The claim about the specific goods referenced is not intended by the author as a limited concession, but rather to show that such goods can be affected by times of economic recession.

Answer choice (E): This is an Opposite answer choice. The information about the changes to consumer spending habits is provided not to support the assertion that such goods are recession-proof, but instead to exemplify the fact that even goods that are perceived as necessities can experience changes in sales during times of economic recession.

Chapter Eleven:
Parallel Reasoning Questions

Chapter Eleven: Parallel Reasoning Questions

Parallel Reasoning Questions 295

Parallel Flaw Questions... 295

The Peril of Abstraction 296

Solving Parallel Reasoning Questions 297

What To Do If All Else Fails 305

Parallel Reasoning Question Review 306

Parallel Reasoning Question Problem Set 307

Parallel Reasoning Questions

Parallel Reasoning questions ask you to identify the answer choice that contains reasoning most similar in structure to the reasoning in the stimulus. Since this task requires you to first identify the method of argumentation used by the author and then to match that reasoning to the reasoning presented in each answer choice, these questions can be quite time consuming (a fact known to and exploited by the test makers).

Like Method of Reasoning and Flaw in the Reasoning questions, Parallel Reasoning questions are in the First Family and have the same information structure. However, because of the abstract nature of these questions, comparing the stimulus to the answer choices takes on a different dimension, and we will address this issue in a moment in the section entitled *Solving Parallel Reasoning Questions*.

Question stem examples:

> "Which of the following is most closely parallel in its reasoning to the reasoning in the argument above?"

> "Which of the following exhibits a pattern of reasoning most similar to that exhibited by the argument above?"

> "Which of the following arguments is most similar in its logical features to the argument above?"

> "Which of the following arguments is most similar in its pattern of reasoning to the argument above?"

> "The structure of the reasoning in the argument above is most parallel to that in which of the following?"

Parallel Flaw Questions

The stimulus for a Parallel Reasoning question can contain either valid or invalid reasoning. When a Parallel Reasoning stimulus contains flawed reasoning, we identify it as a Parallel Flaw question. Like Flaw in the Reasoning questions, Parallel Flaw questions use many of the common forms of erroneous reasoning.

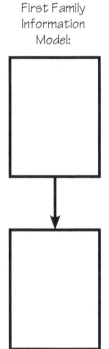

First Family Information Model:

Parallel Reasoning questions appear infrequently on the GMAT, but as with all the rare question types, they appear more frequently if you are doing well.

CHAPTER ELEVEN: PARALLEL REASONING QUESTIONS

If the reasoning is flawed, the question stem will state that the reasoning is bad by using words such as "flawed" or "questionable."

Here are two Parallel Flaw question stem examples. They are virtually identical to the previous Parallel Reasoning questions stems with the exception that they contain a term indicating that the reasoning in the stimulus is invalid:

> "The flawed reasoning in which of the following is most similar to the flawed reasoning in the argument above?"

> "The questionable pattern of reasoning in the argument is most similar to that in which of the following?"

The Peril of Abstraction

Parallel Reasoning questions are challenging because they are the most abstract type of question on the GMAT. Not only must you understand the structure of the argument in the stimulus, you must also understand the structure of the arguments in each of the five answer choices. Juggling all this abstract information is difficult, and you will learn how to effectively approach Parallel Reasoning questions in the following pages.

Parallel Reasoning questions force you to evaluate six different arguments.

We will address several effective ways to handle the abstract nature of these questions, but first you must understand what approach *not* to take. Some companies recommend that you make general abstract diagrams for the elements in each stimulus and do the same for each answer choice. This "general symbolization" approach involves representing the premises and conclusion as "A," "B," "C," etcetera, and writing them next to the stimulus. This approach, while well-meaning, is hopelessly flawed. Parallel Reasoning questions are difficult *because* they involve a great deal of abstraction. The use of non-specific symbols such as "A," "B," and "C" further abstracts the stimulus elements, increasing the difficulty instead of alleviating it.

Please note that the method described above is different from the symbolization described in the causal reasoning chapter of this book. In that chapter, we recommend diagramming in response to specific logical formations, and we strongly recommend using symbols that directly represent elements in the stimulus. That approach, when properly used, makes the questions easier to attack.

Solving Parallel Reasoning Questions

Because you must find the answer with a similar pattern of reasoning to that in the stimulus, using the details of the stimulus to attack the answer choices works differently in Parallel Reasoning questions than in other First Family questions. For example, The Fact Test plays a minimal role in Parallel questions because the details (topic, etc.) of the stimulus and each answer choice are different. Instead, the structural basis of these questions forces you to compare the big-picture elements of the argument: intent of the conclusion, force and use of the premises, the relationship of the premises and the conclusion, and the soundness of the argument. Comparing these elements is like using an Abstract Fact Test—you must examine the general features of the argument in the answer choice and match them to the argument in the stimulus.

Parallel Reasoning questions are a continuation of Method of Reasoning questions: first you must identify the reasoning in the argument, and then you must find the answer with the same reasoning.

First, let us examine the elements of an argument that do *not* need to be paralleled in these questions:

1. Topic of the stimulus

   In Parallel Reasoning questions, the topic or subject matter in the stimulus and the answer choices is irrelevant because you are looking for the argument that has a similar pattern of *reasoning*. Often, same-subject answer choices are used to attract the student who fails to focus on the reasoning in the stimulus. For example, if the topic of the stimulus is banking, you need not have an answer choice that is also about banking.

2. The order of presentation of the premises and conclusion in the stimulus

   The order of presentation of the premises and conclusion in the stimulus is also irrelevant. As long as an answer choice contains the same general parts as the stimulus, they need not be in the same order because the order of presentation does not affect the logical relationship that underlies the pieces. So, for example, if the stimulus has an order of conclusion-premise-premise, you need not have the same order in the correct answer.

Answer choices with the same subject matter as the stimulus are almost always incorrect, and are generally used to lure students who fail to consider the reasoning in the stimulus. You should still consider answer choices with the same topic as the stimulus, but be wary.

Neither of the elements above has any bearing on the correctness of an answer choice. Now, let's look at the elements that must be paralleled, and how to use these elements to eliminate wrong answer choices:

1. The Method of Reasoning

   It may sound obvious, but the type of reasoning used in the stimulus must be paralleled. When you see an identifiable form of reasoning present—for example, causal reasoning or conditional reasoning—you can proceed quickly and look for the answer that matches the form of the stimulus. Given the numerous forms of reasoning we have examined (both valid and invalid), you now have a powerful arsenal of knowledge that you can use to attack these questions. First and foremost, if you recognize the form of reasoning used in the stimulus, immediately attack the answers and search for the answer with similar reasoning.

2. The Validity of the Argument

   The validity of the reasoning in the correct answer choice must match the validity of the reasoning in the stimulus.

   Often, answer choices can be eliminated because they contain reasoning that has a different logical force than the stimulus. If the stimulus contains valid reasoning, eliminate any answer choice that contains invalid reasoning. If the stimulus contains invalid reasoning, eliminate any answer choice that contains valid reasoning.

3. The Conclusion

   Every Parallel Reasoning stimulus contains an argument and therefore a conclusion. Because your job is to parallel the argument, you must parallel the subcomponents, including the premises and conclusion. You can use this knowledge to attack specific answer choices: if an answer has a conclusion that does not "match" the conclusion in the stimulus, then the answer is incorrect. Using this approach is especially helpful if you do not see an identifiable form of reasoning in the stimulus.

   When matching conclusions, you must match the *certainty level* or *intent* of the conclusion in the stimulus, not necessarily the specific wording of the conclusion. For example, a stimulus conclusion containing absolutes ("must," "never," "always") will be matched by a conclusion in the correct answer choice using similar absolutes; a stimulus conclusion that gives an opinion ("should") will be matched by the same idea in the correct answer choice; a conditional conclusion in the stimulus will be matched by a conditional conclusion in the correct answer choice, and so on. This knowledge allows you to quickly narrow down the answer choices to the most likely candidates. This advice can initially be confusing, so let us discuss it in more detail.

Because Parallel Reasoning questions contain six different arguments, they are often lengthy.

First, answers that have identical wording to the conclusion are Contenders (assuming there is no other reason to knock them out of contention). Identical wording for our purposes means answers where the controlling modifiers (such as "must," "could," "many," "some," "never," etcetera) are the same. For example, if the conclusion of the argument stated, "The reactor can supply the city power grid," an answer that had similar wording, such as "The bank can meet the needs of customers," would be a Contender. In brief, the advice in this paragraph is fairly simple: if the conclusion in the answer choice has similar wording to the conclusion in the stimulus, then the answer is *possibly* correct.

Second, because there are many synonyms available for the test makers to use, do not eliminate answers just because the wording is not identical. For example, an answer could state, "The majority of voters endorsed the amendment." The quantity indicator in the sentence—"majority"—has several synonyms, such as "most" and "more than half." Make sure that when you examine each sentence you do not eliminate an answer that has wording that is functionally identical to the wording in the stimulus.

Third, remember that the English language has many pairs of natural opposites, so the presence of a negative term in the stimulus is *not* grounds for dismissing the answer when the stimulus has positive language (and vice versa). For example, a conclusion could state, "The councilmember must be present at the meeting." That conclusion could just as easily have been worded as, "The councilmember must not be absent from the meeting." In the same way, an answer choice can use opposite language (including negatives) but still have a meaning that is similar to the stimulus.

If the stimulus has a positive conclusion, then the presence of negative terms in the conclusion is not grounds for eliminating the answer; if the stimulus has a negative conclusion, then the lack of a negative term in the conclusion is not grounds for eliminating the answer.

4. The Premises

   Like the conclusion, the premises in the correct answer choice must match the premises in the stimulus, and the same wording rules that were discussed in *The Conclusion* section apply to the premises.

   Matching premises is a step to take after you have checked the conclusion, unless you notice that one (or more) of the premises has an unusual role in the argument. If so, you can immediately look at the answer choices and compare premises.

CHAPTER ELEVEN: PARALLEL REASONING QUESTIONS

Because the four components above must be paralleled in the correct answer choice, the test makers have an array of options for making an answer *incorrect*. They can create answer choices that match several of the elements but not all of the elements, and to work through each answer choice in traditional fashion can be a painstaking process. However, since each element must be matched, you can analyze and attack the answer choices by testing whether the answer choice under consideration matches certain elements in the stimulus. If not, the answer is incorrect.

Upon hearing this advice, most students say, "Sounds good. In what order should I examine the elements?" Although the process can be reduced to a step-by-step procedure, a better approach is to realize that examining the elements is like a waterfall and that everything will happen very quickly. Performing well on the GMAT is about flexibility and correctly responding to the clues provided. Rigidly applying the methods below will rob you of the opportunity to accelerate through the problem. Therefore, in Parallel Reasoning questions your job is to identify the features of the argument most likely to be "points of separation"—those features that can be used to divide answers into Losers and Contenders. Sometimes matching the conclusion will knock out several answer choices, other times matching the premises will achieve that same goal. The following list outlines the four tests you can use to evaluate answers, in rough order of their usefulness:

Be wary of Parallel Flaw question stems that ask you to identify both the logical flaws in the stimulus. When this occurs, there is always an incorrect answer that contains only one of the flaws.

This section of four tests for Parallel Reasoning questions describes the unique and original Elemental Attack™ used in all of the PowerScore GMAT Courses.

1. Match the Method of Reasoning

   If you identify an obvious form of reasoning (use of analogy, circular reasoning, conditional reasoning, etc.), move quickly to the answer choices and look for the answer with an identical form of reasoning.

2. Match the Conclusion

   If you cannot identify the form of reasoning, or if you still have two or more answer choices in contention after matching the reasoning, or if the conclusion seems to have unusual language, examine the conclusion of each answer choice and match it against the conclusion in the stimulus. Matching the conclusion can be a critical time-saver because it often eliminates one or more answers. On occasion, all five conclusions in the answer choices will be identical to that in the stimulus. That is not a problem—it just means that the other elements must be used to knock out the wrong answers.

   The key to successfully matching the conclusion is that you must be able to quickly pick out the conclusion in each answer choice.

This is where the conclusion identification skills discussed in Chapter Two come into play.

3. Match the Premises

    If matching the method of reasoning and conclusion does not eliminate the four wrong answer choices, try matching the premises. The more complex the argument structure in the stimulus, the more likely you will have to match the premises to arrive at the correct answer. The less complex the argument, the more likely that matching the conclusion will be effective.

4. Match the Validity of the Argument

    Always make sure to eliminate any answer choice that does not match the logical force (valid or invalid) of the argument. This test rarely eliminates all four answers, but it can often eliminate one or two answer choices.

Different methods can be used to eliminate different answers, and the process should be fluid and based on the signals you derive from the stimulus. This question required a combination of checking the reasoning, the conclusion, and the validity of the argument. Other problems will require different combinations. Remember that you have four basic tests at your disposal, and be prepared to use them when you encounter a Parallel Reasoning problem.

CHAPTER ELEVEN: PARALLEL REASONING QUESTIONS

Parallel Reasoning Decision time: suppose you complete answer choice (A) and you are virtually certain that you have the correct answer. Should you read the remaining answer choices, or should you skip to the next problem? The answer, in part, depends on the time remaining in the section. If it is late in the section, most students are pressed for time and it would not be unreasonable to make a calculated choice to move on without reviewing answer choices (B) through (E). Before doing so, you would be well-advised to make sure that you are certain about the reasoning in the stimulus.

On the other hand, if this question were to appear early in the section, it would be worthwhile to quickly check the remaining answer choices because early in the section one of your goals is to accumulate as many correct answers as possible.

Please take a moment to complete the following problem:

1. The amount of time required to process the application forms before the deadline is more time than Jones currently has available. In addition, Jones needs at least one assistant to help him with the processing of the forms, and currently no one is available to assist him nor will anyone be available prior to the deadline. Thus, it cannot be the case that Jones will complete the processing of the forms by the deadline.

The pattern of reasoning displayed in the argument above is most closely parallel to that in which of the following arguments?

(A) Every employee of the Altierra Corporation receives three weeks of vacation, and since Maya is an employee of the Altierra Corporation, she must have receive three weeks of vacation.

(B) The building on State Street owned by Jared should be demolished. Up until last year the building was in excellent shape, but since that point the building has become uninhabitable and a danger to the public.

(C) All of the students that attend Chase Elementary live in the area immediately surrounding the school. Kofi lives within sight of Chase Elementary, and therefore Kofi must attend the school.

(D) To approve a resolution in the town of Livington, it must have the mayor's signature, and Resolution 27 lacks that signature. Moreover, successful resolutions must also have the approval of a majority of the council members, and Resolution 27 lacks that as well. Thus, Resolution 27 will not be approved by the town.

(E) To be awarded the Certificate of Merit at this school, you must maintain a perfect grade point average. Tomas has not maintained a perfect grade point average at this school, so he cannot receive the Certificate of Merit.

The structure of the stimulus is as follows:

> Premise: The amount of time required to process the application forms before the deadline is more time than Jones currently has available.
>
> Premise: In addition, Jones needs at least one assistant to help him with the processing of the forms, and currently no one is available to assist him nor will anyone be available prior to the deadline.
>
> Conclusion: Thus, it cannot be the case that Jones will complete the processing of the forms by the deadline.

The more complex the argument structure, the more important it is to match the premises. The more simple the argument, the more important it is to match the conclusion.

First note that the reasoning is valid. If you are uncertain, check the question stem.

Most people find that there is no clearly identifiable (or easily described) form of reasoning used to draw the conclusion, and each of the answer choices except (B) contains a conclusion with similar language to the conclusion in the stimulus. Thus, you must look elsewhere for the factor that separates the answer choices. Take a moment to consider each premise and how it relates to the conclusion: the argument is unusual in that both premises independently prove the conclusion, and this structure must be paralleled in the correct answer.

Now examine each premise:

> Premise: The amount of time required to process the application forms before the deadline is more time than Jones currently has available.

The premise indicates that Jones does not have enough time to process the application forms before the deadline, a fact that is then reflected in the language of the conclusion.

> Premise: In addition, Jones needs at least one assistant to help him with the processing of the forms, and currently no one is available to assist him nor will anyone be available prior to the deadline.

CHAPTER ELEVEN: PARALLEL REASONING QUESTIONS

If Jones needs an assistant to process the forms and there is no assistant available, then that also shows that the forms cannot be processed by the deadline. Thus, each premise alone is enough to show that the conclusion is true.

Turning to the answers, you should look for the answer that has two independent premises that both prove the conclusion. Because there are two premises, this "premise test" will take longer to apply and this is one reason we typically look at the conclusion in a Parallel Reasoning question before examining the premises.

Answer choice (A): This answer contains a conditional Repeat form, and as such, the two premises work together. Since the structure of the answer is different from that of the stimulus, the answer choice is incorrect.

Answer choice (B): Only the second premise in this answer choice proves the conclusion; the first premise is irrelevant to the conclusion. Therefore, this answer is incorrect.

As mentioned before, this answer choice is also suspect because the conclusion is different from that in the stimulus (it uses "should" instead of "cannot").

Answer choice (C): There are two excellent reasons to eliminate this answer choice:

1. The answer choice contains invalid reasoning.

2. The two premises work together and are not independent as in the stimulus.

Answer choice (D): This is the correct answer. As with the argument in the stimulus, each premise in this answer choice separately supports the conclusion.

Answer choice (E): This answer is very similar to answer choice (A), and contains a valid form of conditional reasoning based on the contrapositive. Since the two premises work together and neither proves the conclusion alone, this answer choice is incorrect.

This problem is difficult because you must go deeper in your analysis of the argument structure to find the point of separation. If you see that the reasoning is not easy to identify, and the conclusions in most of the answer choices are similar to the conclusion in the stimulus, carefully examine the premises as they are likely to be the part of the argument that will allow you to find the correct answer.

What To Do If All Else Fails

If none of the four tests of analysis reveals the answer, or if nothing stands out to you when you examine the argument, you can always fall back on describing the stimulus in abstract terms. Although less precise than the previous tests, this Test of Abstraction for the stimulus allows for one last shot at the problem.

To abstract the structure of the stimulus, create a short statement that summarizes the "action" in the argument without referring to the details of the argument. For example, if the argument states, "The bank teller had spotted a thief once before, so she was certain she could do it again," turn that argument into an abstract description such as "she had done it once, so she knew it could be done again." Then, take the abstraction and compare it to each argument. Does it match your generalized version of the stimulus? If not, the answer is incorrect. Your description should be a reasonable approximation of what occurred in the stimulus, but it does not have to be perfect.

In creating the abstraction above, the "it" in the short summary is purposely left indefinite so that when you attack the answer choices, you can plug in the "action" to the abstraction and see if it fits.

Creating an abstract description of the stimulus is just one more weapon in your arsenal. As with the previous four tests in this section, you should use it when you feel it is most applicable. Thinking on your feet is important when attacking any GMAT question, but never more so than with Parallel Reasoning questions. You have a variety of techniques at your disposal; you just need to logically think through each stimulus to decide which ones are most applicable.

Here is another example of creating an abstract statement: if the argument states, "I nearly won the marathon several times so I have a good idea of how it feels to win the race," turn that argument into an abstract description such as "I was close, so I know what it is really like."

Parallel Reasoning Question Review

Parallel Reasoning questions ask you to identify the answer choice that contains reasoning most similar in structure to the reasoning in the stimulus.

Parallel Flaw questions are Parallel Reasoning questions where the stimulus contains flawed reasoning.

The following elements do *not* need to be paralleled:

1. Topic of the stimulus

2. The order of presentation of the premises and conclusion in the stimulus

Instead, you must parallel *all* of these elements:

1. The Method of Reasoning

2. The Validity of the Argument

3. The Conclusion

4. The Premises

Because each element must be matched, you can analyze and attack the answer choices by testing whether the answer choice under consideration matches certain elements in the stimulus. If not, the answer is incorrect. The following list outlines the four tests you can use to evaluate answers, in rough order of how useful they are:

1. Match the Method of Reasoning

2. Match the Conclusion

3. Match the Premises

4. Match the Validity of the Argument

If all else fails, use the Test of Abstraction: create a short statement that summarizes the "action" in the argument. Then, take the abstraction and compare it to each argument. Does it match your generalized version of the stimulus? If not, the answer is incorrect.

Parallel Reasoning Question Problem Set

Please complete the problem set and review the answer key and explanations. *Answers on page 308*

1. Oil companies argue strenuously that no further restrictions should be placed on offshore drilling due to our country's need for energy resources, and the possible serious consequences if new energy reserves are not located and explored now. Of course, the vast sums of money the oil companies stand to reap as a result of these drilling efforts completely invalidates any such arguments.

    The questionable pattern of reasoning above is most similar to which of the following?

    (A) Everyone in town was wearing boots yesterday, and everyone in town was also carrying an umbrella. Based on this evidence it is obvious that wearing boots causes one to carry an umbrella.
    (B) The owner of a local gas station claims to be losing money, but everyone knows that the oil industry is earning record profits, which undoubtedly proves that the gas station's owner must be lying.
    (C) The mayor has argued strenuously in favor of a government housing subsidy. Since such a move would benefit some town residents more than others, this plan should not be implemented.
    (D) Although the board claims that their vote in favor of the merger is in the best interest of all shareholders, the fact that the merger will be most beneficial to the board's members themselves shows that other shareholders should object to the board's decision.
    (E) The individual who cheated on yesterday's test surely could have answered every question correctly. Mary answered every question on the test correctly, so she must have been the student who cheated.

2. Most residents of Brookville have lived in the small town for at least twenty-five years, although the majority of Brookville's residents have expressed an interest in moving away from the area. Based on this information one can safely conclude that at least one resident has lived in Brookville for at least twenty-five years but has expressed an interest in moving away from the area.

    The pattern of reasoning used to draw the conclusion above is most similar to that found in which of the following?

    (A) Some people who live in the town of Southdown are long term residents, and many enjoy living there. Based on this information one can safely conclude that some long term residents enjoy living in Southdown.
    (B) Most people who live in Stapleton are friendly, and many of Stapleton's friendliest residents have just recently moved to town. Based on this information one can safely conclude that Stapleton's least friendly resident has lived in town for the longest amount of time.
    (C) Most of the students in Beth's class studied for yesterday's test, and some of those who studied did quite well. From this information one can safely conclude that most of the students who didn't study performed poorly on the test.
    (D) Every member of the football team is required to attend this week's practice, despite the fact that some members of the team are not eligible to play in the next game. From this information one can safely conclude that at least one member will quit the team prior to the next game.
    (E) Although most people believe that fast food is unhealthy, most people eat fast food on a regular basis. Based on this information one can safely conclude that there is at least one person who eats fast food on a regular basis despite the belief that fast food is unhealthy.

Parallel Reasoning Question Problem Set Answer Key

Question #1: Parallel Flaw. The correct answer choice is (D)

In this stimulus, which contains a type of Source argument, the author points to fact that oil companies stand to gain a lot of money from unrestricted offshore drilling, and concludes based on this premise that all oil company arguments must be baseless:

Premise: The oil companies stand to gain financially if no further restrictions are imposed.

Conclusion: Their arguments in favor of such drilling are therefore *completely invalidated*.

While it is true that the financial incentives could potentially lead oil companies to be deceptive, this argument is flawed because the author leaps to the rather extreme and unwarranted conclusion that such arguments are *completely invalidated* by the presence of a strong financial incentive.

The stimulus is followed by a Parallel Flaw question, which means that we need to find the answer choice which employs the same flawed reasoning. The correct answer in this case will likely reflect a similarly flawed assertion, that any conflicting incentives take away all credibility from an argument or decision.

Answer choice (A): The causal flaw represented here is different from that reflected in the stimulus. In this answer choice, the author mistakenly presumes a causal relationship where only a correlation has been shown. Clearly there is probably a third variable (such as the weather) that might cause one both to wear boots and to carry an umbrella.

Answer choice (B): Although this answer also deals with the oil industry, this choice reflects a flaw that is different from that found in the stimulus. The mistake here is in the presumption that a successful industry must mean success for everyone involved with that industry. What is true of the whole, in this case, is not necessarily true of each component part. Note also that answers that deal with the same topic as the stimulus tend to be incorrect.

Answer choice (C): The author of this answer asserts that a subsidy which benefits some more than others is not a good idea. The implication of this questionable argument is that such a subsidy would be justified only in cases where everyone benefits exactly equally. While this argument is indeed questionable, it does not reflect the same flaw as that found in the stimulus, so this answer choice should be eliminated.

Answer choice (D): This is the correct answer choice, displaying a similarly flawed line of reasoning based on a Source argument. The board members may benefit more than other shareholders from the merger approval, and that may provide some reason to scrutinize the board's decision, but it still does not prove that the decision lacks all reasonable basis or should be rejected outright.

Answer choice (E): This choice is incorrect because the flaw represented here is the classic conditional flaw of Mistaken Reversal: Just because the cheater would have known all the answers, this obviously doesn't mean that those who know all the answers are necessarily cheaters.

Parallel Reasoning Question Problem Set Answer Key

Question #2: Parallel Reasoning. The correct answer choice is (E)

This stimulus applies a rather advanced concept involving numbers and percentages. In any given population, two majorities would result in some point of overlap. For example, if in a town of 100 residents the majority (at least 51) owned a dog, and the majority (at least 51) owned a cat, this would require at least one point of overlap: at least one resident of the town would have to own both a cat and a dog. If you try to come up with a scenario that does not reflect this overlap, you will see that there is no way to avoid it.

In this case, the discussion involves the small town of Brookville, in which the majority are long-term residents (of at least 25 years), and the majority have expressed an interest in moving. Based on this information, the author draws the conclusion that at least one long-term resident has expressed in interest in leaving town. The valid reasoning can be broken down as follows:

Premise: *Most* (over 50%) town residents have lived in Brookville for at least 25 years.

Premise: *Most* (over 50%) town resident have expressed an interest in leaving town.

Conclusion: *At least one* resident has both attributes (that is, there is at least one long-term resident who has expressed an interest in leaving town.

Since the question is followed by a Parallel Reasoning question stem, the correct answer choice will likely apply this same overlapping-majority principle, and use a similar "most...most...at least one" construction for the two premises and conclusion.

Answer choice (A): Unlike the two overlapping majorities discussed in the stimulus, this choice provides limited information with vague terms such as "some" and "many." Since the conclusion drawn in this choice is not even logically valid, it cannot parallel the valid reasoning displayed in the stimulus.

Answer choice (B): This answer choice starts out in the right direction, with the word "most," but quickly goes off track with the vague reference to "many" of the town's friendliest residents, followed by an invalid conclusion. "Many," while possibly similar to "most," does not have to be the same as "most."

Answer choice (C): This choice may look tempting at first glance, based on the presence of two "mosts," but, one of the "mosts" appears in a premise and the other "most" appears in the conclusion. This construction is different from the stimulus where both "mosts" appeared in premises and the conclusion used "at least some." Thus, this answer fails to Match the Conclusions and is incorrect.

Answer choice (D): This incorrect answer choice fails on two counts: it lacks the concept of the overlapping majority (rather than "most…most," we see "most…some"), and the conclusion drawn is clearly not justified by the premises presented.

Parallel Reasoning Question Problem Set Answer Key

Answer choice (E): This is the correct answer choice; the valid parallel reasoning found in this answer choice deals with the majority of the population who believes fast food to be unhealthy, and the majority who eats it on a regular basis. Based on this overlapping majority, the author validly concludes that there must be at least one person who both subscribes to the popular belief that fast food is unhealthy, and eats fast food on a regular basis regardless.

The familiar construction of this argument can be broken down simply as follows:

> Premise: *Most* people believe that fast food is unhealthy.
>
> Premise: *Most* people eat fast food on a regular basis.
>
> Conclusion: *At least one* person both believes fast food is unhealthy and consumes it regularly.

This choice might have been quickly located by matching the premises: if you happened to notice that this was the only choice that provided the "most...most" construction, you were probably able to answer this question more quickly than expected.

Chapter Twelve:
Numbers and Percentages

Chapter Twelve: Numbers and Percentages

Numbers and Percentages 313

Must Be True Questions and Numbers and Percentages 319

Markets and Market Share 322

Numbers and Percentages Review 323

Numbers and Percentages Practice Drill 325

Numbers and Percentages Problem Set 329

Numbers and Percentages

Like Cause and Effect Reasoning, the concept of Numbers and Percentages is featured in many GMAT stimuli. Although most people are comfortable working with numbers or percentages because they come up so frequently in daily life (for example in balancing a checking account, dividing a bar tab, or adding up a grocery bill), the makers of the GMAT often prey upon several widely-held misconceptions:

> Misconception #1: Increasing percentages automatically lead to increasing numbers.

When identifying problems that contain numbers or percentages as part of the reasoning, we use a "#%" notation, as in "Must-#%."

Most people assume that if a percentage becomes larger, the number that corresponds to that percentage must also get larger. This is not necessarily true because the overall size of the group under discussion could get smaller. For example, consider the following argument: "Auto manufacturer X increased their United States market share from 10% last year to 25% this year. Therefore, Company X sold more cars in the United States this year than last." This is true if the size of the U.S. car market stayed the same or became larger. But if the size of the U.S. car market decreased by enough, the argument would not be valid, as in the following example:

	Last Year	This Year
Total number of cars sold in the United States	1000	200
X's market share	10%	25%
X's total car sales in the United States	100	50

Of course, if the overall total remains constant, an increasing percentage does translate into a larger number. But on the GMAT the size of the total is usually not given.

Thus, even though auto manufacturer X's market share increased to 25%, because the size of the entire market decreased significantly, X actually sold fewer cars in the United States.

If the percentage increases but the corresponding number decreases, then the overall total must have decreased.

CHAPTER TWELVE: NUMBERS AND PERCENTAGES

If the percentage decreases but the corresponding number increases, then the overall total must have increased.

Misconception #2: Decreasing percentages automatically lead to decreasing numbers.

This misconception is the opposite of Misconception #1. Just because a percentage decreases does not necessarily mean that the corresponding number must become smaller. Reversing the years in the previous example proves this point.

Misconception #3: Increasing numbers automatically lead to increasing percentages.

If the number increases but the corresponding percentage decreases, then the overall total must have increased.

Just as increasing percentages do not automatically translate into increasing numbers, the reverse is also true. Consider the following example: "The number of bicycle-related accidents rose dramatically from last month to this month. Therefore, bicycle-related accidents must make up a greater percentage of all road accidents this month." This conclusion can be true, but it does not have to be true, as shown by the following example:

	Last Month	This Month
Number of bicycle-related accidents	10	30
Total number of road accidents	100	600
Percentage of total accidents that are bicycle-related	10%	5%

In each of the first four misconceptions the makers of the test attempt to lure you into making an assumption about the size of the overall total.

Thus, even though the number of bicycle-related accidents tripled, the percentage of total road accidents that were bicycle-related dropped because the *total number* of road accidents rose so dramatically.

Misconception #4: Decreasing numbers automatically lead to decreasing percentages.

If the number decreases but the corresponding percentage increases, then the overall total must have decreased.

This misconception is the opposite of Misconception #3. Just because a number decreases does not necessarily mean that the corresponding percentage must become smaller. Reversing the months in the previous example proves this point.

Misconception #5: Large numbers automatically mean large percentages, and small numbers automatically mean small percentages.

In 2003, Porsche sold just over 18,000 cars in the United States. While 18,000 is certainly a large number, it represented only about 1/5 of 1% of total U.S. car sales in 2003. Remember, the size of a number does not reveal anything about the percentage that number represents unless you know something about the size of the overall total that number is drawn from.

Misconception #6: Large percentages automatically mean large numbers, and small percentages automatically mean small numbers.

This misconception is the reverse of Misconception #5. A figure such as 90% sounds impressively large, but if you have 90% of $5, that really isn't too impressive, is it?

Numerical situations normally hinge on three elements: an overall total, a number within that total, and a percentage within the total. GMAT problems will often give you one of the elements, but without at least two elements present, you cannot make a definitive judgment about what is occurring with another element. When you are given just percentage information, you cannot make a judgment about numbers. Likewise, when you are given just numerical information you cannot make a judgment about percentages.

In a moment, we will explore this idea by examining several GMAT questions. But first, you must be able to recognize number and percentage ideas when they appear on the GMAT:

Words used to introduce numerical ideas:

- Amount
- Quantity
- Sum
- Total
- Count
- Tally

Knowledge of a percentage is insufficient to allow you to make a determination about the size of the number because the exact size of the overall total is unknown, and changes in the overall total will directly affect the internal numbers and percentages.

CHAPTER TWELVE: NUMBERS AND PERCENTAGES   315

The makers of the GMAT know that numbers and percentages, like science-oriented topics, tend to confuse and frustrate test takers. By knowing the misconceptions that the test makers prey upon, you can turn these questions into quick and easy triumphs.

Words used to introduce percentage ideas:

    Percent
    Proportion
    Fraction
    Ratio
    Incidence
    Likelihood
    Probability
    Segment
    Share

Three words on the percentage list—"incidence," "likelihood," and "probability"—bear further discussion. Each of these words relates to the chances that an event will occur, and when the GMAT makers uses phrases such as "more likely" or "less likely" they are telling you that the percentage chances are greater than 50% or less than 50%, respectively. In fact, a wide variety of phrases can be used to introduce percentage ideas, including such disparate phrases as "more prone to" or "occurs with a high frequency."

With these indicators in mind, please take a moment to complete the following question:

1. An automobile dealership's two car lots have produced remarkably consistent sales figures over the last four years: in each of those years, the new car lot has contributed 25 percent of dollar sales and 50 percent of profits, and the used car lot has accounted for the balance.

   Which of the following regarding the past four years is most strongly supported by the statements above?

   (A) The used car lot produced lower profits per dollar of sales than the new car lot produced.
   (B) There is greater competition in the new car market than there is in the used car market.
   (C) The total profits for the dealership have remained constant for the past four years.
   (D) There is a greater selection of used cars than there is of new cars.
   (E) Luxury automobiles accounted for a higher percentage of new car sales than of used car sales.

We are given a comparison in this stimulus between two car lots at an automobile dealership and their respective percentage contributions to total sales and profitability in each of the last four years:

	Sales (% of Total)	Profits (% of Total)
New Car Lot	25%	50%
Used Car Lot	75%	50%

Since the used car lot has contributed ¾ of the total dollar sales, and the new car lot has contributed only ¼ of the total dollar sales, one might expect the used car to be substantially more profitable. However, we are told that both car lots contributed equally percentage-wise to the overall profits of the dealership. Let's consider what that means by using some hypothetical numbers. If we assume the total dollar sales for the dealership was $4,000,000 for the previous year, then the new car lot produced $1,000,000 in sales and the used car lot produced $3,000,000 in sales:

	Sales ($)	Profits (% of Total)
New Car Lot	1 mil	50%
Used Car Lot	3 mil	50%

Now, let's say that $4,000,000 in total sales yielded a profit of $1,000,000. Since both car lots accounted for 50% of the profits, then both lots produced $500,000 in total profits:

	Sales ($)	Profits ($)
New Car Lot	1 mil	500K
Used Car Lot	3 mil	500K

As we look at these numbers it becomes immediately clear that the new car lot was significantly more profitable for every dollar in sales than the used car was. In fact, the used car lot had to sell three times as much as the new lot dollar-wise to produce the same amount of profit. And this statistic is exactly what the correct answer choice states.

CHAPTER TWELVE: NUMBERS AND PERCENTAGES

Note that this stimulus is only about percentages of dollar sales and profits for both lots, and never references numbers or "amount" of sales/profit. Be wary of answer choices that make factual claims about numbers, as they likely go beyond the information provided.

Answer choice (A): This is the correct answer. As mentioned above, for every dollar in sales, the used car lot was much less profitable than was the new car lot.

Answer choice (B): This goes beyond the facts in the stimulus, as the amount of competition between new and used car markets is never mentioned.

Answer choice (C): This stimulus only tells us that the sales figure *percentages* have stayed consistent over the past four years. That does not mean that the numerical amount of either total sales or total profit has stayed constant. Again, be wary of answer choices that attempt to derive numerical truths from percentage information, or vice versa.

Answer choice (D): This answer choice, like (B), goes beyond the scope of the stimulus and introduces information that cannot be know from the facts provided. There is never any mention of the amount of selection in either the used or new car markets.

Answer choice (E): There is never any reference to "luxury automobiles" in the stimulus, nor to what percentage they might have accounted for in either lot's sales, so this answer is incorrect.

Must Be True Questions and Numbers and Percentages

Because the misconceptions discussed earlier have a predictable effect when you try to make inferences, you can use the following general rules for Must Be True questions:

1. If the stimulus contains percentage or proportion information only, avoid answers that contain hard numbers.

    Example Stimulus Sentence:

    > The car market share of Company X declined this year.

    Avoid answers which say:

    > Company X sold a smaller number of cars this year.

    > Company X sold a greater amount of cars this year.

2. If the stimulus contains only numerical information, avoid answers that contain percentage or proportion information.

    Example Stimulus Sentence:

    > Company Y sold fewer computers this year.

    Avoid answers which say:

    > Company Y now has a lower share of the computer market.

    > Company Y now possesses a greater proportion of the computer market.

3. If the stimulus contains both percentage and numerical information, any answer choice that contains numbers, percentages, or both *may* be true.

The rules to the left address the classic combination of a stimulus with numbers and percentages information and a Must Be True question.

Please keep in mind that these rules are very general. You must read the stimulus closely and carefully to determine exactly what information is present because the makers of the GMAT are experts at camouflaging or obscuring important information in order to test your ability to understand complex argumentation.

CHAPTER TWELVE: NUMBERS AND PERCENTAGES

Please take a moment to complete the following question:

2. The cost of manufacturing microchips in Country K is 15 percent greater than the cost of manufacturing the same microchips in Country P. Even after customs taxes and delivery fees are considered, it is still cheaper for Country K to import microchips from Country P than to have the microchips manufactured domestically.

The claims above, if true, most strongly support which of the following conclusions?

(A) Customs taxes are less in Country K than they are in Country P.
(B) It takes 15 percent more time to manufacture a microchip in Country K than it does in Country P.
(C) The taxes and fees associated with importing microchips from Country P to Country K are less than 15 percent of the cost of manufacturing those microchips in Country K.
(D) Importing microchips from Country P will reduce employment opportunities in manufacturing by 15 percent in Country K.
(E) Manufacturing costs are the primary consideration for countries when considering whether to import foreign goods.

This stimulus contains a fairly straightforward fact set, as follows:

Fact 1: It is 15% more expensive to manufacture microchips in Country K than it is to manufacture them in Country P.

Fact 2: Despite the fees involved, it is still cheaper for Country K to import the microchips from Country P than to manufacture them domestically.

When we consider these two facts together, it must be the case that the customs taxes and the delivery fees associated with importing the microchips from Country P are still less than the additional 15% that it costs Country K to manufacture the chips itself.

Consider these facts with some hypothetical numbers:

> Fact 1: It costs $115 for Country K to manufacture a microchip; it costs $100 for Country P to manufacture that same microchip.
>
> Fact 2: It is still cheaper per microchip for Country K to import them from Country P than to simply make the microchips domestically.

So, following the logic of these two facts, the importation costs themselves must be less than $15/chip (less than the 15% difference in the manufacturing costs).

Answer choice (A): There is no information given in the stimulus that would allow us to accurately know or compare the customs taxes in the two countries.

Answer choice (B): The stimulus is only about a cost comparison, so an answer choice that attempts to compare manufacturing *time* goes beyond the information provided.

Answer choice (C): This is the correct answer. As demonstrated previously, the importation taxes and fees must be less than the additional 15% cost of manufacturing the chips in Country K as opposed to Country P. Otherwise it would not be cheaper to import them than it is for Country K to make them domestically.

Answer choice (D): Not only can we not conclude anything about this practice's effects on employment in either country, but to presume that there will be an exact 15% decline in manufacturing-industry employment is far too presumptuous given the limited information in the stimulus.

Answer choice (E): Once again, we cannot know how various countries prioritize certain factors (costs or otherwise) when considering whether to import foreign goods. This answer choice goes well beyond the facts provided.

Markets and Market Share

Entire books have been written about market operations, so a lengthy discussion of this topic is beyond the scope of this book.

The makers of the GMAT expect you to understand the operation of markets and the concept of market share. Market operation includes supply and demand, production, pricing, and profit. None of these concepts should be unfamiliar to you as they are a routine part of business.

Market share is simply the portion of a market that a company controls. The market share can be measured either in terms of revenues (sales) or units sold. For example:

>Heinz has a 60% market share of the $500 million ketchup market.

>Jif brand peanut butter sold 80 million units last year, a 30% market share.

Like all numbers and percentages problems, market share is a comparative term, as opposed to an absolute term. Thus, many market share questions hinge on one of the Misconceptions discussed in this chapter.

Because market share is a numbers and percentages concept, market share can change when factors in the market change. For example, a company can gain market share (percentage) if the market shrinks and they maintain a constant size, or if they grow in an unchanging market. However, a company losing market share does not mean that their sales decreased, only that they became a smaller entity in the market relative to the whole (for example, the market grew and they stayed the same size). Similarly, a company could lose sales and still gain market share if the overall market became smaller.

Regardless of the size of a market and even though the total amount of the market can shift, the total market share must always add up to 100%.

Numbers and Percentages Review

The makers of the GMAT often prey upon several widely-held misconceptions:

> Misconception #1: Increasing percentages automatically lead to increasing numbers.
>
> Misconception #2: Decreasing percentages automatically lead to decreasing numbers.
>
> Misconception #3: Increasing numbers automatically lead to increasing percentages.
>
> Misconception #4: Decreasing numbers automatically lead to decreasing percentages.
>
> Misconception #5: Large numbers automatically mean large percentages, and small numbers automatically mean small percentages.
>
> Misconception #6: Large percentages automatically mean large numbers, and small percentages automatically mean small numbers.

Words that introduce numerical ideas:

> Amount
> Quantity
> Sum
> Total
> Count
> Tally

Words that introduce percentage ideas:

> Percent
> Proportion
> Fraction
> Ratio
> Incidence
> Likelihood
> Probability
> Segment
> Share

Use the following general rules for Must Be True questions:

1. If the stimulus contains percentage or proportion information only, avoid answers that contain hard numbers.

2. If the stimulus contains only numerical information, avoid answers that contain percentage or proportion information.

3. If the stimulus contains both percentage and numerical information, any answer choice that contains numbers, percentages, or both *may* be true.

Use the following general rules for Weaken and Strengthen questions:

To weaken or strengthen an argument containing numbers and percentages, look carefully for information about the total amount(s)—does the argument make an assumption based on one of the misconceptions discussed earlier?

Market share is simply the portion of a market that a company controls. Market share can be measured either in terms of revenues (sales) or units sold. Regardless of the size of a market, total market share must always add up to 100%.

Numbers and Percentages Practice Drill

The scenarios below are each followed by three statements, any or all of which may be possible. After considering the limited information presented in each case, select *all* statements that apply. *Answers on page 327*

1. The Mercantile Corporation increased its national market share last year by 5% compared to its market share two years ago.

   Which of the following could be true of the overall unit sales of the Mercantile Corporation? Select all that apply.

   I. Mercantile Corporation sold fewer units last year than it had sold the prior year.
   II. Mercantile Corporation sold the same number of units each of the last two years.
   III. Mercantile Corporation sold more units last year than it had sold the prior year.

2. In today's mayoral election, West received 1500 votes, compared with the 1000 votes that he had received in last year's election.

   Which of the following could be true of the percentage of the vote West won in today's election compared to the percentage he won in the last election? Select all that apply.

   I. West received a greater percentage of the vote today than in the last election.
   II. West received a smaller percentage of the vote today than in the last election.
   III. West received the same percentage of the vote today as in the last election.

3. Halstead's and McGrady's are competing furniture stores, each of which carries exactly one type of couch. Next week Halstead's will have its annual holiday sale, during which every piece of furniture in the store is to be marked down by 60%. McGrady's has just announced a competing sale, in which various products will be marked down by 30%.

   Which of the following could be true of Halstead's couch price compared with McGrady's during next week's sale? Select all that apply.

   I. A couch purchased at Halstead's will cost less than a couch at McGrady's.
   II. A couch purchased at Halstead's will cost more than a couch at McGrady's.
   III. A couch purchased at Halstead's will cost the same as a couch at McGrady's.

Numbers and Percentages Practice Drill

4. In response to brisk sales, a certain car dealership increased the price of the Cheetah, its best-selling sport utility vehicle, by 25% on January 1. In February, after no other price changes had been implemented, the dealership held a special sale during which the price of every car was marked down by 20%.

   Which of the following could be true of the price of the Cheetah during the February sale compared with the price on December 31 (just prior to the January 1 price change)?

   I. The price of the Cheetah was higher during the sale than it had been on December 31.
   II. The price of the Cheetah was lower during the sale than it had been on December 31.
   III. The price of the Cheetah was the same during the sale as it had been on December 31.

5. Last year, Davis, Acme Company's top salesperson, was responsible for 25% of Acme's total sales. This year Davis is credited with 35% of Acme's total sales, which have decreased overall compared to last year's total sales.

   Which of the following could be true of Davis' sales this year as compared with Davis' sales from last year? Select all that apply.

   I. Davis' total sales were greater this year.
   II. Davis' total sales were greater last year.
   III. Davis' total sales were the same over the last two years.

Numbers and Percentages Practice Drill Answer Key

1. All three scenarios listed are plausible. The only information provided is a comparison of the corporation's market share from one year to the next. Without further information regarding either the size of the overall market or Mercantile's unit sales, any of the scenarios presented are plausible.

    Statement I Hypothetical:
    Two years ago Mercantile Corporation had a 30% market share, having sold 30,000 out of a total 100,000 units sold by all producers nationally. Last year Mercantile had a 35% market share, having sold 3,500 out of a total of only 10,000 units sold by all producers nationally. In this scenario, thanks to a significant decrease in the overall market, the Mercantile Corporation's higher market share represented lower unit sales.

    Statement II Hypothetical:
    Two years ago Mercantile Corporation had a 20% market share, having sold 20,000 of 100,000 units sold by all producers nationally. Last year, Mercantile increased its market share to 25%, having sold 20,000 of 80,000 units sold by all producers nationally.

    Statement III Hypothetical:
    If the total number of units sold by all producers nationally remained constant over the past two years, e.g., the 5% increase in market share would clearly translate to a greater number of unit sales.

2. The information provided is limited to the number of votes West received. Without further information about either the total number of residents who voted, or alternatively the number of votes received by the other candidates, I, II and III are all possible.

    Statement I Hypothetical:
    If the same number of residents voted in the two elections, then today's total of 1500 would, of course, represent a higher percentage of the total vote for West.

    Statement II Hypothetical:
    Today, West received 1500 out of 15000 total votes, representing 10% of all votes cast. In last years election, he received 1000 out of 2000 total votes cast, representing 50% of all votes cast.

    Statement III Hypothetical:
    Today, West received 1500 out of 15000 total votes, representing 10% of all votes cast. In last year's election, West received 1000 out of 10000 total votes, requiring fewer votes to earn 10% of all votes cast.

CHAPTER TWELVE: NUMBERS AND PERCENTAGES

Numbers and Percentages Practice Drill Answer Key

3. Once again, of course, with such limited information, all things are possible. As we see in the real world, an impressive sounding sale doesn't always provide the best deal. Halstead's sale certainly sounds impressive; if the two stores normally charge the same prices, then of course Halstead's couch price will be lower during the sale. But if Halstead's prices generally start out significantly higher, then the 60% sale might result in a price that is equal to, or possibly even greater than, the price of McGrady's couch at 30% off.

4. Statement III presents the only plausible scenario given the information provided. Regardless of the price on December 31, a 25% increase followed by a 20% decrease has no net effect—the price charged for the Cheetah during the sale will be the same as the price charged on December 31. For example, if the Cheetah was $10,000 on December 31st, the 25% price increased raised the price to $12,500. The 20% decrease then lowered the price back to $10,000, a net change of $0 after all price changes.

5. Without knowing more about the decrease in total sales from last year to this year, once again all scenarios listed are plausible.

Numbers and Percentages Problem Set

Please complete the problem set and review the answer key and explanations. *Answers on page 330*

1. Student: The majority of the 50 students in our class answered at least 80% of the questions correctly on last year's Algebra I final exam. If these final exam scores do accurately measure a student's level of understanding, Marc must have learned less about algebra last year than most other students in our class, because he answered only 75% of the questions correctly on last year's Algebra I final exam.

   Which of the following, if true, most seriously weakens the student's argument?

   (A) Seven students answered less than 75% of the questions correctly on the final exam in Algebra I last year.
   (B) Marc is one of four students in the class who did not take an introductory-level algebra course offered by the school two years ago.
   (C) Marc is one of three students who answered exactly 75% of the questions correctly on the final exam in Algebra I last year.
   (D) The teacher estimated that last year's ninth-grade Algebra I final exam was roughly twice as difficult as this year's Algebra I final exam.
   (E) Only three students spent less time than Marc spent answering the questions on last year's Algebra I final exam.

2. Constructing new office buildings in downtown Carterville's financial district is notoriously difficult due to the extremely limited amount of available construction space. The number of new businesses requiring office space in Carterville is expected to increase by nearly 30 percent over the next five years. In response to this projected growth, Carterville will expand its financial district by an additional four percent during this time period. City officials are confident that this increase in available space will be sufficient to guarantee that the current space availability problems do not worsen.

   Which of the following, if true, provides the most support for the city officials' beliefs?

   (A) The additional four percent of space for the financial district is to come from adjacent land currently designated as a public park.
   (B) Officials plan to closely regulate new construction to ensure that all structures meet city building ordinances.
   (C) Some of the proposed construction will take several years to complete.
   (D) Most of the new businesses requiring office space will be headquarted outside of the financial district, where space for new construction is much more plentiful.
   (E) The new businesses moving to Carterville will provide significant tax revenue for the city.

Numbers and Percentages Problem Set Answer Key

Question #1: Weaken—#% The correct answer choice is (B)

The student argues that since more than half of the students in the class scored an 80% or better on the Algebra exam, and since Marc only scored a 75%, then Marc must have "learned less" about Algebra than most of the other students in the class. Unfortunately for the student, this requires a dangerous assumption: because Marc ended the year slightly behind most other students in terms of percentage score (75% to 80%), he must have made less progress during the year than most other students. In other words, the phrase "learned less" implies that someone makes less progress over time, and that may not necessarily be the case here.

Let's consider an example:

> Say you were to ask five people to train for a one-mile race for two months. At the end of those two months, you time them as they run the mile and you record their results. Runners 1, 2, 3, and 4 each finish in exactly 6 minutes. Runner 5, however, takes 10 minutes to complete the race. Would it be fair to conclude that Runner 5 was the least improved runner over the course of those two months? Not necessarily. What if Runners 1-4 could already run a mile in 7 minutes prior to any training, whereas Runner 5 needed 30 minutes to run a mile two months ago? Now it seems clear that, while Runner 5 can still be described as the slowest runner in the group, saying that he or she is the *least improved* would be inaccurate. So the key when trying to gauge progress is to have a starting point to reference so you can truly measure how far someone has come.

And the same is true of Marc in the stimulus. Certainly he was outscored on the exam by most of the students, but does that mean he learned less over the course of the year? We cannot conclude that unless we know where he started relative to everyone else. So to weaken this student's claim that Marc learned less, we need an answer choice that suggests he made more progress (started further back) than the majority of his classmates.

Answer choice (A): This answer choice places Marc fairly low in the group of 50 students (only 7 of 50 scored worse than him), but this still does not impact the idea of how much he learned. Hence, this answer does not weaken the argument.

Answer choice (B): This is the correct answer. If Marc and three other students did not take the introductory-level Algebra course, and the other 46 students all did, then it seems likely that Marc would have started the Algebra I class knowing less about the subject than his classmates. If that is the case then his final score of 75% could certainly represent much more learned (greater progress) over the course of the year than his classmates who scored 80% or better.

Numbers and Percentages Problem Set Answer Key

Again, numbers can often make these ideas easier to grasp. Say that Marc, having missed the introductory course, began the year only knowing 10% about Algebra I and finished with a 75% (65% improvement). Most of his classmates however, having taken the introductory course, started the year at 50%. Even if they all finished at 90%, that's still only a 40% improvement, which pales in comparison to Marc's 65% increase. Clearly, even though Marc may not have finished in the top-half of his class, he still could have *learned* more than those who outscored him.

Answer choice (C): This answer choice, like (A), only addresses where Marc finished relative to some of his classmates. Since we need an answer choice related to Marc's progress over the course of the year, this answer cannot be correct.

Answer choice (D): The overall difficulty of the exam relative to other exams is completely irrelevant to Marc performance or his progress relative to his classmates.

Answer choice (E): The amount of time that Marc (or anyone else) spent answering questions is also irrelevant to how much he ultimately learned during the course relative to his classmates, so this answer is incorrect.

Numbers and Percentages Problem Set Answer Key

Question #2: Strengthen—#% The correct answer choice is (D)

This stimulus begins with some factual information about Carterville and finishes with a rather unexpected conclusion from the city officials. First, we are told that the number of new business moving to Carterville and requiring office space is expected to increase by nearly 30% over the next five years. Then we are told that in response to this influx of business, Carterville plans to expand its notoriously crowded financial district by only an additional four percent. While this does not seem as though it would be nearly enough expansion to accommodate the large number of new business that will be arriving in Carterville, city officials are confident that this increase will be sufficient to prevent the current space availability issues from getting worse.

The apparent problem here comes from the discrepancy in the numbers: a 30% increase in businesses requiring new office space, and only a 4% expansion of an already overcrowded area. Of course, as we will see in the correct answer, the assumption most people make is that the new businesses will be located in the financial district itself. If instead they are planning to build elsewhere, then it seems likely that the city officials are correct and the 4% financial district expansion could prove to be sufficient.

Answer choice (A): It is irrelevant to the argument *where* the new office space will come from; we need an answer choice that shows that somehow the businesses planning to move to Carterville will not put a further strain on the space limitations in the financial district.

Answer choice (B): Even if the new construction is closely regulated and meets city building ordinances, this answer does not provide any reason why the new construction presumably needed to accommodate the new businesses will not make the current space availability problems worse.

Answer choice (C): This answer choice likely weakens the city officials' argument, since the longer the new construction takes, the more likely it will be that the current space availability worsen.

Answer choice (D): This is the correct answer. If the majority of new businesses coming to Carterville do not plan to build or be headquartered in the financial district, but instead will be located where construction space is plentiful, then there is no reason to think they will put a further strain on the financial district's limited space. This answer choice strongly supports the city officials' belief that the influx of new business can be managed by only a four percent expansion of the financial district.

Answer choice (E): While this answer certainly explains why/how Carterville will benefit from the new businesses, it does not address the new businesses' construction needs and therefore has no effect on the argument in the stimulus.

Chapter Thirteen: Evaluate the Argument, Cannot Be True, and Principle Questions

Chapter Thirteen: Evaluate the Argument, Cannot Be True, and Principle Questions

Evaluate the Argument Questions	335
The Variance Test™	337
Evaluate the Argument Question Type Review	342
Cannot Be True Questions	343
Two Notable Stimulus Scenarios	344
Cannot Be True Question Review	345
Principle Questions	347
Principle Question Review	349
Final Note	349

Evaluate the Argument Questions

Evaluate the Argument questions ask you to consider the question, statistic, or piece of information that would best help determine the logical validity of the argument presented in the stimulus. In other words, you must select the answer choice that decides whether the argument is good or bad.

To better understand this question type, imagine that you are examining an argument and you have to ask one question that—depending on the answer to the question—will reveal whether the argument is strong or weak. By this definition, there must be a flaw in each argument, and your question, if posed correctly, can reveal that flaw or eliminate the flaw. Please note that you are not being asked to prove with finality whether the argument is good or bad—rather, you must simply ask the question that will best help analyze the validity of the argument. For this reason, Evaluate the Argument questions can be seen as a combination of a Strengthen question and a Weaken question: if you ask the best question, depending on the answer to the question the argument could be seen as strong or weak.

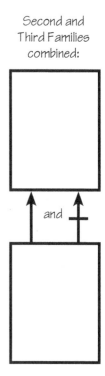

Second and Third Families combined:

As mentioned in Chapter Three, this unusual question type is the only question that does not fall into one of the three question families. Evaluate the Argument questions are actually a combination of the Second and Third Families, and as such you should keep the following considerations in mind:

1. In all Second and Third Family questions the information in the stimulus is suspect, so you should search for the reasoning error present.

2. The answer choices are accepted as given, even if they include "new" information. Your task is to determine which answer choice best helps determine the validity of the argument.

Evaluate the Argument question stems almost always use the word "evaluate" or a synonym such as "judge" or "assess," but the intent is always identical: the question stem asks you to identify the piece of information that would be most helpful in assessing the argument.

Question stem examples:

"The answer to which of the following questions would contribute most to an evaluation of the argument?"

"Clarification of which of the following issues would be most important to an evaluation of the scientists' position?"

"Which of the following would be most important to know in evaluating the hypothesis in the passage?"

"Which of the following would it be most relevant to investigate in evaluating the conclusion of the argument?"

Evaluate the Argument questions have begun to appear more frequently on the GMAT, and the uniqueness of the question type forces students to take a moment to adjust when they do appear. Some question types, such as Must Be True and Weaken, recur so frequently that students become used to seeing them and are comfortable with the process of selecting the correct answer. When a question type appears rarely, test-takers are often thrown off-balance and lose time and energy reacting to the question. The makers of the GMAT are well aware of this, and this is the reason they intersperse different question types in each section (again, imagine how much easier the GMAT would be if the Verbal section was composed of 25 Must Be True questions). One reason we study each type of question is to help you become as comfortable as possible with the questions you will encounter on the test, making your reaction time as fast as possible.

The Variance Test™

Solving Evaluate questions can be difficult. The nature of the answer choices allow for separate interpretations, and deciding on a single answer can be challenging. In order to determine the correct answer choice on an Evaluate the Argument question, apply the Variance Test™.

The Variance Test consists of supplying two polar opposite responses to the question posed *in the answer choice* and then analyzing how the varying responses affect the conclusion in the stimulus. If different responses produce different effects on the conclusion, then the answer choice is correct. If different responses do not produce different effects, then the answer choice is incorrect. For example, if an Evaluate the Argument answer choice states "What is the percentage of people who live near a nuclear plant?" look to test the two most extreme possibilities: first test the response "0%" for its effect on the conclusion and then test the response "100%" for its effect on the conclusion. If the answer choice is correct, one of the percentages should strengthen the argument and one of the percentages should weaken the argument. If the answer choice is incorrect, neither response will have an effect on the argument.

Of course, the answer choice does not have to be about percentages for the technique to work; the Variance Test will work regardless of the nature of the answer choice.

Here are some more example answer choices and Variance Test responses:

> If an answer choice asks "Is the pattern permanent?" first test "Yes" as a response and then test "No" as a response (remember, you *must* test opposite answers). If the answer choice is correct, one response should strengthen the argument and one response should weaken the argument. If the answer choice is incorrect, neither response will have an effect on the argument.

> If an answer choice asks "Are corporate or environmental interests more important?" first test "Corporate interests are more important" as a response and then test "Environmental interests are more important" as a response. If the answer choice is correct, one response should strengthen the argument and one response should weaken the argument. If the answer choice is incorrect, neither response will have an effect on the argument.

Now we will use a question to more fully explore how the question type works and how the correct answer can be determined by applying the Variance Test.

The Variance Test is a very powerful tool for attacking Evaluate the Argument questions. Because of the unique structure of Evaluate questions, the Variance Test can only be used with these questions and the test does not apply to any other question type.

After you have narrowed your answer choices to the Contenders, or to the one answer choice you believe is correct, then apply the Variance Test. Do not apply the Test to all five answers!

Please take a moment to complete the following question:

1. Editorial: This year, the Marionville school board received five textbook proposals submitted by local book publishers. In each instance, the school rejected the proposal on the grounds that the curriculum covered within the textbooks was inadequate, controversial or, surprisingly, too comprehensive. Consequently, because the school board must accept at least one textbook proposal in order to have materials for this upcoming year, the school board has acted negligently in failing to accept at least one of the proposals.

   The answer to which one of the following questions would be most useful in evaluating the truth of the conclusion in the editorial?

   (A) How many of the proposals that were rejected by the school board were rejected on the basis that the curriculum was too comprehensive?
   (B) What was the opinion of the parents' association regarding the five textbook proposals?
   (C) Did any non-local textbook publishers submit a textbook proposal to the Marionville school board?
   (D) Could the school board have accepted multiple proposals that would have, in combination, have provided the appropriate materials?
   (E) In previous years, has the Marionville school board rejected all the textbook proposals submitted by book publishers?

As with all questions, you must identify the structure of the argument.

> Premise: This year, the Marionville school board received five textbook proposals submitted by local book publishers.
>
> Premise: In each instance, the school rejected the proposal on the grounds that the curriculum covered within the textbooks was inadequate, controversial or, surprisingly, too comprehensive.
>
> Premise: because the school board must accept at least one textbook proposal in order to have materials for this upcoming year,
>
> Conclusion: Consequently...the school board has acted negligently in failing to accept at least one of the proposals.

Evaluate the Argument stimuli always contain a conclusion.

The conclusion states that the school board has acted negligently in failing to accept at least one of the proposals. In the question stem, we are asked to evaluate the truth of this conclusion. Each answer choice is then posed in the form of a question. The answer choice that is correct will contain the question that, when answered, will reveal whether the conclusion is strong or weak.

In order to understand the application of the Variance Test, we will look at each answer choice in succession and thus we will not perform an initial analysis of the argument (on the GMAT we would analyze the stimulus closely). Also note that on the test we would *not* apply the Variance Test to each answer choice, only to the Contenders. For teaching purposes, we will apply the Variance Test to each answer in an effort to give you the best possible understanding of how the technique works.

Answer choice (A): This answer asks about how many of the proposals were rejected on the basis that the curriculum was too comprehensive. To apply the Variance Test, we should supply different and opposing answers to the question posed by the answer choice. First, try the answer "One." With this answer, would the fact that one textbook proposal was rejected on the basis of being too comprehensive help us evaluate the conclusion? No—this does not help us evaluate whether the board was negligent in rejecting all the proposals. What if the answer was "Four" (you cannot use five because at least one proposal was rejected for being "inadequate"; four is also possible because the "controversial" tag could be additionally applied to a proposal that was already too comprehensive, or inadequate)?

CHAPTER THIRTEEN: EVALUATE/CANNOT/PRINCIPLE QUESTIONS

Would the fact that four of the textbook proposals were rejected on the basis of being too comprehensive help us evaluate the conclusion? Not at all. So, regardless of how we respond to the question posed in answer choice (A), our view of the conclusion is the same—we do not know whether the conclusion is true or not. According to the Variance Test, if the answer is correct, then supplying opposite answers should yield different views of the conclusion. Since our assessment of the conclusion did not change, the Variance Test tells us that this answer is incorrect.

Answer choice (B): The question in answer choice (B) is, "What was the opinion of the parents' association regarding the five textbook proposals?" Again, apply the Variance Test and supply opposite answers to the question in the answer choice. In this case, try "Positive (liked all five)" and "Negative (disliked all five)." If the parents association liked all five, would that change the fact of whether the school board was negligent in rejecting all five? No, because the motives and goals of the parents association are possibly different from the goals of the school board, and the opinion of one would not establish whether the school board was negligent for rejecting all five local proposals. Let's look at the opposite side: if the parents association disliked all five, would that change the fact of whether the school board was negligent in rejecting all five? No. Because our view of the truth of the conclusion does not change when we consider different responses to the question posed in answer choice (B), the Variance Test tells us that answer choice (B) is incorrect.

Answer choice (C): The question in answer choice (C) is, did any non-local textbook publishers submit book proposals to the school board? Using the Variance Test, supply one response that says, "Yes." If this is true, then the conclusion is unquestionably weakened because the school board could have accepted one of the non-local textbook proposals, meaning that there will be textbooks for the upcoming year. Now supply a response that says, "No." If this is true, then the conclusion is strengthened because there will likely not be any textbooks for the upcoming year. So, depending on the answer supplied to the question posed in answer choice (C), our view of the validity of the argument changes: sometimes we view the conclusion as stronger and other times as weaker. Therefore, according to the Variance Test, this is the correct answer. In this instance, the Variance Test reveals the flaw in the argument: the author simply assumed that the local proposals were the only ones received. Nowhere in the argument did the author mention that anything about other, non-local proposals, and the Variance Test reveals this flaw.

Answer choice (D): For this answer, again supply "Yes" and "No" responses. Neither answer changes our view of the argument because we already know that the school board rejected all five of the proposals. Thus, answer choice (D) is incorrect.

All flawed arguments contain an error of assumption. The correct answer in an Evaluate the Argument question reveals that error.

Answer choice (E): Again, supply "Yes" and "No" responses to the question in this answer choice. Because the editorials is about the current school board and makes an assessment about this board, the actions of previous boards do not have an effect on the conclusion. Hence, answer choice (E) is incorrect.

The key thing to note is that the Variance Test is applied according to the nature of each answer choice. Thus, with some answer choices we might supply responses of "Yes" and "No," and other answer choices might require responses of "0%" and "100%," or "Very Important" and "Not Important." But, in each case, the answers we supply are different, and as opposite as possible, and the correct answer is always the one that changes your view of the validity of the conclusion when those different responses are supplied. If your view of the argument does not change, then the answer choice is incorrect.

Keep in mind that the Variance Test should only be applied to the contending answer choices. In the discussion above we applied it to every answer choice, but we did this simply to show how to effectively apply the Variance Test. During the actual test you would only want to apply the Variance Test to two or three answer choices at most.

Evaluate the Argument Question Type Review

Evaluate the Argument questions ask you to consider the question, statistic, or piece of information that would best help determine the logical validity of the argument presented in the stimulus.

Evaluate the Argument questions are a combination of the Second and Third Families, and as such you should keep the following considerations in mind:

1. In all Second and Third Family questions the information in the stimulus is suspect, so you should search for the reasoning error present.

2. The answer choices are accepted as given, even if they include "new" information.

Evaluate the Argument question stems almost always use the word "evaluate" or a synonym such as "judge" or "assess."

To determine the correct answer choice on an Evaluate the Argument question, apply the Variance Test™ by supplying two opposite responses to the question posed *in the answer choice* and then analyze how the varying responses affect the conclusion in the stimulus. If different responses produce different effects on the conclusion, the answer choice is correct. If different responses do not produce different effects, the answer choice is incorrect.

The Variance Test should only be applied to Contenders (to determine which one is correct) or to the answer choice you believe is correct (to confirm your selection).

Cannot Be True Questions

This question type appears infrequently, but a short review is worthwhile in order to prepare you for every eventuality.

Cannot Be True questions are worded in a variety of ways. The gist of the question type is to show that an answer cannot follow, and this tasks tends to be expressed in three separate ways:

1. Stating that the answer cannot be true or does not follow.

   Question stem examples:

   > "If the statements above are true, which one of the following CANNOT be true?"

   > "The argument can most reasonably be interpreted as an objection to which one of the following claims?"

   > "The statements above, if true, most seriously undermine which one of the following assertions?"

   > "The information above, if accurate, can best be used as evidence against which one of the following hypotheses?"

2. Stating that the answer could be true EXCEPT.

   This construction is frequently used to convey the Cannot Be True concept. If the four incorrect answers could be true, then the one remaining answer must be the opposite, or cannot be true.

   Question stem example:

   > "If all of the claims made above are true, then each of the following could be true EXCEPT: "

3. Stating that the answer choice must be false.

   The phrase "must be false" is functionally identical to "cannot be true." The use of this wording is just one more way for the test makers to present you with unusual phrasing.

   Question stem example:

   > "If the statements above are true, then which one of the following must be false?"

When the word "cannot" is used in question stems, it is typically capitalized.

CHAPTER THIRTEEN: EVALUATE/CANNOT/PRINCIPLE QUESTIONS

Two Notable Stimulus Scenarios

Although Cannot Be True questions are not associated with any particular type of stimulus scenario, two concepts we have discussed appear with some frequency: numbers and percentages, and conditional relationships. Both areas can cause confusion, so let's examine each in more detail:

1. Numbers and Percentages

    As detailed in an earlier chapter, numbers and percentages can be confusing when they appear on the GMAT, and the test makers know how to exploit certain preconceived notions that students bring with them to the test. In Cannot Be True questions, the stimulus will often supply enough information for you to determine that certain outcomes must occur (for example, increasing market share while the overall market size remains constant results in greater sales). The correct answer then violates this outcome.

2. Conditional Statements

    Many different scenarios can occur in Cannot Be True questions featuring conditional statements, except the following:

    > The sufficient condition occurs, and the necessary condition does not occur.

    Thus, when a conditional statement is made in a Cannot Be True question stimulus, you should actively seek the answer that matches the scenario above.

    Incorrect answers often play upon the possibility that the necessary condition occurs but the sufficient condition does not occur. Those scenarios could occur and are thus incorrect.

Cannot Be True Question Review

In Cannot Be True questions your task is to identify the answer choice that cannot be true or is most weakened by the information in the argument. In this sense, this is a reversed First Family question. Answers that could be true are incorrect. The stimulus in a Cannot Be True question rarely contains a conclusion.

For this question type, the following rules apply:

1. Accept the stimulus information and use only it to prove that one of the answer choices cannot occur.

2. If an answer choice contains information that does not appear directly in the stimulus or as a combination of items in the stimulus, then that answer choice could be true, and it is incorrect. The correct answer choice will directly disagree with the stimulus or a consequence of the stimulus.

Cannot Be True questions can be worded in a variety of ways, but the gist of the question type is to show that an answer cannot follow, and this tends to be executed in one of three separate ways:

1. Stating that the answer choice cannot be true or does not follow.

2. Stating that each of the answer choices could be true EXCEPT.

3. Stating that the answer choice must be false.

Cannot Be True questions are tricky because the concept of an answer choice being possibly true and therefore wrong is counterintuitive. When you encounter a Cannot Be True question, you must mentally prepare yourself to eliminate answers that could be true or are possible, and select the one answer choice that cannot be true or is impossible.

In problems that revolve around numbers and percentages, the stimulus will often supply enough information for you to determine that certain outcomes must occur. The correct answer then violates this outcome.

In problems featuring conditional statements, many different scenarios can occur, except the following:

> The sufficient condition occurs, and the necessary condition does not occur.

Thus, when a conditional statement is made in a Cannot Be True question stimulus, you should actively seek the answer that matches the scenario above.

Principle Questions

This is another element that appears on the GMAT infrequently, but we cover this topic briefly in the interests of covering all bases.

Principle question typically appear as an overlay with one of the other questions, as in the following example:

> "Which of the following principles most weakens the author's conclusion?"

Since a principle is by definition a broad rule (usually conditional in nature), the presence of the Principle indicator serves to broaden the scope of the question. The question becomes more abstract, and you must analyze the problem to identify the underlying relationships. Functionally, you must take a broad, global proposition and apply it in a specific manner, either to the answer choices (as in a Must or Parallel question) or to the stimulus (as in a Strengthen or Weaken question). Here is a brief analysis of how this process affects the two question types most likely to appear with a Principle designation:

1. Must Be True/Parallel Principle Questions

   In these questions you must use the principle presented in *the stimulus* and then apply it to the situation in each answer choice (one principle applied to five situations). The presence of the principle designation broadens the question, and the answer choice can address a scenario not specifically included in the stimulus; your job is to find the answer that follows from the application of the principle. If an answer does not match the principle, it is incorrect.

   Since many, if not all, of the principles in these stimuli are conditional, you will often be able to identify that reasoning and make a quick diagram. If you cannot clearly identify the conditional nature of the principle, create an abstraction of the stimulus similar to one you would create in a Parallel Reasoning question. This approach can be useful since it creates an accurate representation of the principle.

   The classification of these questions can sometimes be difficult for students since the relation of the stimulus to the answer choices is so similar to Parallel Reasoning questions (each answer often features a scenario and topic that is entirely different from that in the stimulus). Remember, both Parallel Reasoning and Must Be True questions are in the First Question Family, and they share many of the same characteristics. In the final analysis, when considering the answer choices, ask yourself, "Does this answer match the attributes of the principle in the stimulus?"

2. Strengthen/Justify Principle Questions

In these questions each *answer choice* contains a principle that acts as an additional, broad premise that supports or proves the conclusion. Functionally, five different principles are applied to the situation in the stimulus. While reading the stimulus, you must think in abstract terms and identify an underlying idea or belief that can be used to draw the conclusion in the stimulus. Then, as you analyze the answer choices, tie this idea or belief to the structure of the author's argument and ask yourself, "If this answer is true, does it support or prove the conclusion?"

When you encounter a Principle designator in the question stem, prepare to apply the principle to a situation that falls under the purview of the principle but is not necessarily directly addressed by the principle. This process of abstraction consumes more time that the average question and contributes to lengthening the problem completion time. Regardless, if you use the skills you developed while examining other question types (such as Must Be True and Strengthen), you can successfully navigate Principle questions.

Principle Question Review

Principle questions (PR) are not a separate question type but are instead an "overlay" that appears in a variety of question types.

A principle is a broad rule that specifies what actions or judgments are correct in certain situations. The degree of generality of principles can vary considerably, and some are much narrower than others.

Since a principle is by definition a broad rule (usually conditional in nature), the presence of the Principle indicator serves to broaden the scope of the question. The question becomes more abstract, and you must analyze the problem to identify the underlying relationships. Functionally, you must take a broad, global proposition and apply it in a specific manner, either to the answer choices (as in a Must or Parallel question) or to the stimulus (as in a Strengthen or Justify question).

In Must-PR questions you must use the principle presented in the stimulus and then apply it to the situation in each answer choice (one principle applied to five situations). The presence of the principle designation broadens the question, and the answer choice can address a scenario not included in the stimulus.

In Strengthen-PR questions each answer choice contains a principle that acts as an additional, broad premise that supports or proves the conclusion (functionally, five different principles are applied to the situation in the stimulus).

When you encounter a Principle designator in the question stem, prepare to apply the principle to a situation that falls under the purview of the principle but is not necessarily directly addressed by the principle. This process of abstraction consumes more time than the average question and contributes to lengthening the problem.

Final Note

Because the question types discussed in this chapter appear relatively infrequently on the GMAT, no problem set accompanies this section.

Chapter Fourteen:
Test Readiness

Chapter Fourteen: Test Readiness

The day before the test 353

The morning of the test 353

At the test center 354

After the test 354

Afterword 355

The day before the test

On the day before your GMAT appointment, we recommend that you study very little, if at all. The best approach for most students is to simply relax as much as possible. Read a book, go see a movie, or play a round of golf. If you feel you must study, we recommend that you only briefly review each of the concepts covered in the book.

If you are not familiar with the location of your test center, drive by or visit the test center and survey the situation. This will alleviate anxiety or confusion on the day of the test.

Eat only bland or neutral foods the night before the test and try to get the best sleep possible.

The morning of the test

Attempt to follow your normal routine on the morning of the test. For example, if you read the paper every morning, do so on the day of the test. If you do not regularly drink coffee, do not start on test day. Constancy in your routine will allow you to focus on your primary objective: performing well on the test.

Dress in layers, so you will be warm if the test center is cold, but also able to shed clothes if the test center is hot.

You are encouraged to arrive at the test center approximately 30 minutes before your scheduled appointment time.

We strongly believe that performing well requires confidence and a belief that you can perform well. As you prepare to leave for the test, run though the test in your head, visualizing an exceptional performance. Imagine how you'll react to each math problem, essay question, and verbal problem. Many athletes use this same visualization technique to achieve optimal performance.

The following pages contain general notes on preparing for the day of the GMAT.

Do not study hard the day before the test. If you haven't learned it by then, that final day won't make much difference.

CHAPTER FOURTEEN: TEST READINESS

At the test center

Upon check-in, test supervisors will ask you to provide acceptable personal identification (typically a current driver's license or passport). Supervisors are instructed to deny admission to anyone who does not present a photo ID with signature. They will also take a palm vein scan, photograph you, and typically videotape you.

The test supervisors will assign each examinee a work station. You are not permitted to choose your own station.

Once you are seated, testing will begin promptly.

Food and drink are not allowed in the testing room.

You may not leave your work station during the timed portions of the test.

If you engage in any misconduct or irregularity during the test, you may be dismissed from the test center and may be subject to other penalties for misconduct or irregularity. Actions that could warrant such consequences are creating a disturbance; giving or receiving help; removing noteboards from the testing room; eating or drinking during the test; taking part in an act of impersonation or other forms of cheating; or using books, calculators, ear plugs, headsets, rulers, or other aids. The penalties for misconduct are high: you may be precluded from attending business school.

If you encounter a problem with the test or test center itself, report it to a test administrator. Reportable problems include: power outages, computer malfunctions, and any unusual disturbances caused by an individual.

If you feel anxious or panicked for any reason before or during the test, close your eyes for a few seconds and relax. Think of other situations where you performed with confidence and skill.

After the test

At the end of the test you will be allowed to preview your unofficial score (without your AWA score) and you will be presented with the option of cancelling your score. If you cancel your score, it can be reinstated within a grace period after the exam, for a fee. If you do cancel your score, you do not receive a refund of your test fee.

If you choose to accept your score, you will see your unofficial scores from the multiple choice sections immediately. Official test results will be delivered to you within several weeks after the test.

Afterword

Thank you for choosing to purchase the *PowerScore GMAT Critical Reasoning Bible*. We hope you have found this book to be both useful and enjoyable, but most importantly we hope this book helps raise your GMAT score.

In all of our publications we strive to present the material in the clearest and most informative manner. If you have any questions, comments, or suggestions, please do not hesitate to email us at:

We love to receive feedback and we do read every email that comes in!

Also, if you haven't done so already, we strongly suggest you visit the website for this book at:

This free online resource area contains supplements to the book material, provides updates as needed, and answers questions posed by students. There is also an official evaluation form that we encourage you to use.

If we can assist you in any way in your GMAT preparation or in the business school admissions process, please do not hesitate to contact us. We would be happy to help.

Thank you and best of luck on the GMAT!

Complete Chapter Answer Key

Notes

Answers to every question used in this book are found in the text of the chapter or in the chapter explanations. The consolidated answer key in this section contains three parts: the first part provides a question description legend, the second part provides an identification of the Three Question Families, and the third part provides a quick chapter-by-chapter answer key for students who need to find the answers quickly.

Question Description Legend

Question Type Designations
Must = Must Be True
MP = Main Point
Assumption = Assumption
Strengthen = Strengthen/Support
Resolve = Resolve the Paradox
Weaken = Weaken
Method = Method of Reasoning
Flaw = Flaw in the Reasoning
Parallel = Parallel Reasoning
Evaluate = Evaluate the Argument
FIB = Fill in the blank
AP = Argument Part
X = Except question

Problem Type Designations
CE = Cause and Effect
#% = Numbers and Percentages

Question Family Categorization

Family #1, also known as the Must Be or Prove Family, consists of the following question types:

(1) Must Be True
(2) Main Point
(7) Method of Reasoning
(8) Flaw in the Reasoning
(9) Parallel Reasoning

Family #2, also known as the Help Family, consists of the following question types:

(3) Assumption
(4) Strengthen/Support
(5) Resolve the Paradox

Family #3, also known as the Hurt Family, consists of the following question type:

(6) Weaken

Evaluate the Argument questions are a combination of the Second and Third Families.

Complete Chapter Answer Keys

Notes

The chapter-by-chapter answer key lists every problem in this book in chronological order and identifies the classification of the question. You can use this answer key as a quick reference when you are solving problems. Each problem is explained in more detail in the text of the chapter.

Chapter-by-Chapter Answer Key

Chapter 2: Critical Reasoning Basics Chapter Text

    1. Must   (B)

Chapter 4: Must Be True Chapter Text

    1. Must   (A)
    2. Must   (D)

Chapter 4: Must Be True Problem Set

    1. Must   (B)
    2. Must   (A)
    3. Must   (C)
    4. Must   (C)

Chapter 5: Main Point Chapter Text

    1. MP   (E)

Chapter 5: Main Point Problem Set

    1. MP   (E)
    2. MP   (B)

Chapter-by-Chapter Answer Key

Chapter 6: Weaken Chapter Text

    1. Weaken   (D)
    2. Weaken   (C)

Chapter 6: Weaken Problem Set

    1. Weaken   (E)
    2. Weaken   (A)
    3. Weaken   (D)
    4. Weaken   (D)

Chapter 7: Cause and Effect Chapter Text

    1. Weaken—CE   (E)
    2. Weaken—CE   (D)

Chapter 7: Cause and Effect Problem Set

    1. Weaken—CE   (D)
    2. Weaken—CE   (D)
    3. Weaken—CE   (C)
    4. Weaken—CE   (D)

Chapter 8: Strengthen and Assumption Chapter—Strengthen Text

    1. Strengthen   (D)
    2. Strengthen   (B)

Chapter 8: Strengthen and Assumption Chapter—Strengthen Problem Set

    1. Strengthen—CE   (C)
    2. Strengthen   (E)

Chapter-by-Chapter Answer Key

Chapter 8: Strengthen and Assumption Chapter—Assumption Text

    1. Assumption   (D)
    2. Assumption   (E)

Chapter 8: Strengthen and Assumption Chapter—Assumption Problem Set

    1. Assumption—FIB   (B)
    2. Assumption   (D)

Chapter 9: Resolve Chapter Text

    1. Resolve   (C)
    2. Resolve   (C)

Chapter 9: Resolve Problem Set

    1. Resolve   (C)
    2. Resolve   (D)

Chapter 10: Method of Reasoning and Flaw in the Reasoning Chapter Text

    1. Method   (A)
    2. Method—AP   (C)

Chapter 10: Method of Reasoning and Flaw in the Reasoning Problem Set

    1. Flaw   (E)
    2. Flaw—CE   (B)
    3. Method—AP   (B)

Chapter-by-Chapter Answer Key

Chapter 11: Parallel Reasoning Chapter Text

    1. Parallel   (D)

Chapter 11: Parallel Reasoning Problem Set

    1. Parallel Flaw   (D)
    2. Parallel   (E)

Chapter 12: Numbers and Percentages Chapter Text

    1. Must—#%   (A)
    2. Must—#%   (C)

Chapter 12: Numbers and Percentages Problem Set

    1. Weaken—#%   (B)
    2. Strengthen—#% (D)

Chapter 13: Evaluate the Argument Chapter Text

    1. Evaluate   (C)

Glossary and Index

Alphabetical Glossary

#%: See Numbers and Percentages.

Additional Premise: Page 33

Additional premises are premises that may be central to the argument or they may be secondary. To determine the importance of the premise, examine the remainder of the argument.

Answer Choices: Page 82

All GMAT questions have five answer choices and each question has only one correct response.

Appeal Fallacies: Page 263

A common error of reasoning that attempts to "appeal" to various insubstantial viewpoints of the reader (emotion, popular opinion, tradition, authority, etc.). However the appeal is not valid, and concrete evidence is needed to support the argument.

Argument: Pages 25, 38, 42

A set of statements wherein one statement is claimed to follow from or be derived from the others. An argument requires a conclusion.

Argument Part (AP) Questions: Page 273

A subset of Method of Reasoning questions. In Argument Part questions, the question stem cites a specific portion or two bolded portions of the stimulus and then asks you to identify the role the cited portion plays in the structure of the argument, or how the two portions relate to each other.

Assumption: Pages 44, 206

An assumption is an unstated premise of the argument. Assumptions are an integral component of the argument that the author takes for granted and leaves unsaid.

Assumption Questions: Pages 59, 63, 206

These questions ask you to identify an assumption of the author's argument.

Assumption Negation Technique™: Page 215

This technique requires you to logically negate the answer choice under consideration, which results in a negated answer choice that attacks the argument. If the negated answer does not attack the argument, then it is incorrect. The purpose of this technique is to take an Assumption question, which is generally difficult for most students, and turn it into a Weaken question, which is easier for most students. This technique can only be used on Assumption questions.

Bolded Argument Part (AP) Questions: Page 273

This is a specific type of Method of Reasoning question, wherein there are two bolded portions of the stimulus, and you are asked to identify the relationship between the two bolded portions.

C:

In diagramming Logical Reasoning questions, "C" indicates Cause. Also see Cause.

Cannot Be True Questions: Page 343

Ask you to identify the answer choice that cannot be true or is most weakened based on the information in the stimulus.

Causality: See Causal Reasoning

Causal Reasoning: Pages 169, 261

Asserts or denies that one thing causes another, or that one thing is caused by another. On the GMAT, cause and effect reasoning appears in many Logical Reasoning problems, often in the conclusion where the author mistakenly claims that one event causes another.

Cause (C):

The event that makes another occur.

Cause and Effect (CE): Page 169

When one event is said to make another occur. The cause is the event that makes the other occur; the effect is the event that follows from the cause. By definition, the cause must occur before the effect, and the cause is the "activator" or "ignitor" in the relationship. The effect always happens at some point in time after the cause.

CE: See Cause and Effect.

Circular Reasoning: Page 259

A flaw where the author assumes as true what is supposed to be proved. The premise supports the conclusion, but the conclusion equally supports the premise, creating a "circular" situation where you can move from premise to conclusion, and then back again to the premise, and so on.

Commonly Used Construction: Page 40

One of the most frequently used argument constructions raises a viewpoint at the beginning of the stimulus and then disagree with it immediately thereafter. This efficiently raises two opposing views in a very short paragraph. These stimuli are recognizable because they often begin with the phrase, "Some people claim..." or one of the many variations of this phrase.

Complex Argument: Page 38

Arguments that contain more than one conclusion. In these instances, one of the conclusions is the main conclusion, and the other conclusions are subsidiary conclusions (also known as sub-conclusions). In basic terms, a complex argument makes an initial conclusion based on a premise. The author then uses that conclusion as the foundation (or premise) for another conclusion, thus building a chain with several levels.

Conclusion: Pages 26, 37

A statement or judgment that follows from one or more reasons. Conclusions, as summary statements, are supposed to be drawn from and rest on the premises.

Conclusion/Premise Indicator Form: Page 29

The test makers will sometimes arrange premise and conclusion indicators in a way that is designed to be confusing. One of their favorite forms places a conclusion indicator and premise indicator back-to-back, separated by a comma, as in the following examples:

"Therefore, since..."
"Thus, because..."
"Hence, due to..."

Conclusion Identification Method™: Page 37

Take the statements under consideration for the conclusion and place them in an arrangement that forces one to be the conclusion and the other(s) to be the premise(s). Use premise and conclusion indicators to achieve this end. Once the pieces are arranged, determine if the arrangement makes logical sense.

Conditional Reasoning: Pages 106, 260

The broad name given to logical relationships composed of sufficient and necessary conditions. Any conditional statement consists of at least one sufficient condition and at least one necessary condition. In everyday use, conditional statements are often brought up using the "if...then" construction. Conditional reasoning can occur in any question type.

Contender: Page 83

An answer choice that appears somewhat attractive, interesting, or even confusing. Basically, any answer choice that you cannot immediately identify as incorrect.

Contrapositive: Page 110

Denies the necessary condition, thereby making it impossible for the sufficient condition to occur. Contrapositives can often yield important insights in Logic Games.

Correlation: Pages 172, 261

A positive correlation is a relationship where the two values move together. A negative correlation is one where the two values move in opposite directions, such as with age and eyesight (the older you get, the worse your eyesight gets).

Counter-premise: Page 34

A premise that actually contains an idea that is counter to the argument. Counter-premises, also called adversatives, bring up points of opposition or comparison.

Critical Reasoning Primary Objectives™: See Primary Objectives

Defender: Page 208

In the Supporter/Defender Assumption Model™, the Defender assumptions contain statements that eliminate ideas or assertions that would undermine the conclusion. In this sense, they "defend" the argument by showing that a possible source of attack has been eliminated.

E: In diagramming, indicates Effect. See Effect.

Effect: Pages 169, 261

The event that follows from the cause.

Elemental Attack™: Page 300

When attacking Parallel Reasoning questions, compare the big-picture elements of the argument: intent of the conclusion, force and use of the premises, the relationship of the premises and the conclusion, and the soundness of the argument. The four tests you can use to evaluate answers are Match the Method of Reasoning, Match the Conclusion, Match the Premises, and Match the Validity of the Argument.

Errors in the Use of Evidence: Page 254

A common error of reasoning that involves the misuse of evidence in one of these ways:
   1. Lack of evidence for a position is taken to prove that position is false.
   2. Lack of evidence against a position is taken to prove that position is true.
   3. Some evidence against a position is taken to prove that position is false.
   4. Some evidence for a position is taken to prove that position is true.

Errors of Composition and Division: Page 267

A common error of reasoning that involves judgments made about groups and parts of a group. An error of composition occurs when the author attributes a characteristic of part of the group to the group as a whole or to each member of the group. An error of division occurs when the author attributes a characteristic of the whole (or each member of the whole) to a part of the group.

Errors of Conditional Reasoning: Page 260

A common error of reasoning that involves confusing the sufficient condition with the necessary condition. Note that the authors can either mistake a necessary condition for a sufficient condition, or mistake a sufficient condition for a necessary condition.

Evaluate the Argument Questions: Pages 61, 64, 335

With Evaluate the Argument questions you must decide which answer choice will allow you to determine the logical validity of the argument. Use the Variance Test™ to prove or disprove answers as needed.

Exaggerated Answer: Page 103

In Must Be True and Method questions, Exaggerated Answers take information from the stimulus and then stretch that information to make a broader statement that is not supported by the stimulus.

Except: Page 76

When "except" is placed in a question it negates the logical quality of the answer choice you seek. It turns the intent of the question stem upside down.

Exceptional Case/Overgeneralization: Page 255

A common error of reasoning that involves taking a small number of instances and treating those instances as if they support a broad, sweeping conclusion.

F

Fact Set: Page 25

A collection of statements without a conclusion. Fact sets make a series of assertions without making a judgment.

Fact Test™: Page 91

The correct answer to a Must Be True question (and other First Family questions) can always be proven by referring to the facts stated in the stimulus. An answer choice that cannot be substantiated by proof in the stimulus is incorrect.

False Analogy: Page 268

A common error of reasoning that involves an author using an analogy that is too dissimilar to the original situation to be applicable.

False Dilemma: Page 269

A common error of reasoning that involves assuming that only two courses of action are available when there may be others (for example, "You are either rich or impoverished"). Do not confuse a False Dilemma with a situation where the author legitimately establishes that only two possibilities exist. Phrases such as "either A or B will occur, but not both" can establish a limited set of possibilities, and certain real-world situations yield only two possibilities, such as "you are either dead or alive."

First Family: Page 66

Consists of question types that use the stimulus to prove that one of the answer choices must be true. No information outside the sphere of the stimulus is allowed in the correct answer choice. Includes the following question types: Must Be True, Main Point, Method of Reasoning, Flaw in the Reasoning, and Parallel Reasoning.

Fill in the Blank (FIB) Questions: Page 136

Questions that contain a stimulus that ends with a blank space. The question stem asks you to fill in the blank with an appropriate answer.

Flaw in the Reasoning Questions: Pages 60, 63, 248

Flaw in the Reasoning questions ask you to describe, in abstract terms, the error of reasoning committed by the author.

General Lack of Relevant Evidence for the Conclusion: Page 254

Some authors misuse information to such a degree that they fail to provide any information to support their conclusion or they provide information that is irrelevant to their conclusion.

Guessing: Page 9

Because the GMAT typically assesses a scoring penalty for unanswered questions, you should always guess on any question that you cannot complete during the allotted time.

H

Half Right, Half Wrong Answer: Page 251

In Must Be True, Method, and Flaw questions, the makers of the GMAT love to present answers that start out by describing something that in fact occurred in the stimulus. Unfortunately, these answers often end by describing something that did *not* occur in the stimulus.

I

Idea Umbrella™: Page 96

A concept first introduced in Must Be True questions, but one which can play a role in other question types as well. Certain concepts act as an umbrella, and as such they automatically imply other things. For example, a discussion of "all animals" thereby includes cats, zebras, lizards, etc. In this way, elements that are not explicitly mentioned in the stimulus can still validly appear in the right answer choice.

Inference: Page 44

In logic, an inference can be defined as something that must be true. If you are asked to identify an inference of the argument, you must find an item that must be true based on the information presented in the argument.

Internal Contradiction: Page 255

A common error of reasoning (also known as a self-contradiction) that occurs when an author makes conflicting statements.

L

Least: Page 76

When "least" appears in a question stem you should treat it exactly the same as "except." Note: this advice holds true only when this word appears in the question stem! If you see the word "least" elsewhere on the GMAT, consider it to have its usual meaning of "in the lowest or smallest degree."

Logical Opposition: See Opposition Construct™

Loser: Page 83

An answer choice which immediately strikes you as incorrect.

M

Main Point (MP) Questions: Pages 59, 63, 131

Main Point questions are a variant of Must Be True questions. As you might expect, a Main Point question asks you to find the primary conclusion made by the author.

Match the Conclusion: Page 300

In Parallel Reasoning questions, the conclusion in the correct answer choice must match the logical force of the conclusion in the stimulus.

Match the Method of Reasoning: Page 300

In Parallel Reasoning questions, if you identify an obvious form of reasoning (use of analogy, circular reasoning, conditional reasoning, etc.), move quickly to the answer choices and look for the answer with an identical form of reasoning.

Match the Premises: Page 301

In Parallel Reasoning questions, the premise(s) in the correct answer choice must match the logical force of the premises) in the stimulus.

Match the Validity of the Argument: Page 301

In Parallel Reasoning questions, always make sure to eliminate any answer choice that does not match the logical force (valid or invalid) of the argument.

Method of Reasoning Questions: Pages 60, 63, 247

Method of Reasoning questions ask you to describe, in abstract terms, the way in which the author made his or her argument.

Mistaken Cause and Effect: Page 261

A common error of reasoning that occurs because arguments that draw causal conclusions are inherently flawed because there may be another explanation for the stated relationship. This can occur by assuming a causal relationship on the basis of the sequence of events or when only a correlation exists. This can also occur due to failure to consider an alternate cause for the effect, an alternate cause for both the cause and the effect, or that the events may be reversed.

Mistaken Negation™: Page 109

Negates both sufficient and necessary conditions, creating a statement that does not have to be true.

Mistaken Reversal™: Page 109

> Switches the elements in the sufficient and necessary conditions, creating a statement that does not have to be true.

MP: See Main Point.

Must Be True Questions: Pages 59, 63, 91

> Must Be True questions ask you to identify the answer choice that is best proven by the information in the stimulus.

N

N: See Necessary Condition.

Necessary Condition (N): Pages 106, 107

> An event or circumstance whose occurrence is required in order for a sufficient condition to occur.

Negation: Pages 109, 215

> Negating a statement consists of creating the logical opposite of the statement. The logical opposite is the statement that denies the truth of the original statement, and a logical opposite is different from the polar opposite.

New Element Answer: Pages 251, 278

> Because correct Method of Reasoning answers must be based on elements of the stimulus, an answer that describes something that did not occur or describes an element new to the argument cannot be correct.

New Information: Page 103

> In Must Be True questions, be wary of answers that present so-called new information—that is, information not mentioned explicitly in the stimulus. Although these answers can be correct when they fall under the umbrella of a statement made in the stimulus, they are often incorrect.

Not Necessarily True: Page 82

> The logical opposite of "Must Be True." When an answer choice is not proven by the information in the stimulus.

Noteboards: Pages 9, 12

During an actual GMAT administration, you are given noteboards to use in place of scratch paper.

Numbers and Percentages (#%): Page 313

Numerical situations normally hinge on three elements: an overall total, a number within that total, and a percentage within the total. GMAT problems will often give you one of the elements, but without at least two elements present, you cannot make a definitive judgment about what is occurring with another element. When you are given just percentage information, you cannot make a judgment about numbers. Likewise, when you are given just numerical information you cannot make a judgment about percentages.

Numbers and Percentages Errors: Page 270

A common error of reasoning that is committed when an author improperly equates a percentage with a definite quantity, or when an author uses quantity information to make a judgment about the percentage represented by that quantity.

Opposite Answer: Page 104

Provides an answer that is completely opposite of the stated facts of the stimulus. Opposite Answers are very attractive to students who are reading too quickly or carelessly and quite frequently appear in Strengthen and Weaken questions.

Opposition Construct™: Page 217

An Opposition Construct efficiently summarizes the logical opposites of subjects within a limited spectrum of possibilities, such as quantity, which falls into *All* vs *Not All*, and *Some* vs *None*.

Out of Scope Answer: Pages 152, 158

These answers simply miss the point of the argument and raise issues that are either not related to the argument or tangential to the argument.

Parallel Flaw Questions: Page 295

A Parallel Reasoning stimulus that contains flawed reasoning is known as a Parallel Flaw question.

Parallel Reasoning Questions: Pages 61, 63, 295

Parallel Reasoning questions ask you to identify the answer choice that contains reasoning most similar in structure to the reasoning presented in the stimulus.

Polar Opposite: Pages 216, 217

A statement that is the extreme opposite of another. "Hot" and "cold" are polar opposites.

Premise: Pages 26, 30

A fact, proposition, or statement from which a conclusion is made. Literally, the premises give the reasons why the conclusion should be accepted.

Prephrasing: Pages 81, 92

One of the most effective techniques for quickly finding correct answer choices and avoiding incorrect answer choices, prephrasing an answer involves quickly speculating on what you expect the correct answer will be based on the information in the stimulus.

Primary Objectives™: Pages 25, 28, 42, 46, 58, 81, 85, 86

A cohesive strategy for attacking any Critical Reasoning question. By consistently applying the objectives, you give yourself the best opportunity to succeed on each question.

Principle (PR): Page 347

A broad rule that specifies what actions or judgments are correct in certain situations. These are not a separate question type but are instead an "overlay" that appears in a variety of question types and the presence of the Principle indicator serves to broaden the scope of the question.

Question Stem: Pages 18, 57

Follows the stimulus and poses a question directed at the stimulus. Make sure to read the question stem very carefully. Some stems direct you to focus on certain aspects of the stimulus and if you miss these clues you make the problem much more difficult.

R

Repeat Form: Page 108

Simply restates the elements of a conditional statement in the original order they appeared. This creates a valid argument.

Resolve the Paradox Questions: Pages 60, 63, 233

Every Resolve the Paradox stimulus contains a discrepancy or seeming contradiction. You must find the answer choice that best explains the situation.

Reverse Answer: Page 104

Occurs when an answer choice contains familiar elements from the stimulus, but rearranges those elements to create a new, unsupported statement.

S

S: See Sufficient Condition

Scope: Page 47

The range to which the premises and conclusion encompass certain ideas. An argument with a narrow scope is definite in its statements, whereas a wide scope argument is less definite and allows for a greater range of possibility.

Second Family: Page 67

Consists of question types that take the answer choices as true and uses them to help the stimulus. Information outside the sphere of the stimulus is allowed in the correct answer choice. Includes the following question types: Assumption, Justify the Conclusion, Strengthen/Support, and Resolve the Paradox.

Secondary Conclusion: See Sub-conclusion

Shell Game: Page 104

An idea or concept is raised in the stimulus, and then a very similar idea appears in the answer choice, but the idea is changed just enough to be incorrect but still attractive. This trick is called the Shell Game because it abstractly resembles those street corner gambling games where a person hides a small object underneath one of three shells, and then scrambles them on a flat surface while a bettor tries to guess which shell the object is under.

Source Argument: Page 258

A common error of reasoning that attacks the person (or source) instead of the argument they advance. Because the GMAT is concerned solely with argument forms, a speaker can never validly attack the character or motives of a person; instead, a speaker must always attack the argument advanced by a person.

Statement Negation: Page 216

Negating a statement means to alter the sentence so the meaning is logically opposite of what was originally stated. Negation largely consists of taking a "not" out of a sentence when one is present, or putting a "not" in a sentence if one is not present.

Stimulus: Page 18

A short passage containing arguments taken from a variety of topics reflecting a broad range of academic disciplines (including letters to the editor, speeches, advertisements, newspaper articles and editorials, informal discussions and conversations, as well as articles in the humanities, the social sciences, and the natural sciences) that presents all of the necessary information to answer the subsequent question stem.

Straw Man: Page 262

A common error of reasoning that occurs when an author attempts to attack an opponent's position by ignoring the actual statements made by the opposing speaker and instead distorts and refashions the argument, making it weaker in the process.

Strengthen/Support Questions: Pages 59, 63, 193

These questions ask you to select the answer choice that provides support for the author's argument or strengthens it in some way.

Sub-conclusion: Page 38

A conclusion that is then used as a premise to support another conclusion. This is also known as a secondary or subsidiary conclusion.

Subsidiary Conclusion: See Sub-conclusion

Sufficient: Page 106

A sufficient condition can be defined as an event or circumstance whose occurrence indicates that a necessary condition must also occur.

Sufficient Condition (S): Page 106

> An event or circumstance whose occurrence indicates that a necessary condition must also occur. The sufficient condition does not make the necessary condition occur, it is simply an indicator.

Support: See Strengthen or Must Be True, depending on usage

Supporter: Page 208

> In the Supporter/Defender Assumption Model™, the Supporter Assumptions link together new or rogue elements in the stimulus or fill logical gaps in the argument.

Supporter/Defender Assumption Model™: Page 208

> Assumptions play one of two roles—the Supporter or the Defender. The Supporter role is the traditional linking role, where an assumption connects the pieces of the argument. The Defender role is entirely different, and Defender assumptions protect the argument by eliminating ideas that could weaken the argument.

Survey Errors: Page 265

> A common error of reasoning that occurs when a survey uses a biased sample, the survey questions are improperly constructed or the respondents to the survey give inaccurate responses. Surveys, when conducted properly, produce reliable results. However, surveys can be invalidated when any of these errors occur.

T

Test of Abstraction™: Page 305

> A last resort method for attacking Parallel Reasoning and Parallel Flaw questions. To use the Test of Abstraction, create a short abstract description that summarizes the "action" in the argument without referring to the details of the argument. Then compare that summary to each answer choice, eliminating the answers that are different.

Third Family: Page 68

> Consists of question types that take the answer choices as true and uses them to hurt the stimulus. Information outside the sphere of the stimulus is allowed in the correct answer choice. Includes the following question type: Weaken.

Three Question Families™: Page 63

> All question types are variations of three main question "families," and each family is comprised of question types that are similar to each other.

Time Shift Errors: Page 270

A common error of reasoning that involves assuming that conditions will remain constant over time, and that what was the case in the past will be the case in the present or future.

Uncertain Use of a Term or Concept: Page 268

A common error of reasoning that occurs when the author uses a term or concept in different ways instead of using each term or concept in a constant, coherent fashion. This error is inherently confusing and undermines the integrity of the argument.

Uniqueness Rule of Answer Choices™: Page 82

This rule states that "Every correct answer has a unique logical quality that meets the criteria in the question stem. Every incorrect answer has the opposite logical quality."

Validity: Page 41

Validity reflects the logical relationship of the pieces of an argument, and how well do the premises, if accepted, prove the conclusion.

Variance Test™: Page 337

Consists of supplying two polar opposite responses to the question posed in the answer choice and then analyzing how the varying responses affect the conclusion in the stimulus. If different responses produce different effects on the conclusion, then the answer choice is correct. If different responses do not produce different effects, then the answer choice is incorrect. The Variance Test can only be used with Evaluate the Argument questions.

Weaken Questions: Pages 60, 63, 147

Weaken questions ask you to attack or undermine the author's argument.